BUILDING BASIC
VOCABULARY A

Robert J. Marzano

NATIONAL
GEOGRAPHIC
LEARNING | CENGAGE
Learning

Australia • Brazil • Japan • Korea • Mexico • Singapore • Spain • United Kingdom • United States

Building Basic Vocabulary A
Robert J. Marzano

Publisher: Sherrise Roehr

Executive Editor: Carmela Fazzino-Farah

Managing Editor: Kellie Cardone

Development Editors: Cécile Engeln and
Marissa Petrarca

Marketing Manager: Emily Stewart

Director of Content and Media Production:
Michael Burggren

Senior Content Project Manager: Daisy Sosa

Manufacturing Manager: Marcia Locke

Manufacturing Buyer: Marybeth Hennebury

Cover Design: Page 2 LLC

Interior Design: Muse Group, Inc.

Composition: PreMediaGlobal

Contributing Writers: Karen Haller Beer,
Jackie Counts, and Wendy Criner

For permission to use material from this text or product,
submit all requests online at **cengage.com/permissions**
Further permissions questions can be emailed to
permissionrequest@cengage.com

Library of Congress Control Number: 2012936056

ISBN-13: 978-1-133-30849-2

ISBN-10: 1-133-30849-X

National Geographic Learning
20 Channel Center St.
Boston, MA 02210
USA

Cengage Learning is a leading provider of customized learning solutions with
office locations around the globe, including Singapore, the United Kingdom,
Australia, Mexico, Brazil, and Japan. Locate your local office at:
international.cengage.com/region

Cengage Learning products are represented in Canada by Nelson Education, Ltd.

Visit National Geographic Learning online at **ngl.cengage.com**
Visit our corporate website at **www.cengage.com**

Printed in the United States of America
1 2 3 4 5 6 7 16 15 14 13 12

Renee M. Belvis
Dunedin Highland Middle
School
Dunedin, FL

Brian Cerda
Sabina Magnet School
Chicago, IL

Ashley Cimo
Amos Alonzo Stagg High
School
Palos Hills, IL

Fred Cochran
Lincoln Unified School District
Stockton, CA

Raquel Cruz
Country Club Middle School
Miami, FL

Meg Daniewicz
New Millennium Academy
Minneapolis, MN

Amber Driscoll
March Middle School
Moreno Valley, CA

Annie Duong
San Joaquin COE
Stockton, CA

Jill Hoffmann
Victor J. Andrew High School
Tinley Park, IL

Laura Hook
Howard County Public School
System
Ellicott City, MD

Tara Kim
March Middle School
Moreno Valley, CA

Alice Kos
Minneapolis Public Schools
Minneapolis, MN

Elizabeth Koutny
Ames Middle School
Berwyn, IL

Mary Lein
Rochester ISD
Rochester, MN

Sam Nofziger
The English Learner Group
Fresno, CA

Esmeralda Placencia
Chicago Public Schools
Chicago, IL

Maria Rivera
Richard Edwards Elementary
School
Chicago, IL

Mytzy Rodriguez-Kufner
Round Lake Area Schools
Round Lake, IL

Nathalie Rumowicz
Seminole Middle School
Plantation, FL

Susan Sharko
Old Quarry Middle School
Lemont, IL

Dr. LaWanna Shelton
Trevecca Nazarene University
Nashville, TN

Gwen Snow
Jefferson County Public Schools –
ESL Newcomer Academy
Louisville, KY

Claudia Viloria
South Ft. Myers High School
Ft. Myers, FL

Brenda Ward
Lafayette School Corporation
Lafayette, IN

Bryn Watson
Hough Street Elementary
School
Barrington, IL

Jennifer White
ESOL Program, Charleston
County School District
Charleston, SC

Vicki Writsel
Bowling Green Independent
Schools
Bowling Green, KY

CONTENTS

Book C Super Clusters

Note: This Contents section provides information on how to find the first instance of each super cluster. For information on where specific clusters can be found, please refer to the Appendix on pages 292 to 295.

1. Modals

Check (✔) the words you already know. Then, listen and repeat.

🎧 Tracks 1–10

☐ **may**
TR 1

She **may** say, "Yes."

☐ **shall**
TR 2

We **shall** marry.

☐ **might**
TR 3

He **might** go to the dance.

☐ **will**
TR 4

She **will** graduate.

☐ **can**
TR 5

He **can** run fast.

☐ **cannot**
TR 6

She **cannot** walk.

☐ **could**
TR 7

When she was young, she **could** sing well.

☐ **must**
TR 8

He **must** clean his room.

☐ **would**
TR 9

He **would** read ten books a day when he was young.

☐ **should**
TR 10

Everyone **should** recycle bottles and cans.

Definitions*

can ability/possibility; permission; polite request

cannot lack of ability; impossibility; prohibition

could past ability/possibility; polite request; suggestion; permission

may possibility; permission

might possibility

must necessity; conclusion

shall future; suggestion

should advice; prediction

will future; prediction; volunteer

would repeated action in past; polite request; preference

*Modals are helping verbs. They don't have their own meaning. They help verbs, or action words.

Check Your Understanding

A. Circle the word in each group that does not belong.

1. will	may	would
2. could	must	shall
3. may	might	can
4. cannot	could	might
5. should	can	cannot

B. Choose the sentence that correctly uses the underlined word.

1. a. After exercising for six months, I <u>can</u> run three miles.

   b. Since Alex didn't study last night, he <u>can</u> pass his test.

2. a. Harry has a lot of friends because he <u>cannot</u> talk to anyone.

   b. Janis <u>cannot</u> go out to eat tonight because she is too busy.

3. a. Chris <u>could</u> play the piano very well when he was young.

   b. It was very cloudy last night, so we <u>could</u> see the stars.

4. a. Erin <u>may</u> take the train home because the tire on her bike is flat.

   b. I want a car, so I <u>may</u> take the train.

5. a. Mark <u>might</u> ask Linda to help him with his homework because he doesn't understand it.

   b. Michael went to sleep at <u>might</u>.

6. a. Kim <u>must</u> wear a hat and coat today because it is snowing.

   b. Danny <u>must</u> keep his eyes closed when he drives.

7. a. Sam <u>shall</u> go shopping because he does not have time.

   b. We <u>shall</u> be married in the spring.

8. a. The baseball players <u>should</u> make it to the game on time if there is no traffic.

   b. Michael <u>should</u> take his dog for a walk because his leg is broken.

9. a. Jack said he <u>will</u> work yesterday.

   b. Mary <u>will</u> go to the doctor on Monday.

10. a. Melissa said she <u>would</u> go to the party if her parents gave her permission.

    b. Nate <u>would</u> pick his aunt up at the airport.

Challenge Words

Check (✔) the words you already know.

☐ ought   ☐ used to

3. Primary Auxiliary Verbs

Check (✔) the words you already know. Then, listen and repeat.

 Tracks 1–6

Definitions*

Subject	Auxiliary Verb	Main Verb
I / you / we / they	**do**	like, go, watch, eat
he / she / it	**does**	need, start, make, walk
I / you / we / they he / she / it	**did**	eat, take, arrive
I / you / we / they	**have**	been, learned, eaten, enjoyed
he / she / it	**has**	forgotten, visited, taken, stopped
I / you / we / they he / she / it	**had**	put, lived, made, stayed

Oh no! I **had** put my homework in my bag before I left the house…

☐ **have**
TR 2

☐ **had**
TR 1

They **have** been wonderful students.

☐ **do**
TR 4

☐ **does**
TR 5

Do you like dogs?

Sorry, but I **do** not like dogs.

Does Sparky need a walk?

Yes, he **does**.

☐ **did**

Did he eat yet?
TR 6

Yes, he **did**.

Teri **has** forgotten her homework.

☐ **has**
TR 3

*Primary auxiliary verbs are helping verbs. They don't have their own meaning. They help verbs, or action words.

Check Your Understanding

A. Circle the correct word to complete each sentence or question.

1. Maria and Karen _____ do their chores.

   a. doing   b. did   c. have

2. You _____ have baseball practice tomorrow.

   a. doing   b. has   c. do

3. _____ Miguel like to do homework in his room?

   a. Does   b. Do   c. Have

4. Tara _____ visited this museum many times.

   a. have   b. has   c. did

5. I _____ been listening to my MP3 player for three hours before she arrived.

   a. do   b. had   c. does

6. They _____ spent the afternoon washing the car.

   a. doing   b. have   c. has

B. Underline the correct word to complete each sentence or question.

1. Alexandra (**had / have**) gone to bed by the time her sister got home.

2. (**Do / Does**) Fred need to wash his dog today?

3. I (**do / doing**) not dance salsa anymore.

4. Tina (**does / did**) have to drive her sister to school yesterday.

5. I (**has / have**) enjoyed my aunt's visit.

6. Toby (**has / have**) waited a long time to get his driver's license.

4. Auxiliary Verbs

Check (✔) the words you already know. Then, listen and repeat.

 Tracks 1–8

Definitions

Be is the most common verb in the English language. It can be used as an auxiliary, or helping, verb. When used as an auxiliary verb, it does not have meaning. The main verb provides meaning.

Be is the base form. The other forms are:

Present form = **am / is / are**

I **am** going to school.
  ↑   ↑
Auxiliary Verb Main Verb

He **is** starting his homework.
 ↑   ↑
Auxiliary Verb Main Verb

They **are** eating lunch.
  ↑   ↑
Auxiliary Verb Main Verb

Past form = **was / were**

I **was** dancing and singing.
 ↑   ↑
Auxiliary Verb Main Verb

We **were** studying for the exam.
  ↑   ↑
Auxiliary Verb Main Verb

When **been** and **being** are used as auxiliary verbs, they are added to the main verb and become part of a verb phrase.

They <u>are</u> **being** asked a lot of questions.
   ↑   ↑
Auxiliary Verb Main Verb

I <u>have</u> **been** playing soccer all afternoon.
   ↑   ↑
Auxiliary Verb Main Verb

We **are** folding towels.

All of the dryers are **being** used.

He **is** making a mess!

I have **been** sitting here since 8 AM!

This washer **was** not working last week.

But the rest **were** working well.

I **am** doing laundry.

☐ **am**	TR 1
☐ **are**	TR 2
☐ **be**	TR 3
☐ **been**	TR 4
☐ **being**	TR 5
☐ **is**	TR 6
☐ **was**	TR 7
☐ **were**	TR 8

Check Your Understanding

A. Circle the correct word to complete each sentence.

1. Marta _____ reading a book.

   a. am   b. is   c. be

2. Tina and Chris _____ studying for a test.

   a. are   b. been   c. is

3. Ben and I _____ watching television.

   a. was   b. is   c. were

4. I _____ riding the bus to school today.

   a. am   b. are   c. were

5. Luke _____ practicing the violin yesterday.

   a. is   b. was   c. were

6. Jessica has _____ studying for two hours.

   a. was   b. been   c. were

7. The computer is _____ used right now.

   a. were   b. are   c. being

8. Theo will _____ leaving early today.

   a. be   b. been   c. am

B. Complete each sentence with the correct word from the word bank.

be	are	was	is
am	were	been	being

1. The baby _____ crying, but now she is happy.

2. We will _____ coming to the party at 6 o'clock.

3. Eric _____ practicing the clarinet right now.

4. The music was _____ enjoyed by everyone at the concert.

5. You _____ sleeping when I came home.

6. I _____ eating lunch with Sarah now.

7. Theresa had _____ hoping to go to the gym today.

8. They _____ having a great time with their friends right now.

1 AUXILIARY AND HELPING VERBS

342. Linking Verbs

Check (✔) the words you already know. Then, listen and repeat.

Tracks 1–2

☐ **seem**

TR 1

He **seems** happy.

☐ **become**

TR 2

Definitions

If people or things **become** a particular thing, they change to be that thing.

If people or things **seem** a particular way, they appear to be that way.

Check Your Understanding

A. Fill in each blank with *became* or *seemed*.

Frida wanted to buy a new bicycle. She had $200 to spend, so she went to a store to look for one. She (1) _____ very excited when she saw a blue bicycle on display. Blue was her favorite color. The bicycle (2) _____ perfect. It had sturdy wheels, it was a good size, and it was a beautiful color. But then Frida looked at the price. It was $500! She (3) _____ very sad.

A salesperson saw Frida. He asked Frida if he could help her find anything. He smiled and (4) _____ like he really wanted to help her. Frida told him that she wanted a blue bicycle. She said that there (5) _____ to be only expensive blue bicycles. The salesperson told Frida that he would be right back.

In a few minutes, the salesperson returned with an even more beautiful bicycle than the one on display. And, it was blue! Frida asked him how much it cost. The salesperson said it cost $180. Frida (6) _____ happy again.

B. Match each description to the correct word. Each word will have two answers.

1. _____ become
2. _____ seem

a. to appear a certain way
b. to come to be
c. to turn into something
d. to give the impression

Challenge Words

Check (✔) the words you already know.

☐ appear   ☐ remain

411. Semi-Auxiliary Verbs

Check (✔) the words you already know. Then, listen and repeat.

Track 1

I **have to** clean this mess.

☐ **have to**

TR 1

Definition

You use **have to** when you are saying that someone must do something or that something must happen. If you do not **have to** do something, it is not necessary that you do it.

Check Your Understanding

A. In order for these people to do their jobs well, they <u>have to</u> do certain things. Create four sentences by choosing one item from each column. Write each complete sentence on the lines below.

1. A firefighter	a. has to	i. protect people.
2. A doctor		ii. teach students.
3. A police officer		iii. save people from fires.
4. A teacher		iv. help sick people.

1. _____

2. _____

3. _____

4. _____

B. Write **T** for **true statements** and **F** for **false statements**.

1. _____ I have to exercise and eat right to stay healthy.

2. _____ You have to talk to your friends every day to stay healthy.

3. _____ Martha has to go to work to make money.

4. _____ The farmer has to feed his animals every day.

Challenge Words

Check (✔) the words you already know.

☐ had best   ☐ had better

6. Pronouns / Reflexive Pronouns

Check (✔) the words you already know. Then, listen and repeat.

Tracks 1–12

□ she
TR 1

□ it
TR 2

□ he
□ him
TR 5 and TR 6

□ I
□ me
TR 3 and TR 4

You look nice today.

□ myself
TR 7

I first learned to dress **myself** when I was four.

□ you
TR 8

□ us
□ we
□ them
□ they
TR 9, TR 10, TR 11, and TR 12

Definitions

You use **he** to talk about a man, a boy, or a male animal as the subject of a sentence.

You use **him** to talk about a man, a boy, or a male animal.

You use **I** to talk about yourself as the subject of a sentence.

You use **it** when you are talking about an object, an animal, a thing, or a situation that you have already mentioned.

A speaker uses **me** when talking about himself or herself.

A speaker uses **myself** when talking about something done to oneself.

You use **she** to talk about a woman, a girl, or a female animal as the subject of a sentence.

You use **them** to talk about more than one person, animal, or thing.

You use **they** when you are talking about more than one person, animal, or thing as the subject of a sentence.

You use **us** to talk about yourself and the person or people with you.

A speaker or writer uses **we** to talk about both himself or herself and about one or more other people as a group. It is used as the subject of a sentence.

A speaker or writer uses **you** to refer to the person or people being spoken to or written to.

Check Your Understanding

A. Write the words from the word bank in the correct column. One word will be used more than once.

I	us	it	we
he	me	him	them
they	she	you	myself

WORDS USED TO TALK ABOUT ONLY YOURSELF	WORDS USED TO TALK ABOUT A GROUP THAT INCLUDES YOU	WORDS USED TO TALK ABOUT A GROUP THAT DOES NOT INCLUDE YOU	SOMEONE YOU ARE TALKING TO

MALE PERSON OR ANIMAL	FEMALE PERSON OR ANIMAL	SOMETHING THAT ISN'T LIVING

B. Underline the correct words to complete each sentence.

1. (**Him / I**) heard the puppy barking, so I took (**it / myself**) for a walk.

2. (**She / Him**) told (**me / myself**) to write my name on the paper.

3. After the ceremony, (**they / it**) ran to show (**us / we**) their awards.

4. Before (**us / we**) ate dinner, my mom said, "(**You / They**) need to wash your hands."

5. (**He / Him**) loved to read stories to (**they / them**) before they went to sleep.

6. Before my presentation, (**me / I**) told (**myself / me**) not to be scared.

7. "(**You / Them**) can't do that!" I yelled at (**us / him**).

8. Every year, (**it / she**) bought (**us / we**) new outfits for the first day of school.

Challenge Words

Check (✔) the words you already know.

☐ herself   ☐ himself   ☐ itself   ☐ yourself

7. Possessive Pronouns

Check (✔) the words you already know. Then, listen and repeat.

 Tracks 1–12

☐ **our**   **Our** food

TR 1

The food is **ours**.   ☐ **ours**

TR 2

☐ **his**

TR 5

His MP3 player

☐ **its**

TR 6

Its house

☐ **their**

TR 9

Their food
The food is **theirs**.

☐ **theirs**

TR 10

12

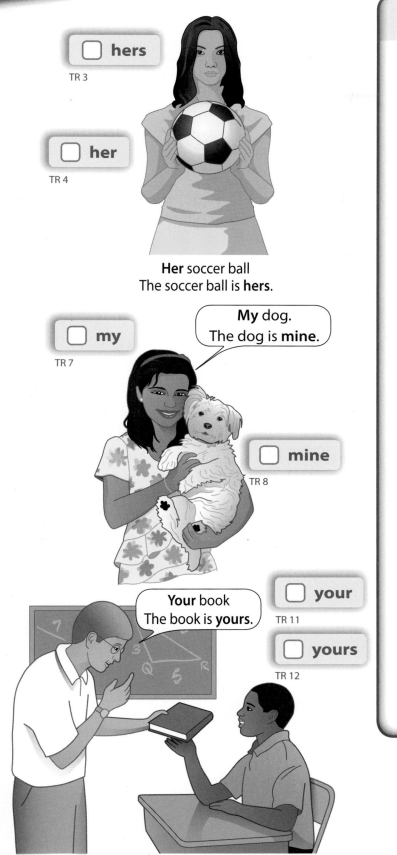

hers
TR 3

her
TR 4

Her soccer ball
The soccer ball is **hers**.

My dog.
The dog is **mine**.

my
TR 7

mine
TR 8

Your book
The book is **yours**.

your
TR 11

yours
TR 12

Definitions

You use **her** to show that something belongs to or relates to a girl or a woman.

You use **hers** to show that something belongs to a woman or a girl.

You use **his** to show that something belongs to or relates to a man or a boy.

You use **its** to show that something belongs or relates to a thing, a place, or an animal that has just been mentioned.

Mine means belonging to me.

You use **my** to show that something belongs or relates to yourself.

You use **our** to show that something belongs or relates both to you and to one or more other people.

You use **ours** when you are talking about something that belongs to you and one or more other people.

You use **their** to show that something belongs to or relates to the group of people, animals or things that you are talking about.

You use **theirs** to show that something belongs to or relates to the group of people, animals, or things that you are talking about.

You use **your** to show that something belongs to or relates to the person or people that you are talking or writing to.

You use **yours** when you mean something that belongs to or relates to the person or people that you are talking to.

13

Check Your Understanding

A. Write the words from the word bank in the correct category. Some words are used more than once.

my	her	his	ours
its	mine	our	their
yours	your	hers	theirs

BELONGS TO YOU	BELONGS TO A FEMALE	BELONGS TO A MALE	BELONGS TO A PERSON YOU ARE TALKING TO

BELONGS TO A GROUP YOU ARE PART OF	BELONGS TO A GROUP YOU ARE NOT A PART OF	BELONGS TO A THING OR AN ANIMAL

B. Underline the correct word to complete each sentence.

1. Marie found (**her / hers**) wallet under her bed.

2. After I walked home in the rain, (**my / mine**) hair was very wet.

3. Is that notebook (**your / yours**)?

4. (**Their / Theirs**) jackets are by the front door.

5. That ball is (**our / ours**).

6. My cat loves sleeping on (**it / its**) bed in the sun.

7. John drove (**his / her**) father's car to the store.

8. WH-question Words

Check (✔) the words you already know. Then, listen and repeat.

 Tracks 1–4

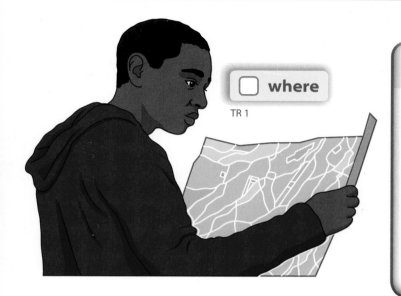

☐ **where**
TR 1

Definitions

You use **what** in questions when you ask for information.

You use **when** to ask questions about the time at which things happen or happened.

You use **where** to ask questions about the place someone or something is in.

You use **which** to talk about a choice between two or more possible people or things.

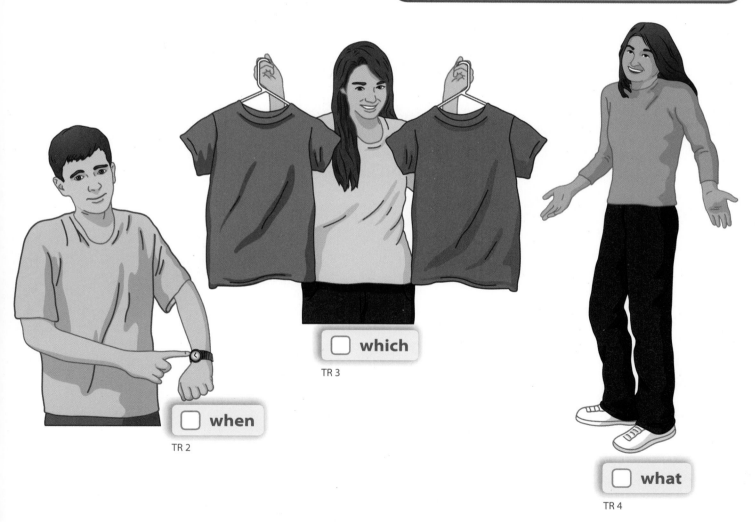

☐ **which**
TR 3

☐ **when**
TR 2

☐ **what**
TR 4

Check Your Understanding

A. Underline the correct word to complete each question.

1. (**Where / When**) is the library?

2. (**When / What**) is your address?

3. (**Which / When**) does the meeting start?

4. (**Where / Which**) color do you like the best?

B. Match each word to the correct description. One description will not be used.

1. _____ what
2. _____ when
3. _____ where
4. _____ which

a. the time something happens

b. the place something is located

c. the way something works

d. choice between two or more things

e. information

Challenge Words

Check (✔) the word you already know.

☐ whichever

11. Relative Pronouns

Check (✔) the words you already know. Then, listen and repeat.

 Tracks 1–3

The house **that** I live in is over there.

☐ **that**

TR 1

Definitions

You use **that** to show which person or thing you are talking about.

You use **which** when you want to show the exact thing that you are talking about.

You use **who** to talk about the identity of a person or a group of people.

KNOCK KNOCK KNOCK

The woman **who** lives next door is knocking.

☐ **who**

TR 2

The red house, **which** I lived in for five years, is now for sale.

☐ **which**

TR 3

Check Your Understanding

A. Underline the correct word to complete each sentence.

1. That is the girl (**who** / **which**) was working at the grocery store yesterday.

2. Nelson has a jacket (**that** / **who**) he only wears on special occasions.

3. My car, (**which** / **who**) is parked between the two black cars, is very old.

4. Our coach, (**who** / **which**) will soon retire, has been at our school for 20 years.

B. Match each word to the correct description. One description will not be used.

1. _____ who

2. _____ that

3. _____ which

a. shows the name of a person or a group of people

b. shows which person or thing you are talking about

c. shows the exact thing that you are talking about

d. shows the identity of a person or a group of people

Challenge Words

Check (✔) the word you already know.

☐ whom

12. Indefinite/Interrogative Adverbs

Check (✔) the words you already know. Then, listen and repeat.

Tracks 1–2

How did this happen?

☐ **how**
TR 1

Why are you crying?

☐ **why**
TR 2

Definitions

You use **how** to ask about the way that something happens or is done.

You use **why** in questions when you ask about the reasons for something.

Check Your Understanding

A. Underline the correct word to complete each question.

1. **a:** (**How** / **Why**) did you learn to swim?

   b: I took swimming lessons.

2. **a:** (**How** / **Why**) are you crying?

   b: I am crying because I hurt myself.

3. **a:** (**How** / **Why**) did you build that birdhouse?

   b: I built it with my uncle. He told me what to do.

4. **a:** (**How** / **Why**) do you need to leave early?

   b: I need to leave early because I have a doctor's appointment.

B. Write **T** for **true statements** and **F** for **false statements**.

1. _____ You use *why* in a question when you want to know the reason for something.

2. _____ You use *why* in a question when you want directions to a location.

3. _____ You use *how* in a question when you want to know the way something happens.

4. _____ You use *how* in a question when you want to know the way something is done.

Challenge Words

Check (✔) the words you already know.

☐ somehow   ☐ someway   ☐ whenever   ☐ wherever

34. Indefinite Pronouns

Check (✔) the words you already know. Then, listen and repeat.

Tracks 1–13

There is **something** in the box.

☐ **something**

TR 5

☐ **no one**
☐ **nobody**

TR 1 and TR 2

☐ **somebody**
☐ **someone**

TR 3 and TR 4

Yes, **anybody** can go.

Can **anyone** go?

There is **nothing** in the box.

☐ **nothing**

TR 11

☐ **enough**

TR 8

☐ **anybody**
☐ **anyone**

TR 9 and TR 10

$5.00
any item

☐ any

TR 6

I am not hungry. I do not want to eat **anything**.

☐ anything

TR 7

☐ some

TR 12

Definitions

You use **any** when you are referring to any person or thing in a group.

You use **anybody** and **anyone** to talk about someone when the exact person is not important.

You use **anything** to talk about something when the exact thing is not important.

You use **each** to talk about every person or thing.

Enough means as much as you need.

No one and **nobody** mean not a single person.

Nothing means not a single thing.

You use **some** to talk about an unidentified amount of something or number of people.

You use **somebody** and **someone** to talk about a person without saying exactly who you mean.

You use **something** to talk about an unknown thing or a situation.

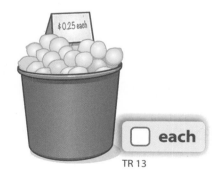

$ 0.25 each

☐ each

TR 13

Check Your Understanding

A. Write each word from the word bank by the correct description. More than one word may apply to a definition.

anyone	any	each	some
no one	someone	nobody	enough
anything	something	somebody	nothing
anybody			

1. _____ : used to talk about an unknown thing or situation

2. _____ : not a single person

3. _____ : something when the exact thing is not important

4. _____ : an unidentified amount of things or people

5. _____ : not a single thing

6. _____ : a person that is not specific

7. _____ : the amount that is needed

8. _____ : used to talk about any person or thing in a group

9. _____ : used to talk about every person or thing

B. Underline the correct word to complete each sentence or question.

1. Sonia had (**nothing / something**) to write with, so she borrowed a pen from Caitlin.
2. Daisy showed Ann (**some / any**) pictures from her vacation.
3. (**Nobody / Somebody**) wanted dessert because they were too full.
4. There is a notebook and a pencil on (**each / any**) desk.
5. Does (**anybody / anything**) want to play hockey tonight?
6. I will ask (**some / someone**) for directions if I get lost.
7. Joanne can play (**any / enough**) sport and have a good time.
8. Jonathan's dog will eat (**anything / enough**) that is put in his bowl.
9. (**Someone / No one**) spoke during the test, so the classroom was very quiet.
10. There is (**anything / something**) I need to discuss with you.
11. Samantha heard (**somebody / anyone**) knocking at the door.
12. There are (**enough / each**) people here to play a game of basketball.
13. Does (**anyone / each**) need me to repeat the instructions?

Challenge Words

Check (✔) the word if you already know it.

☐ whoever

10. Cause / Effect (Relationship Markers)

Check (✔) the words you already know. Then, listen and repeat.

Tracks 1–10

I have this umbrella **because** it's raining.

☐ **because**
TR 1

This letter is **from** my grandma.

☐ **from**
TR 2

Definitions

You use **because** when you are giving the reason for something.

If an event or situation happens **because of** something, that thing is the reason or cause.

If something is done **by** a person or thing, that person or thing does it.

You use **for** to talk about the purpose or reason for something.

If something comes **from** a particular person or thing, that person or thing is the source of it.

You use **if** to talk about the result or effect of things that might happen or be true.

You use **since** when you are giving the reason for something.

You use **so** to introduce the result of a situation.

You use **then** to say that one thing happens after another.

You use **to** when you are talking about how something changes.

These are **for** art class.

☐ **for**
TR 3

If I practice every day, I'll play very well.

☐ **if**
TR 4

We won the game **because of** the goal you scored!

☐ **because of**
TR 5

☐ **to**
TR 6

It changed from a caterpillar **to** a butterfly.

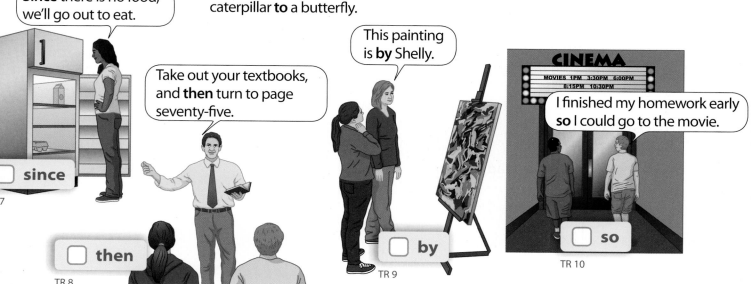

Since there is no food, we'll go out to eat.

☐ **since**
TR 7

Take out your textbooks, and **then** turn to page seventy-five.

☐ **then**
TR 8

This painting is **by** Shelly.

☐ **by**
TR 9

CINEMA
MOVIES 1PM 3:30PM 6:00PM
8:15PM 10:30PM

I finished my homework early **so** I could go to the movie.

☐ **so**
TR 10

Check Your Understanding

A. Underline the correct word to complete each sentence.

1. Maria needs glasses (**because / for**) driving at night.

2. Raphael switched from the baseball team (**to / so**) the basketball team.

3. Andre went to the store (**because / so**) he needed to buy a new pair of jeans.

4. We can leave now (**then / if**) you are ready.

5. Tina folded the blankets, and (**then / from**) she put them in the closet.

6. Liza was late to work (**because of / since**) the traffic on the freeway.

7. These peaches come (**for / from**) the tree in our backyard.

8. Danny and Aaron wanted to go swimming, (**so / by**) they went to the pool.

9. This play is written (**because / by**) a very famous writer.

10. (**Then / Since**) Melanie cannot drive, her dad drove her to her friend's house.

B. Write **T** for **true statements** and **F** for **false statements**.

1. _____ The word *from* tells who receives something.

2. _____ The word *to* tells how something changes.

3. _____ The word *for* tells the purpose of something.

4. _____ The word *by* tells who something is for.

5. _____ The words *because of* tell the reason something happened.

6. _____ The word *because* means the same thing as the word *from*.

7. _____ The word *so* tells the cause of a situation.

8. _____ The word *if* tells the result of something that might happen.

9. _____ The word *since* tells the reason for something.

10. _____ The word *then* tells that one thing happened before another thing.

Challenge Words

Check (✔) the words you already know.

☐ if only   ☐ if … then

273. Cause / Effect

Check (✔) the words you already know. Then, listen and repeat.

Tracks 1–7

I want to **change** my hairstyle.

☐ **change**
TR 1

☐ **cause**
TR 2

☐ **effect**
TR 3

Definitions

The **cause** of an event is what makes it happen.

A **change** is when something becomes different.

The **effect** is the result of something.

The **outcome** of an activity is the situation that exists at the end of it.

The **purpose** of something is the reason why you do it.

The **reason** for something is the purpose for doing it.

A **result** is the consequence for an action.

☐ **purpose**
TR 4

☐ **outcome**
☐ **result**
TR 5 and TR 6

I am putting on sun block to protect my skin.

☐ **reason**
TR 7

Check Your Understanding

A. Match each word to the correct description. One description will not be used.

1. _____ cause
2. _____ change
3. _____ effect
4. _____ outcome
5. _____ purpose
6. _____ reason
7. _____ result

a. something that makes something happen
b. the result of something
c. the reason why you do something
d. the consequence of an action
e. to cause something to change in some way
f. the purpose for doing something
g. the situation at the end of an event
h. to become different

B. Circle the word that occurs first.

1. outcome   purpose
2. effect   cause
3. reason   result
4. cause   change

Challenge Words

Check (✔) the words you already know.

- ☐ affect
- ☐ consequence
- ☐ impact
- ☐ impress
- ☐ incentive
- ☐ influence
- ☐ initiate
- ☐ intent
- ☐ motive
- ☐ vary

9. Direction To and From

Check (✔) the words you already know. Then, listen and repeat.

Tracks 1–3

☐ **at**

TR 1

Definitions

You use **at** to say where something happens or is located.

If you move **from** a place, you leave it.

If you move **to** a place, you move in its direction or toward it.

☐ **to**

TR 2

☐ **from**

TR 3

Check Your Understanding

A. Choose the correct word from the word bank to complete each sentence. Some words will be used more than once.

at	to	from

1. Marta traveled _____ Australia to Argentina.

2. I was _____ school on Monday.

3. Tim came _____ our house after he finished his homework.

4. Shelly went _____ the doctor this morning.

5. Matt and Ray are _____ the post office.

B. Choose the sentence that correctly uses the underlined word.

1. a. Gabe came <u>from</u> Brazil to the United States.

   b. He went <u>from</u> Florida on vacation.

2. a. They are <u>to</u> her office.

   b. My mom went <u>to</u> my school and talked to my teacher.

3. a. Please give your test <u>at</u> me.

   b. Please write your name <u>at</u> the top of the paper.

4. a. They walked <u>to</u> Paul's Pizza after the movie.

   b. They are <u>to</u> the movies.

5. a. Leila moved <u>from</u> Chicago to Boston.

   b. She is <u>from</u> the store right now.

Challenge Words

Check (✔) the words you already know.

☐ bound for   ☐ hither

17. Directions

Check (✔) the words you already know. Then, listen and repeat.

 Tracks 1–6

☐ **left**
TR 1

☐ **right**
TR 2

Definitions

The **east** is the direction in front of you when you are watching the sun rise.

Your **left** arm, hand, or leg is the one that is on or by the side of the body containing the heart.

The **north** is the direction to your left when you are watching the sun rise.

Your **right** arm, hand, or leg is the one that is on the right side of your body.

The **south** is the direction to your right when you are watching the sun rise.

The **west** is the direction in front of you when you are watching the sun set.

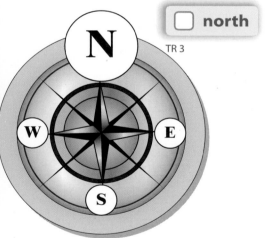

☐ **north**
TR 3

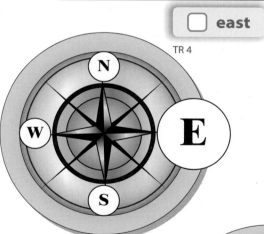

☐ **east**
TR 4

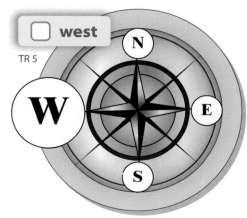

☐ **west**
TR 5

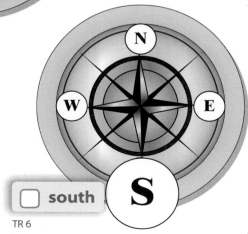

☐ **south**
TR 6

Check Your Understanding

A. Choose the sentence that correctly uses the underlined word.

1. a. Turn <u>right</u> at Main Street.

    b. The sun sets in the <u>right</u> every evening.

2. a. A lot of birds fly <u>south</u> for the winter.

    b. The library will be on your <u>south</u> side.

3. a. The sun rises in the <u>east</u>.

    b. There is dirt on your <u>east</u> shoe.

4. a. Make a <u>north</u> turn when you see the restaurant.

    b. There are some good restaurants <u>north</u>
       of the city.

5. a. I write with my <u>west</u> hand.

    b. Drive <u>west</u> on the highway.

6. a. The kitchen is on the <u>left</u> side of the apartment.

    b. We are going down <u>left</u> for vacation.

B. Circle the words that are the opposite of each other.

1. left   right   east

2. east   north   west

3. left   north   south

Challenge Words

Check (✔) the words you already know.

- ☐ midwest
- ☐ northeast
- ☐ northeastern
- ☐ northern
- ☐ northwest
- ☐ southeast
- ☐ southeastern
- ☐ southern
- ☐ southwest

20. Distances

Check (✔) the words you already know. Then, listen and repeat.

Tracks 1–16

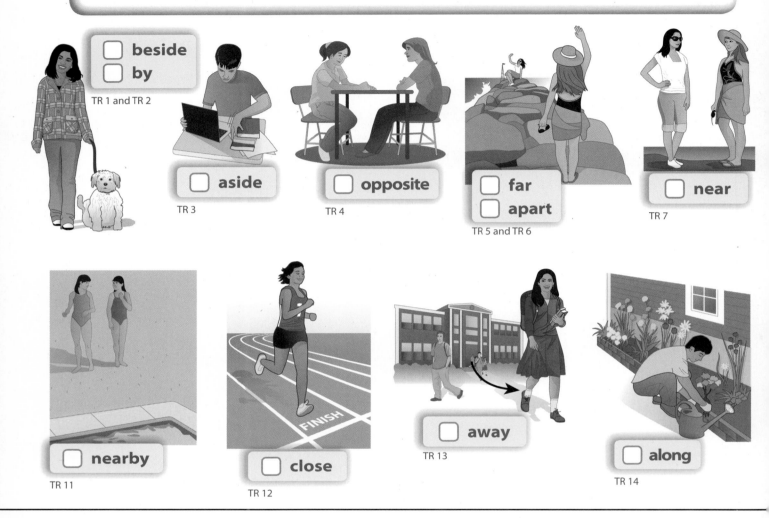

- ☐ beside
- ☐ by

TR 1 and TR 2

- ☐ aside

TR 3

- ☐ opposite

TR 4

- ☐ far
- ☐ apart

TR 5 and TR 6

- ☐ near

TR 7

- ☐ nearby

TR 11

- ☐ close

TR 12

- ☐ away

TR 13

- ☐ along

TR 14

Check Your Understanding

A. Circle the word in each group that does not belong.

1. away	between	far
2. beside	by	toward
3. apart	close	near
4. beyond	nearby	past
5. outer	by	near
6. opposite	along	aside

☐ **past**

TR 8

She drove **past** the exit.

☐ **toward**

R 9

☐ **between**

TR 10

☐ **outer**

TR 16

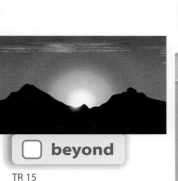

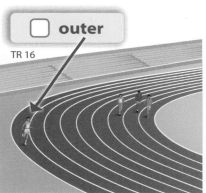

☐ **beyond**

TR 15

Definitions

If something is **along** a place or thing, it is beside it.

When people or things are **apart**, they are some distance from each other.

If you move something **aside**, you move it to one side of you.

If someone or something moves **away** from a place, they move so that they are no longer there.

Something that is **beside** something else is next to it.

If something is **between** two people or things, it is in the space separating the two.

Something that is **beyond** a place is on the other side of it, or farther away from it.

Someone or something that is **by** something else is beside it.

Something that is **close** to something else is near to it.

If one place, thing, or person is **far** from another, there is a great distance between them.

If one place, thing, or person is **near** another, there is a short distance between them.

If something is **nearby**, it is close to something or someone.

If one person or thing is **opposite** another, it is across from that person or thing.

The **outer** parts of something are farthest from the center.

If you go **past** someone or something, you pass that person or thing.

If you move **toward** something or someone, you move in the direction of that thing or person.

B. Circle the correct word to complete each sentence.

1. Sit across from me on the _____ side of the table.

   a. outer   b. opposite   c. along

2. The cat slept _____ the bed and the dresser.

   a. between   b. close   c. apart

3. The dog sat _____ the door with a leash in its mouth.

   a. aside   b. far   c. by

4. The restaurant was _____ to the mall, so Lanie and Jill walked there.

    a. by   b. close   c. away

5. Jonathan walked _____ us when he saw us arrive.

    a. toward   b. aside   c. along

6. Jay's grandparents live _____ from him, so he hardly gets to see them.

    a. near   b. far   c. beyond

7. Liz and I live 20 minutes _____ from each other.

    a. toward   b. nearby   c. apart

8. Nelson sat _____ the front of the classroom to see the board better.

    a. near   b. beside   c. past

9. Tania pushed the sandwich _____ and said she would eat it later.

    a. close   b. aside   c. beyond

10. Scott walked _____ from school and headed home.

    a. toward   b. along   c. away

11. There is a grocery store _____, so we can just walk there.

    a. nearby   b. far   c. aside

12. John sat _____ Cindy to show her pictures from his vacation.

    a. beside   b. between   c. past

13. The lake is _____ these trees.

    a. aside   b. away   c. beyond

14. Bill drove _____ the house quickly.

    a. along   b. past   c. far

15. Kevin lives in the _____ part of the city, away from the center.

    a. away   b. apart   c. outer

16. Linda walked _____ the shore slowly.

    a. along   b. close   c. away

Challenge Words

Check (✔) the words you already know.

- ☐ abreast
- ☐ abroad
- ☐ closeness
- ☐ contact
- ☐ distant
- ☐ homeward
- ☐ local
- ☐ overseas
- ☐ remote
- ☐ yonder

21. Front / Middle / Back

Check (✔) the words you already know. Then, listen and repeat.

Tracks 1–14

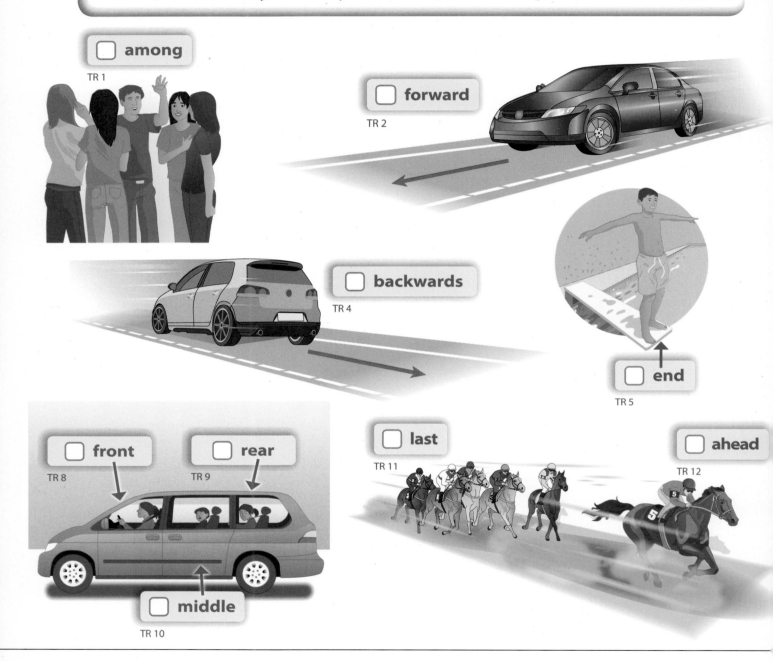

☐ **among**
TR 1

☐ **forward**
TR 2

☐ **backwards**
TR 4

☐ **end**
TR 5

☐ **front**
TR 8

☐ **rear**
TR 9

☐ **middle**
TR 10

☐ **last**
TR 11

☐ **ahead**
TR 12

Check Your Understanding

A. Circle the word in each group that does not belong.

1. front   middle   center
2. last   ahead of   end
3. behind   front   back

back

TR 3

center

TR 6

backward

TR 7

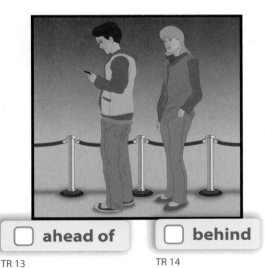

ahead of

TR 13

behind

TR 14

Definitions

Someone or something that is **ahead** is in front of you.

If someone is **ahead of** you, that person is in front of you.

Someone or something that is **among** a group of things or people is surrounded by them.

The **back** of something is the side or part of it that is farthest from the front.

A **backward** movement or look is in the direction that your back is facing.

If you move **backwards**, you move in the direction that your back is facing.

If something is **behind** a thing or person, it is at the back of that thing or person.

The **center** of something is the middle of it.

The **end** of an object is the tip or farthest part of it.

If you move or look **forward**, you move in the direction that is in front of you.

The **front** of something is the part of it that faces you, or that faces forward.

The **last** thing or person is the only one that is left.

The **middle** of something is the part of it that is farthest from its edges or ends.

The **rear** of something is the back part of it.

4. back   among   rear

5. ahead   front   center

6. backwards   last   forward

B. Write **T** for **true statements** and **F** for **false statements**.

1. _____ If you move backwards, you move in the direction the front part of your body is facing.

2. _____ Someone who is ahead of you is far behind you.

3. _____ The back of something is the part farthest from the front.

4. _____ If you are behind something, you are at the front of it.

5. _____ The end of a road is the farthest part of it.

6. _____ If you move forward, you move in the direction that is in front of you.

7. _____ The front of something is the part that faces forward.

8. _____ The middle of something is the part that is closest to its edges.

9. _____ If you are last in line, no one is standing in front of you.

10. _____ If people are ahead of you, they are in front of you.

11. _____ The center of something is the middle of it.

12. _____ If you look backward, you look in the direction your back is facing.

13. _____ The rear of something is the front part of it.

14. _____ If you are standing among people, they are surrounding you.

Challenge Words

Check (✔) the words you already know.

☐ background   ☐ core   ☐ forth   ☐ intermediate   ☐ midst

☐ central   ☐ fore   ☐ hind   ☐ medium   ☐ midway

22. In / Out

Check (✔) the words you already know. Then, listen and repeat.

Tracks 1–13

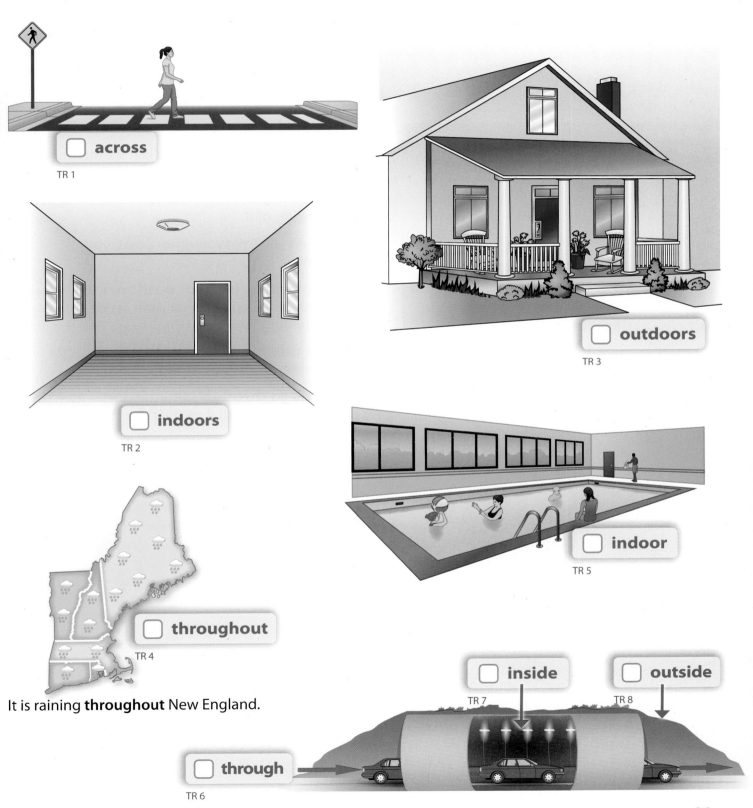

☐ **across**

TR 1

☐ **indoors**

TR 2

☐ **outdoors**

TR 3

☐ **indoor**

TR 5

☐ **throughout**

TR 4

It is raining **throughout** New England.

☐ **inside**

TR 7

☐ **outside**

TR 8

☐ **through**

TR 6

39

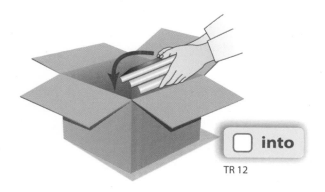

enter

TR 9

within

TR 10

out

TR 11

into

TR 12

in

TR 13

Definitions

If you go **across** a place, you go from one side of it to the other.

When you **enter** a place such as a room or a building, you go into it.

You use **in** when you are describing the location within something.

Indoor activities happen inside a building and not outside.

If something happens **indoors**, it happens inside a building.

The **inside** of something is the inner part of it.

If you put one thing **into** another thing, it is inside of it.

When you take something **out**, you remove it from a place.

If something happens **outdoors**, it happens outside rather than inside a building.

The **outside** of something is the outside or exterior surface of something.

If you go **through** something, you go from one side of it to the other side.

If something happens or exists **throughout** a place, it happens or exists in all parts of that place.

If something is **within** a place, area, or object, it is inside it or surrounded by it.

Check Your Understanding

A. Circle the word in each group that does not belong.

1. within   through   across

2. outside   inside   outdoors

3. indoor   across   indoors

4. enter   throughout   into

5. in   inside   out

B. Complete the sentence by unscrambling the word in parentheses.

1. We _____ (trnee) the house through the garage when it is raining.

2. The ship sailed _____ (scaros) the ocean.

3. He took the laptop _____ (tou) of his bag.

4. She put the keys _____ (snidei) her purse.

5. Allen walked _____ (rothugh) the hall and into the kitchen.

6. Lana put the berries _____ (tino) a basket.

7. We are playing _____ (dronoi) hockey in the gym today.

8. Ms. Andrews told her class to stay _____ (winith) the boundaries of the playground.

9. George likes to be _____ (todorsuo) on sunny days.

10. The paint on the _____ (distuoe) of the house is peeling.

11. Please put litter _____ (ni) the trash can.

12. We should go _____ (nidrsoo) if it starts to rain.

13. There are many farms _____ (rogthohutu) this part of the country.

Challenge Words

Check (✔) the words you already know.

- ☐ embark
- ☐ external
- ☐ inner
- ☐ internal
- ☐ outward
- ☐ exterior
- ☐ inland
- ☐ interior
- ☐ inward
- ☐ overboard

23. Down / Under

Check (✔) the words you already know. Then, listen and repeat.

Tracks 1–10

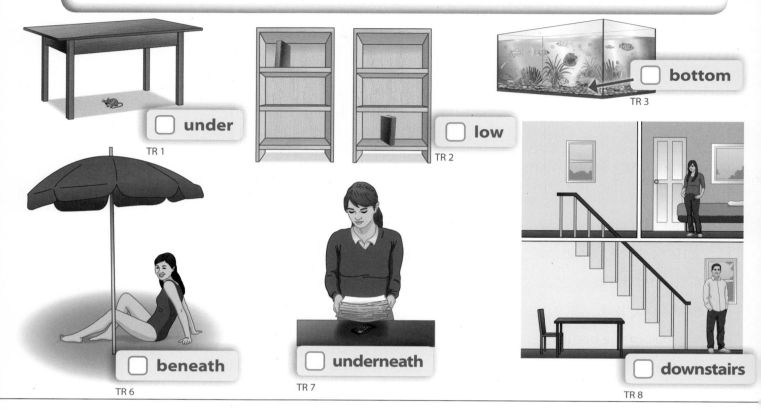

☐ **under**
TR 1

☐ **low**
TR 2

☐ **bottom**
TR 3

☐ **beneath**
TR 6

☐ **underneath**
TR 7

☐ **downstairs**
TR 8

Check Your Understanding

A. Circle the word that matches each description.

1. to be on a lower floor in a building	a. down	b. downstairs	c. underneath
2. to move or look toward a lower location	a. low	b. downward	c. downhill
3. to move down a slope	a. under	b. down	c. downhill
4. toward a lower level	a. down	b. low	c. beneath
5. below	a. under	b. bottom	c. downstairs
6. close to the ground	a. low	b. beneath	c. downward
7. under	a. downhill	b. bottom	c. beneath
8. in a lower position	a. low	b. underneath	c. below
9. below or under	a. down	b. underneath	c. bottom
10. the lowest or deepest part	a. bottom	b. downward	c. below

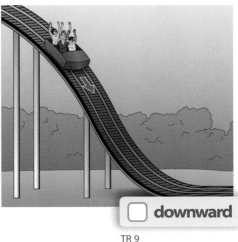

☐ **down**
TR 5

☐ **downhill**
TR 4

☐ **below**
TR 10

☐ **downward**
TR 9

Definitions

If something is **below** something else, it is in a lower position.

Something that is **beneath** another thing is under it.

The **bottom** of something is the lowest or deepest part of it.

Down means toward a lower level, or in a lower place.

If something or someone is moving **downhill**, that thing or person is moving down a slope.

If someone or something is **downstairs** in a building, that person or thing is on a lower floor than you.

If you move or look **downward**, you move or look toward the ground or a lower level.

If something is **low**, it is close to the ground or floor.

If a person or a thing is **under** something, that person or thing is below it.

If one thing is **underneath** another, it is below or under it.

B. Underline the correct word to complete each sentence.

1. Lisa left her shoes at the (**bottom** / **down**) of the stairs.

2. I am wearing a T-shirt (**low** / **underneath**) my sweater.

3. Michelle went (**below** / **downstairs**) to help her father with dinner.

4. Andy keeps a spare key (**downward** / **under**) a rock by the front door.

5. The old house had very (**downhill** / **low**) ceilings.

6. Natalie and her friends raced (**downhill** / **under**) on their sleds.

7. There are fish swimming (**low** / **beneath**) the surface of the water.

8. Jon happily pointed (**beneath** / **downward**) to the dollar on the sidewalk.

9. Emma put the baby (**down** / **bottom**) in the crib after he fell asleep.

10. Anna's apartment is (**below** / **downstairs**) Leo's apartment.

Challenge Words

Check (✔) the words you already know.

☐ downwind ☐ underfoot ☐ underground ☐ undergrowth

25. Locations (Nonspecific)

Check (✔) the words you already know. Then, listen and repeat.

Tracks 1–7

Meet me **here** in 2 hours.

☐ here

TR 1

We are going **there**.

☐ there

TR 2

Where do you want to sit?

Anywhere.

☐ anywhere

TR 5

☐ where

TR 3

Where were we supposed to meet?

Check Your Understanding

A. Circle the correct description for each word.

1. someplace
   a. not in any place
   b. a specific place
   c. a place that is not specific

2. there
   a. a place that is not specific
   b. a place you are referring to
   c. the place where you are

3. nowhere
   a. not in any place
   b. a place in which something happens
   c. the place where you are

4. here
   a. not in any place
   b. a place that is not specific
   c. the place where you are

5. anywhere
   a. a specific place
   b. the exact place is not important
   c. not in any place

6. somewhere
   a. a place that is not specific
   b. a place in which something happens
   c. a specific place

7. where
   a. a place that is not specific
   b. a place in which something happens
   c. not in any place

We should go **somewhere** far away for vacation.

☐ **somewhere**
TR 4

☐ **nowhere**
TR 6

Where do you want to go on vacation?

Someplace warm.

☐ **someplace**
TR 7

Definitions

You use **anywhere** to talk about a place when the exact place is not important.

You use **here** when you are talking about the place where you are.

You use **nowhere** to mean "not in any place" or "not to any place."

You use **someplace** to talk about a place without saying exactly where you mean.

You use **somewhere** to talk about a place without saying exactly where you mean.

You use **there** to talk about a place that you are pointing to or looking at.

You use **where** to talk about a place in which something is situated or happens.

B. Underline the correct word to complete each sentence.

1. The bus was empty so Gloria could sit (**nowhere / anywhere**).

2. The police looked everywhere, but the thief was (**nowhere / somewhere**) to be found.

3. Emily is standing over (**there / anywhere**) with Nelson.

4. Mr. Anderson told the team (**nowhere / where**) to meet before the game.

5. Sarah wants to go (**here / someplace**) special for her birthday dinner.

6. Dylan and Pete went to find (**anywhere / somewhere**) to sit.

7. There is a sandwich and an apple (**here / where**) on the table.

Challenge Words

Check (✔) the words you already know.

☐ all over   ☐ elsewhere

45

26. Up / On

Check (✔) the words you already know. Then, listen and repeat.

 Tracks 1–16

☐ **high**
TR 1

☐ **aboard**
TR 2

☐ **over**
TR 3

☐ **upward**
TR 7

☐ **above**
TR 8

☐ **upstairs**
TR 6

☐ **off**
TR 11

☐ **onto**
TR 12

☐ **upon**
TR 13

top
TR 4

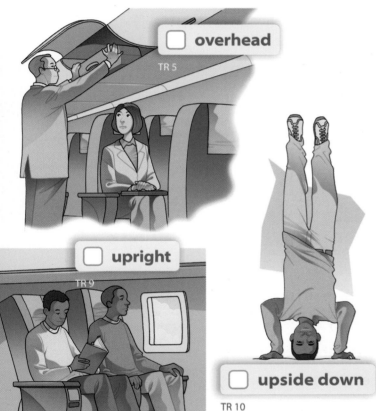
overhead
TR 5

upright
TR 9

upside down
TR 10

Definitions

If you are **aboard** a ship or plane, you are on it or in it.

If one thing is **above** another, it is over it or higher than it.

Something that is **high** extends a long way from the bottom to the top.

If you take something **off** another thing, it is no longer on it.

If you are **on** a surface, you are resting on it.

If something moves **onto** a surface, it moves to a position on that surface.

If something is **over** another thing, it is at a higher level than something else.

Something that is **overhead** is above you.

The **tip** of something long and narrow is the end of it.

The **top** of something is its highest point.

Up means toward a higher place.

Upon means on.

If you are sitting or standing **upright**, you are sitting or standing up straight.

If something is **upside down**, the part that is usually at the bottom is at the top.

If you go **upstairs** in a building, you walk up the stairs to a higher floor.

If someone or something moves **upward**, it moves from a lower place to a higher place.

on
TR 14

tip
TR 15

up
TR 16

Check Your Understanding

A. Circle the word in each group that does not belong.

1. on	upon	up
2. above	high	upside down
3. off	upright	upward
4. high	onto	aboard
5. upward	top	upstairs
6. tip	over	overhead

B. Underline the correct word to complete each sentence.

1. The cat climbed (**above / high**) up into the tree and could not get down.

2. Monique put the food (**on / off**) the table when it was time to eat.

3. The Florida Keys are islands located near the (**tip / upstairs**) of the state of Florida.

4. The helicopter flew (**onto / overhead**) on its way to the airport.

5. We walked (**upright / upstairs**) to the third floor.

6. Gina wants to hike to the (**over / top**) of the mountain.

7. Tim put the book back (**aboard / upon**) the shelf.

8. My little sister loves hanging (**upside down / over**) at the playground.

9. Louis sat (**off / upright**) in his chair.

10. The sand was hot when I stepped (**upstairs / onto**) it, so I put sandals on.

11. Tom looked (**upward / upside down**) toward the sky to see the stars.

12. John took the bowl (**on / off**) the shelf and set it on the table.

13. Elizabeth jumped (**upright / up**) and tried to see over the fence.

14. The plane flew (**up / above**) the clouds.

15. The bird flew (**over / high**) the trees.

16. We climbed (**aboard / overhead**) the plane and took our seats.

Challenge Words

Check (✔) the words you already know.

- [ ] atop
- [ ] peak
- [ ] pinnacle
- [ ] summit
- [ ] upland
- [ ] upper

37. Boundaries

Check (✔) the words you already know. Then, listen and repeat.

 Tracks 1–5

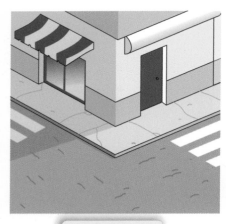

☐ **corner**

TR 1

☐ **margin**

TR 2

☐ **edge**

TR 3

Check Your Understanding

A. Match each word to the correct description. One description will not be used.

1. _____ corner

2. _____ edge

3. _____ limit

4. _____ margin

5. _____ side

a. the farthest point, the border

b. a particular location away from the side

c. a raised line on a flat surface

d. the place where something stops

e. the border where something begins or ends

f. where two sides come together

☐ **side**

TR 4

☐ **limit**

TR 5

Definitions

A **corner** is a point where two sides of something meet, or where one road meets another road.

The **edge** of something is the border where it begins or ends.

A **limit** is the farthest point or the border of an area of land.

A **margin** is the place where something stops or the edge of something.

The **side** of something is a particular location away from the center of it.

B. Underline the correct word to complete each sentence.

1. We rode our bikes all the way to the city (**limit / side**).

2. Linda moved the glass of water away from the (**limit / edge**) of the table.

3. The little girl hit her head on the (**margin / corner**) of the bookshelf and started crying.

4. Fred lives at the (**margin / corner**) of the city, so he's not close to the center.

5. The basketball court is on the left (**limit / side**) of the street.

Challenge Words

Check (✔) the words you already know.

☐ border   ☐ brim   ☐ flank   ☐ perimeter   ☐ rim

☐ bounds   ☐ brink   ☐ horizon   ☐ ridge   ☐ verge

51

49. Location (General)

Check (✔) the words you already know. Then, listen and repeat.

Tracks 1–7

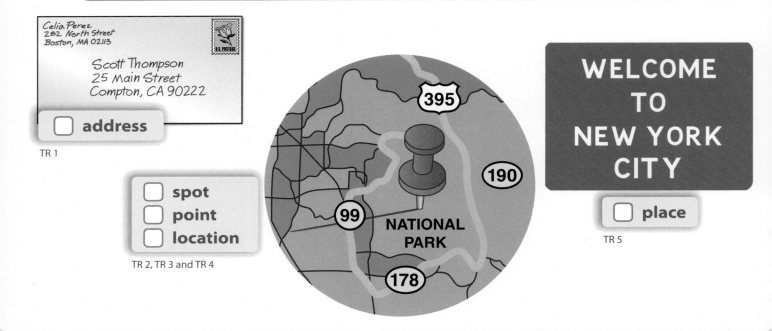

Celia Perez
282 North Street
Boston, MA 02113

Scott Thompson
25 Main Street
Compton, CA 90222

U.S. POSTAGE

☐ **address**

TR 1

☐ **spot**
☐ **point**
☐ **location**

TR 2, TR 3 and TR 4

395

190

99

NATIONAL PARK

178

WELCOME TO NEW YORK CITY

☐ **place**

TR 5

Check Your Understanding

A. Circle the correct word to complete each sentence.

1. We are walking in the _____ of the ocean.

   a. address   b. direction   c. place

2. Alex's _____ is 901 Washington Avenue, Dallas, TX 75246.

   a. spot   b. direction   c. address

3. We met Danny at a _____ halfway between our houses.

   a. point   b. address   c. direction

4. New York City is a popular _____ for tourists to visit.

   a. address   b. spot   c. position

5. I don't like the _____ of that table. Can we move it?

   a. spot   b. point   c. position

6. Amber found a nice, quiet _____ where we can study together.

   a. direction   b. place   c. position

7. What is the _____ of the drama club meeting?

   a. location   b. spot   c. place

Definitions

Your **address** is the number of the place or building, the name of the street, and the town or city and state where you live or work.

A **direction** is the general line that someone or something is moving or pointing in.

A **location** is the place where something is.

A **place** is a particular building, area, town, or country.

A **point** is a particular location or place.

The **position** is the place where someone or something is.

A particular place or area can be called a **spot**.

☐ direction

TR 6

☐ position

TR 7

B. Complete the sentences.

1. *Point* and *spot* are alike because _____.

2. *Location* and *position* are alike because _____.

3. *Place* and *address* are different because _____.

4. *Direction* and *position* are different because _____.

Challenge Words

Check (✔) the words you already know.

☐ altitude

☐ axis

☐ destination

☐ distance

☐ niche

☐ whereabouts

390. Geometric Planes

Check (✔) the word you already know. Then, listen and repeat.

Track 1

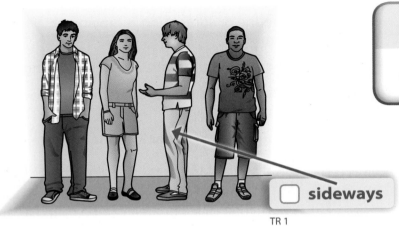

□ sideways

TR 1

Definition

If you do something **sideways**, you do it from or toward the side.

Check Your Understanding

A. Write **T** for **true statements** and **F** for **false statements**.

1. _____ People usually walk sideways.

2. _____ To pour water from a bottle, you must turn it sideways.

3. _____ When you look sideways, you are not looking in front of you.

B. Choose the sentence that correctly uses the underlined word.

1. a. We had to turn the desk <u>sideways</u> to fit it through the door.
   b. Marcus had to <u>sideways</u> through the door.

2. a. I watched the tiny crabs walk <u>sideways</u> across the beach.
   b. Nancy <u>sideways</u> down the beach.

3. a. Drew put the bottle on the table <u>sideways</u> so the juice wouldn't spill.
   b. Mike turned the bottle <u>sideways</u> to pour a glass of juice.

Challenge Words

Check (✔) the words you already know.

□ broadside   □ horizontal   □ perpendicular

□ diagonal   □ lateral   □ vertical

13. Specifiers

Check (✔) the words you already know. Then, listen and repeat.

Tracks 1–11

That bird is colorful.

☐ **that**

TR 1

You can **either** use tape or glue.

☐ **either**

TR 2

Those strawberries are delicious.

☐ **those**

TR 3

☐ **a**

TR 4

A lamp

☐ **this**

TR 5

This magazine is amazing.

☐ **an**

R 6

An armchair

☐ **every**
☐ **each**

TR 7 and TR 8

You can use **these** markers.

☐ **these**

TR 9

Definitions

You use **a** when you are talking about any person or thing of a particular type.

You use **an** when you are talking about any person or thing of a particular type, that begins with the sound of *a, e, i, o,* or *u.*

If you refer to **each** thing or **each** person in a group, you are referring to every member of the group and considering them as individuals.

Either means one or the other.

You use **every** to show that you are talking about all the members of a group.

No means not any or not one person or thing.

You use **that** to show which person or thing you are talking about.

You use **the** before a noun when it is clear which person or thing you are talking about.

You use **these** to talk about people or things that are near you, especially when you touch or point to that person or thing.

You use **this** to talk about a person or a thing that is near you, especially when you touch or point to that person or thing.

You use **those** when you are talking about people or things that are a distance away from you in position or time, especially when you point to them.

The blue mug

☐ **the**

TR 10

☐ **no**

TR 11

Check Your Understanding

A. Underline the correct word to complete each sentence.

1. There is (**a / an**) egg in the nest.

2. (**Each / That**) is the last piece of cake.

3. (**Every / that**) person in my family has brown hair.

4. Jim needs (**a / an**) new car.

5. Kayla filled (**each / either**) basket with fruit.

6. (**These / This**) are my favorite sandals.

7. (**A / No**) food is allowed in the computer lab.

8. Eric loved (**the / those**) movie.

9. Heidi does not like (**these / this**) song.

10. Mr. Joseph said the trip will (**either / each**) be this month or next month.

11. (**This / Those**) dogs across the street are barking too much.

B. Write **T** for **true statements** and **F** for **false statements**.

1. _____ *No* means not one person or thing.

2. _____ *These* refers to people or things that are not near the speaker.

3. _____ *Either* means one or the other.

4. _____ *Every* refers to all the members of a group.

5. _____ *Each* refers to not one person or thing.

6. _____ *The* is used before a noun someone is talking about.

7. _____ *This* refers to more than one person or thing that is near the speaker.

8. _____ *A* is used to talk about any person or thing of a particular type.

9. _____ *An* is used to talk about any person or thing of a particular type that begins with the sound of *a, e, i, o,* or *u.*

10. _____ *That* refers to which person or thing someone is talking about.

11. _____ *Those* refers to one person or thing that is not near the speaker.

15. Intensifiers

Check (✔) the words you already know. Then, listen and repeat.

Tracks 1–10

☐ **well**

It was **such** a damaging storm.

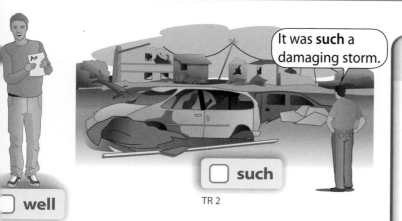

☐ **such**
TR 2

I'm **sure** I have the winning ticket!

☐ **most**
TR 4

☐ **more**
TR 5

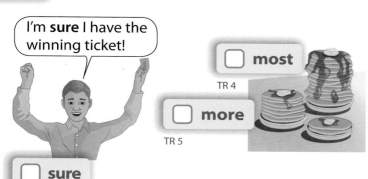

☐ **sure**
TR 3

Definitions

If something is done **badly**, it is done in a seriously bad way.

You use **more** to talk about a greater amount of something.

You use **most** to talk about the largest amount of people or things.

You use **much** to talk about the large amount of something.

You can use **so** in front of adjectives and adverbs to make them stronger.

You use **such** to make a noncount or plural noun stronger in quality, degree, or number.

If you are **sure** that something is true, you are certain about it.

You use **too** to mean very or extremely.

Very is used before an adjective to make it stronger.

If you do **well**, you are successful.

☐ **too**
TR 6

☐ **much**
TR 7

This path is **so** long!

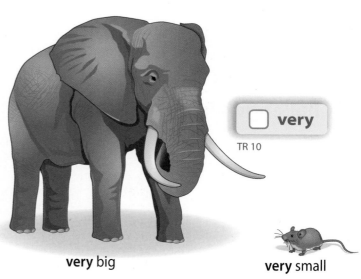

☐ **very**
TR 10

☐ **badly**
TR 9

☐ **so**
TR 8

The arm is **badly** broken.

very big

very small

Check Your Understanding

A. Write **T** for **true statements** and **F** for **false statements**.

1. _____ *Very* is used to make an adjective stronger.

2. _____ *Sure* means certain.

3. _____ *Badly* means that something has been done very successfully.

4. _____ *Such* is used to make some nouns stronger.

5. _____ *Most* means the smallest amount of people or things.

6. _____ *Well* means that something is not very successful.

7. _____ *More* is used to talk about a greater amount of something.

8. _____ *Too* means very or extremely.

9. _____ *Much* is used to talk about the small amount of something.

10. _____ *So* is used to make adjectives and adverbs stronger.

B. Underline the correct word to complete each sentence.

1. Heather needs (**more / most**) time to finish her project.

2. Diana was upset because she played (**well / badly**), and her team lost the game.

3. (**Most / Very**) of Jackie's friends are on vacation.

4. Arthur's parents were happy because he did (**well / sure**) on his exams.

5. Tammy's new perfume smells (**very / most**) good.

6. Jean has so (**such / much**) homework to do tonight.

7. Emily is (**sure / most**) that Nina will be on time.

8. Brandon has (**so / such**) much homework that he doesn't know where to begin.

9. That is (**very / such**) a small dog.

10. My aunt has (**too / such**) many cats.

Challenge Words

Check (✔) the words you already know.

☐ absolute(ly)　　☐ completely　　☐ extreme　　☐ intense　　☐ quite

☐ altogether　　☐ deeply　　☐ highly　　☐ perfectly　　☐ totally

18. Diminishers

Check (✔) the words you already know. Then, listen and repeat.

 Tracks 1–9

☐ **alone**

TR 1

The jar is **nearly** full.

☐ **nearly**

TR 2

☐ **mostly**

TR 3

☐ **simply**

TR 4

Definitions

Almost means nearly, but not completely.

When you are **alone**, you are not with other people.

Enough means as much as you need.

You use **hardly** in expressions such as **hardly any** to mean almost none.

Just means exactly.

Mostly means almost completely.

If something is **nearly** a particular amount, it is very close to that amount, but not exactly.

The **only** person or thing is the one person or thing of a particular type.

You use **simply** to say *only* or *just*.

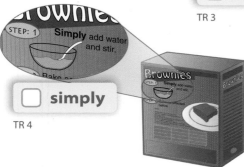

☐ **only**

TR 6

☐ **hardly**

TR 7

☐ **enough**

TR 8

☐ **just**

TR 9

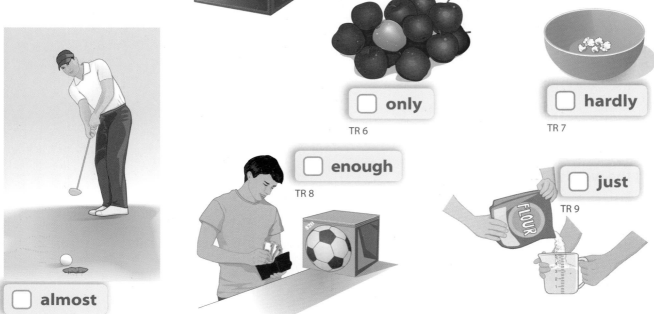

☐ **almost**

TR 5

Check Your Understanding

A. Match each word to the correct description. One description will not be used.

1. _____ enough
2. _____ only
3. _____ alone
4. _____ nearly
5. _____ simply
6. _____ mostly
7. _____ hardly
8. _____ just
9. _____ almost

a. nearly, but not completely
b. good enough
c. as much as is needed
d. one person or thing of a particular type
e. very close to a certain amount, but not exactly
f. almost completely
g. not with other people
h. only or just
i. almost none
j. exactly

B. Complete each sentence by unscrambling the word in parentheses.

1. Josh did not have a date to the dance, so he went _____ (nealo).

2. There was _____ (draylh) any cereal left, so Claire had a muffin instead.

3. _____ (milpsy) click on the start button to begin.

4. There is _____ (yonl) one banana left.

5. My little brother is _____ (smoalt) three feet tall, but not quite.

6. There was _____ (utjs) enough tea left for Chelsie to have one more cup.

7. Carl _____ (ranely) had enough money to buy a new video game.

8. Sophie has _____ (genouh) money to buy a new guitar.

9. During the summer, the weather is _____ (yotsml) warm.

Challenge Words

Check (✔) the words you already know.

☐ a bit   ☐ a little   ☐ at least   ☐ kind of   ☐ more or less
☐ adequate   ☐ as good as   ☐ barely   ☐ mainly   ☐ practically

19. Amounts

Check (✔) the words you already know. Then, listen and repeat.

Tracks 1–24

☐ **more**
TR 1

☐ **less**
TR 2

☐ **half**
TR 3

☐ **whole**
TR 4

☐ **amount**
TR 5

$22.50

☐ **both**
TR 6

☐ **couple**
☐ **two**
TR 7 and 8

☐ **single**
TR 9

☐ **plenty**
TR 10

☐ **few**
TR 11

☐ **several**
TR 12

☐ **many**
TR 13

He called me **twice**.

☐ **little**
TR 14

☐ **a lot**
TR 15

☐ **pair**
TR 16

☐ **twice**
TR 17

extra
TR 19

only
TR 18

most
TR 20

none
TR 21

Do you want the **other** half?

other
TR 22

another
TR 23

I am going to eat **all** of this pizza.

all
TR 24

Definitions

You use **all** to talk about the whole of something.

A lot of something is a large amount of it.

The **amount** is the total number or quantity of something.

Another thing means one more of the same type.

You use **both** to talk about two things.

A **couple** of things means two of them.

An **extra** amount or thing is another one that is added.

A **few** means some, but not many.

Half of an amount or an object is one of two equal parts.

You use **less** to talk about a smaller amount of something.

You use **little** to show that there is only a very small amount of something.

You use **many** to talk about a large number of things.

You use **more** to talk about a greater amount of something.

You use **most** to talk about the largest quantity of people or things.

None of something means not one or not any.

The **only** thing is the one thing of a particular type.

You use **other** when you are talking about a thing that remains out of two or more.

A **pair** of things is two things of the same size and shape that are used together.

If there is **plenty** of something, there is a large amount of it.

You use **several** to talk about a number of things that is not a lot but is greater than two.

You use **single** to talk about only one thing.

If something happens **twice**, it happens two times.

Two is the number 2.

The **whole** of something means all of it.

Check Your Understanding

A. Circle the word in each group that does not belong.

1. both	two	other
2. twice	two	less
3. another	most	many
4. few	single	only
5. amount	pair	couple
6. extra	none	plenty
7. whole	half	all
8. many	little	a lot

B. Underline the correct word to complete each sentence.

1. David has (**less / little**) money than Fred.

2. Lucy has a new (**extra / pair**) of shoes.

3. Ella broke the chalk evenly and gave (**half / little**) of it to her little brother.

4. (**Most / Whole**) of the students were late to class.

5. (**All / Less**) of the flowers in my mother's garden are red.

6. Ricky asked for (**more / only**) glue because the bottle he had was empty.

7. Jasmine needs a (**couple / several**) of pieces of paper.

8. Please put a (**most / single**) slice of cheese on my sandwich.

9. Alex bought a large (**amount / twice**) of food to serve at his party.

10. (**Both / Few**) his mother and father were at the concert last night.

11. Evan could not pour any milk into his cereal because there was (**none / other**) left.

12. He knocked (**many / twice**) on the door and then waited for someone to answer.

13. Natalie finished her glass of water and asked for (**another / half**) one.

14. Jana only had a (**little / single**) money left after she bought a computer.

15. Greta is the (**only / other**) one who does not wear glasses in her family.

16. Pat read the e-mail (**two / twice**) times to make sure he understood it.

17. Tom and Nicky talked for a (**single / few**) minutes after class.

18. There are (**a lot / many**) of pigeons on the sidewalk.

19. There are (**most / many**) movies that are filmed in the United States.

20. Jason has had (**several / couple**) different cell phones.

21. Kelly has (**other / amount**) friends who could not come to the party.

22. Ed put together the (**all / whole**) puzzle without any help.

23. I had an (**only / extra**) baseball glove, so I gave it to my little brother.

24. There are (**plenty / half**) of books to read in the library.

Challenge Words

Check (✔) the words you already know.

☐ additional   ☐ decrease   ☐ excess   ☐ lack   ☐ quantity

☐ capacity   ☐ entire   ☐ increase   ☐ least   ☐ remainder

28. Numbers

Check (✔) the words you already know. Then, listen and repeat.

Tracks 1–43

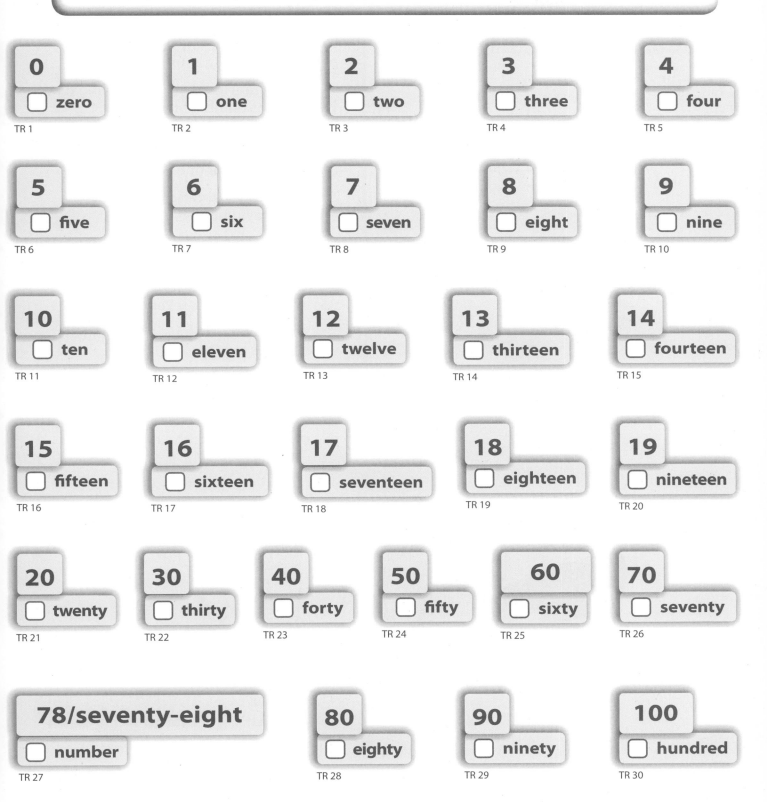

0 ☐ zero
TR 1

1 ☐ one
TR 2

2 ☐ two
TR 3

3 ☐ three
TR 4

4 ☐ four
TR 5

5 ☐ five
TR 6

6 ☐ six
TR 7

7 ☐ seven
TR 8

8 ☐ eight
TR 9

9 ☐ nine
TR 10

10 ☐ ten
TR 11

11 ☐ eleven
TR 12

12 ☐ twelve
TR 13

13 ☐ thirteen
TR 14

14 ☐ fourteen
TR 15

15 ☐ fifteen
TR 16

16 ☐ sixteen
TR 17

17 ☐ seventeen
TR 18

18 ☐ eighteen
TR 19

19 ☐ nineteen
TR 20

20 ☐ twenty
TR 21

30 ☐ thirty
TR 22

40 ☐ forty
TR 23

50 ☐ fifty
TR 24

60 ☐ sixty
TR 25

70 ☐ seventy
TR 26

78/seventy-eight ☐ number
TR 27

80 ☐ eighty
TR 28

90 ☐ ninety
TR 29

100 ☐ hundred
TR 30

1, 8, or 289

☐ numeral

TR 31

1,000

☐ thousand

TR 32

1,000,000

☐ million

TR 33

3.14

☐ decimal

TR 35

1,000,000,000

☐ billion

TR 34

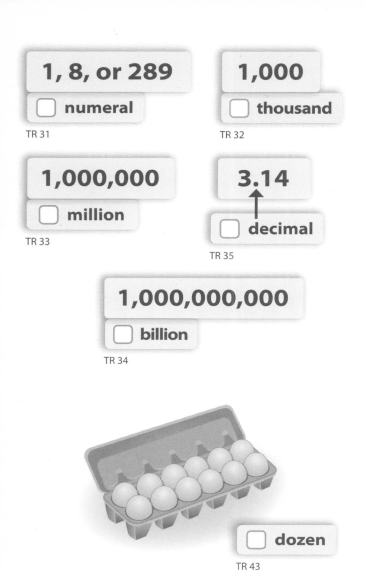

☐ dozen

TR 43

Definitions*

A **decimal** is part of a number that is written in the form of a dot followed by one or more numbers.

A **dozen** means twelve.

The **first** item in a series is the thing or person you count as number one.

The **ninth** item in a series is the thing that you count as number nine.

A **number** is a word such as "two," "nine," or "twelve," or a symbol such as "1", "3", or "47" that is used in counting.

A **numeral** is a written symbol that represents a number.

The **second** item in a series is the thing that you count as number two.

The **seventh** item in a series is the thing that you count as number seven.

The **sixth** item in a series is the thing that you count as number six.

The **tenth** item in a series is the thing that you count as number ten.

The **third** item in a series is the thing that you count as number three.

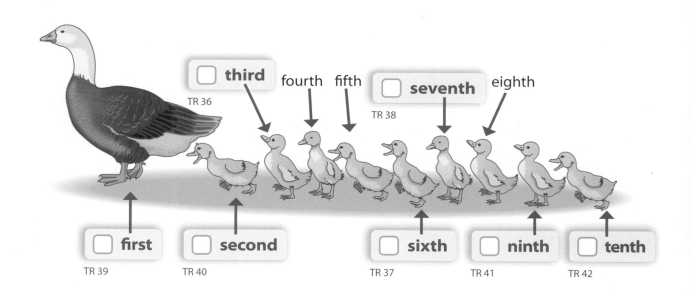

☐ third
TR 36

fourth fifth

☐ seventh
TR 38

eighth

☐ first
TR 39

☐ second
TR 40

☐ sixth
TR 37

☐ ninth
TR 41

☐ tenth
TR 42

*The definitions for the numbers were not included. They are represented by the images.
  For example: "One" is the number 1.

Check Your Understanding

A. Write the words from the word bank in the correct column.

five	six	fifty	sixty	thirty
four	ten	first	third	billion
nine	two	forty	ninth	twelve
sixth	one	tenth	ninety	million
eight	zero	fifteen	sixteen	thirteen
dozen	three	eleven	seventy	thousand
twenty	seven	second	numeral	
seventh	eighty	fourteen	nineteen	
decimal	eighteen	hundred	seventeen	

NUMBERS	WORDS RELATED TO NUMBERS	WORDS TO ORDER ITEMS IN A SERIES

B. Fill in each line below by following the direction or answering the question.

1. Put the following numbers in order from smallest to greatest:

    a. two, zero, one, four, three _____

    b. five, eight, seven, six _____

    c. eleven, nine, ten, twelve _____

    d. fifteen, thirteen, sixteen, fourteen _____

    e. twenty, eighteen, seventeen, nineteen _____

    f. fifty, thirty, sixty, forty _____

    g. eighty, seventy, hundred, ninety _____

    h. thousand, billion, million _____

2. Put the following words in order from first to last.

    a. fourth, second, third, first, fifth _____

    b. ninth, seventh, sixth, tenth, eighth _____

3. What does a decimal look like? _____

4. Write an example of a numeral. _____

5. Write an example of a number. _____

6. What number does a *dozen* mean? _____

Challenge Words

Check (✔) the words you already know.

☐ data	☐ integer	☐ thirteenth	☐ trillion	☐ twelfth
☐ digit	☐ sixtieth	☐ thousandth	☐ triple	☐ twentieth

33. Size and Weight

Check (✔) the words you already know. Then, listen and repeat.

Tracks 1–11

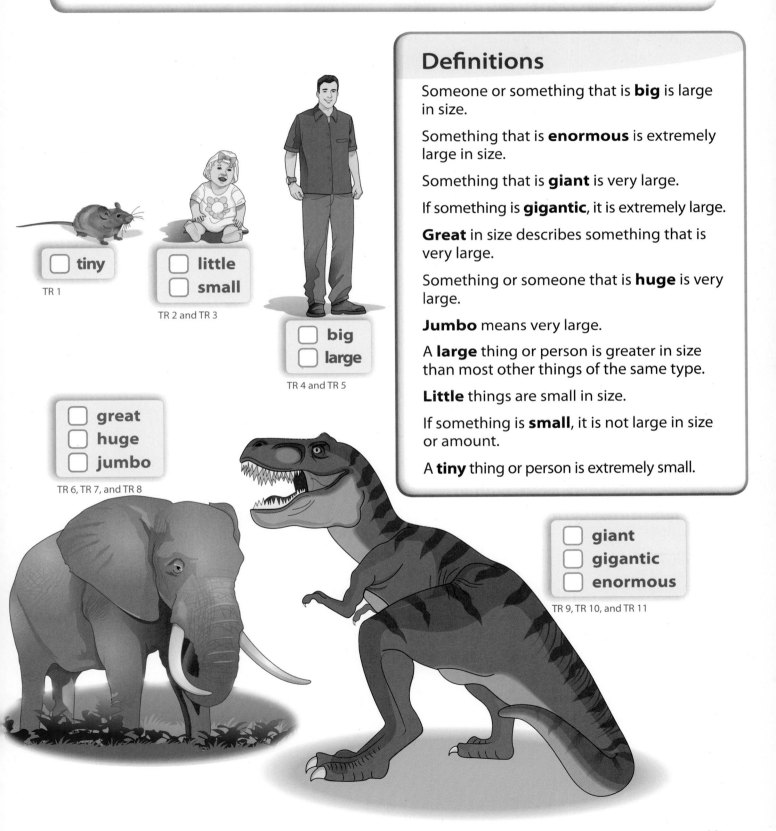

☐ **tiny**
TR 1

☐ **little**
☐ **small**
TR 2 and TR 3

☐ **big**
☐ **large**
TR 4 and TR 5

☐ **great**
☐ **huge**
☐ **jumbo**
TR 6, TR 7, and TR 8

☐ **giant**
☐ **gigantic**
☐ **enormous**
TR 9, TR 10, and TR 11

Definitions

Someone or something that is **big** is large in size.

Something that is **enormous** is extremely large in size.

Something that is **giant** is very large.

If something is **gigantic**, it is extremely large.

Great in size describes something that is very large.

Something or someone that is **huge** is very large.

Jumbo means very large.

A **large** thing or person is greater in size than most other things of the same type.

Little things are small in size.

If something is **small**, it is not large in size or amount.

A **tiny** thing or person is extremely small.

69

Check Your Understanding

A. Write the words in the correct column. One word will not be used.

huge	great	gigantic	giant
jumbo	large	tiny	
medium	little	enormous	

BIG	SMALL

B. Circle the word with a similar meaning.

1. big

   a. tiny   b. large

2. gigantic

   a. enormous   b. small

3. small

   a. little   b. jumbo

4. great

   a. small   b. huge

5. giant

   a. jumbo   b. tiny

Challenge Words

Check (✔) the words you already know.

☐ bulk   ☐ grand   ☐ medium   ☐ monstrous   ☐ vast

☐ compact   ☐ massive   ☐ miniature   ☐ petite

73. Units of Measurement

Check (✔) the words you already know. Then, listen and repeat.

 Tracks 1–11

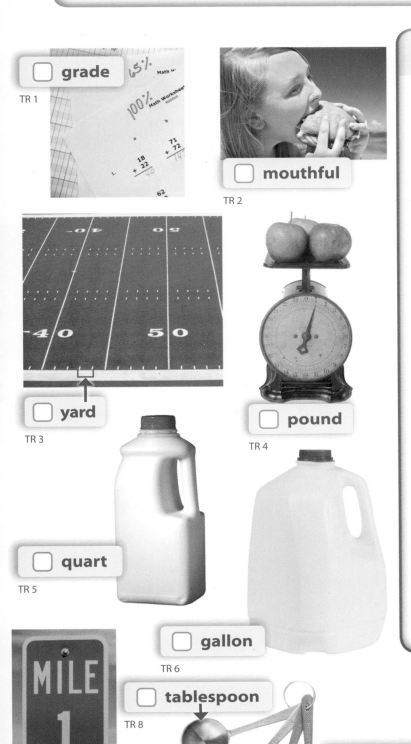

☐ grade
TR 1

☐ mouthful
TR 2

☐ yard
TR 3

☐ pound
TR 4

☐ quart
TR 5

☐ gallon
TR 6

☐ mile
TR 7

☐ tablespoon
TR 8

☐ spoonful
TR 9

☐ foot
TR 10

☐ inch
TR 11

Definitions

A **foot** is a unit for measuring length. A foot is equal to 30.48 centimeters. There are 12 inches in a foot. The plural form is **feet** or **foot**.

A **gallon** is a unit for measuring liquids. A gallon is equal to 128 ounces. There are eight pints in a gallon.

The **grade** of something is its level of quality.

An **inch** is a unit for measuring length. There are 2.54 centimeters in an inch. There are 12 inches in a foot.

A **mile** is a unit for measuring distance. A **mile** is equal to 1.6 kilometers. There are 5,280 feet in a mile.

A **mouthful** of drink or food is the amount that you can put in your mouth at one time.

A **pound** is a unit of weight. One pound is equal to 0.454 kilograms.

A **quart** is a unit for measuring liquid that is equal to thirty-two ounces or two pints.

A **spoonful** of food is an amount of food that a spoon holds.

A **tablespoon** is a large spoon that you use when you are cooking.

A **yard** is a unit for measuring length. There are 91.4 centimeters in a yard.

Check Your Understanding

A. Write each word from the word bank in the correct column.

foot	inch	yard	pound
mouthful	mile	spoonful	quart
grade	tablespoon	gallon	

AMOUNT	QUALITY	WEIGHT	LENGTH

B. Underline the correct word to complete each sentence.

1. Please add a (**spoonful** / **inch**) of salt to the soup.

2. There is a (**mouthful** / **gallon**) of milk in the refrigerator.

3. There are 12 inches in a (**foot** / **mile**).

4. Marissa only wants to cut an (**tablespoon** / **inch**) off her hair.

5. Pablo's car only takes the highest (**quart** / **grade**) of gasoline.

6. I ran a (**pound** / **mile**) this morning.

7. Sally ate a (**mouthful** / **yard**) of blueberries.

8. The pool is only five (**yards** / **grades**) away from the school.

9. Eric lost five (**pounds** / **gallons**) by eating healthy foods and exercising.

10. The batter needs a (**mile** / **tablespoon**) of cinnamon added to it.

11. Jamie used a (**mouthful** / **quart**) of water to make the lemonade.

Challenge Words

Check (✔) the words you already know.

☐ degree ☐ handful ☐ meter ☐ ounce ☐ teaspoon

☐ gram ☐ liter ☐ metric ☐ pint ☐ ton

130. Parts

Check (✔) the words you already know. Then, listen and repeat.

Tracks 1–12

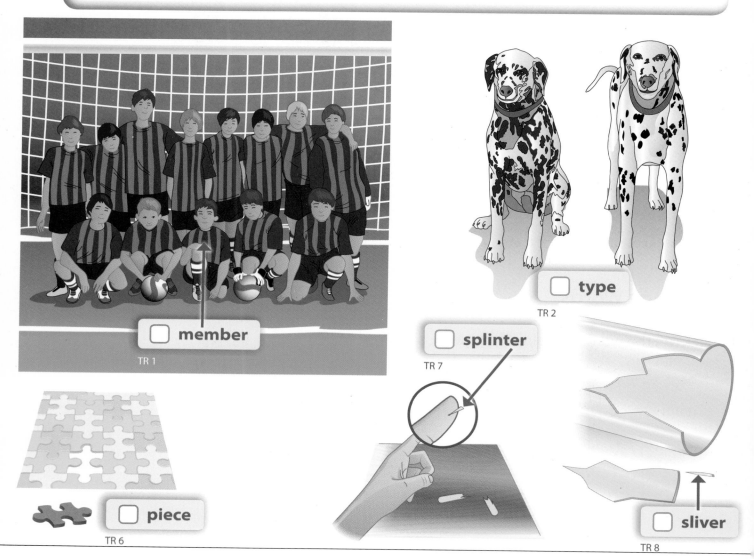

☐ member
TR 1

☐ type
TR 2

☐ piece
TR 6

☐ splinter
TR 7

☐ sliver
TR 8

Check Your Understanding

A. Write **T** for **true statements** and **F** for **false statements**.

1. _____ A bit is a large piece of something.

2. _____ Crumbs are small pieces of bread.

3. _____ A slice is a thin piece of something cut from a large piece.

4. _____ If you are a member of a club, you are part of it.

5. _____ A sliver of something is a large chunk of it.

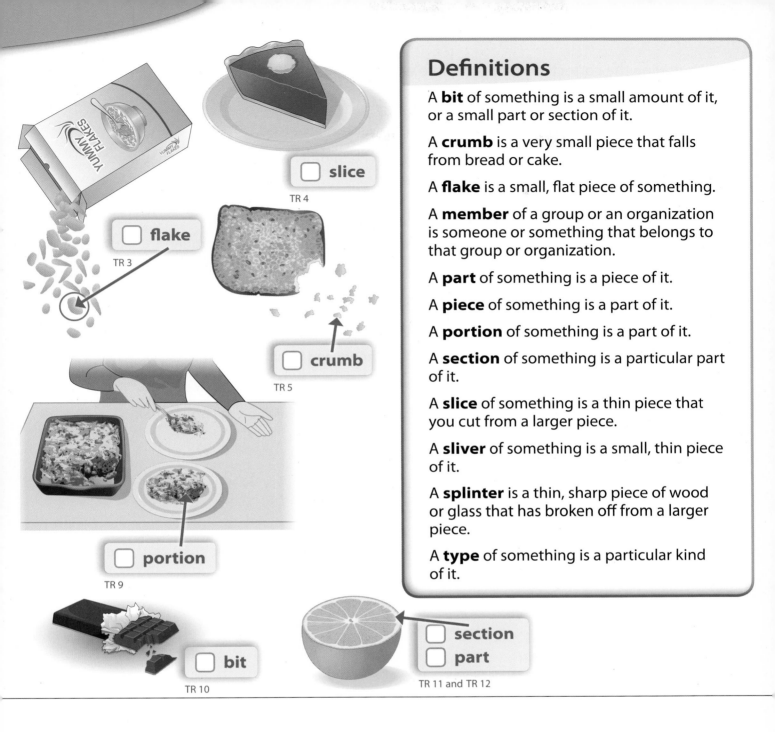

Definitions

A **bit** of something is a small amount of it, or a small part or section of it.

A **crumb** is a very small piece that falls from bread or cake.

A **flake** is a small, flat piece of something.

A **member** of a group or an organization is someone or something that belongs to that group or organization.

A **part** of something is a piece of it.

A **piece** of something is a part of it.

A **portion** of something is a part of it.

A **section** of something is a particular part of it.

A **slice** of something is a thin piece that you cut from a larger piece.

A **sliver** of something is a small, thin piece of it.

A **splinter** is a thin, sharp piece of wood or glass that has broken off from a larger piece.

A **type** of something is a particular kind of it.

slice — TR 4

flake — TR 3

crumb — TR 5

portion — TR 9

bit — TR 10

section / part — TR 11 and TR 12

6. _____ If you ask for a piece of something, it means you want the whole thing.

7. _____ Splinters of glass or wood are not sharp.

8. _____ A flake is a small, flat piece of something.

9. _____ A portion of something is not the whole thing, but a part of it.

10. _____ A type of something is a particular kind of it.

11. _____ A part of something is a small, thin piece of it.

12. _____ A section of something is a particular part of it.

B. Underline the correct word to complete each sentence.

1. Juan cut a (**crumb / slice**) of bread to eat with his soup.

2. That (**type / portion**) of car is known to be very safe on the road.

3. Amber ate a little (**bit / member**) of cake when her mother was looking the other way.

4. The puzzle has 700 (**pieces / sections**).

5. Please serve me a small (**flake / portion**) because I am not very hungry.

6. A glass bottle broke and now there are (**slivers / types**) of glass on the ground.

7. This (**section / slice**) of the city has a lot of restaurants and pastry shops.

8. Danielle left a lot of (**parts / crumbs**) on the table after eating some bread with jam.

9. Ellie spent (**piece / part**) of her allowance on a gift for her sister.

10. Michelle has a (**slice / splinter**) of wood in her finger and it is hurting her.

11. My brother is a (**member / piece**) of the art club because he loves to draw.

12. Mandy and her mom watched the small (**splinters / flakes**) of snow fall from the sky.

Challenge Words

Check (✔) the words you already know.

☐ category   ☐ element   ☐ item   ☐ segment   ☐ species

☐ department   ☐ fragment   ☐ sample   ☐ slab   ☐ version

327. Things That Are Commonly Measured

Check (✔) the words you already know. Then, listen and repeat.

Tracks 1–3

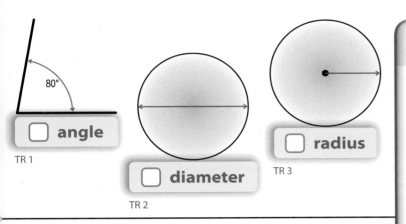

☐ **angle**
TR 1

☐ **diameter**
TR 2

☐ **radius**
TR 3

Definitions

An **angle** is the space between two lines or surfaces that meet in one place. Angles are measured in degrees.

The **diameter** of a round object is the length of a straight line that can be drawn across it, passing through the middle of it.

The **radius** of a circle is the distance from its center to its outside edge.

Check Your Understanding

A. Match each word to the correct description. One description will not be used.

1. _____ angle
2. _____ diameter
3. _____ radius

a. the space between two lines that meet at a point
b. the distance around a circle
c. the length of a line through the center of a circle
d. the length from the center of a circle to its edge

B. Choose the correct word from the word bank to complete each sentence. One word will not be used.

angle	diameter	circumference	radius

1. We only measured halfway across the circle to measure the length of its _____.

2. The _____ measured 30 degrees.

3. The teacher asked the students to measure a straight line across the circle through its middle to find the _____.

Challenge Words

Check (✔) the words you already know.

☐ census
☐ circumference

☐ latitude
☐ longitude

☐ meridian

373. Actions Related to Measurement

Check (✔) the words you already know. Then, listen and repeat.

 Tracks 1–2

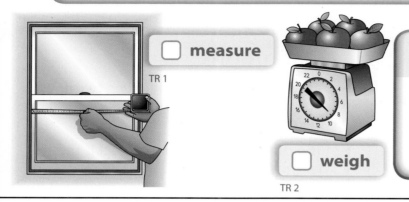

☐ measure

TR 1

☐ weigh

TR 2

Definitions

If you **measure** something, you find out its size.

If you **weigh** something, you measure how heavy it is.

Check Your Understanding

A. Write the phrases from the word bank in the correct column.

| how heavy you are | how long a table is | how heavy apples are |
| how heavy a package is | how tall someone is | how wide a window is |

THINGS YOU CAN MEASURE	THINGS YOU CAN WEIGH

B. Use *measure* or *weigh* to complete each sentence.

1. Hector wanted to _____ the pumpkin to see how heavy it was.

2. Alicia asked if the hairstylist could _____ how long her hair was before she cut it.

3. We need to _____ how wide the door is to make sure the couch will fit through it.

4. The doctor needs to _____ the baby to make sure he is gaining enough weight.

Challenge Words

Check (✔) the word you already know.

☐ fathom

374. Devices Used for Measurement

Check (✔) the words you already know. Then, listen and repeat.

Tracks 1–2

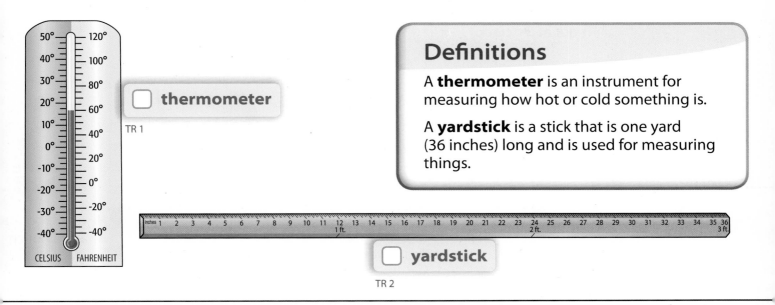

☐ **thermometer**

TR 1

Definitions

A **thermometer** is an instrument for measuring how hot or cold something is.

A **yardstick** is a stick that is one yard (36 inches) long and is used for measuring things.

☐ **yardstick**

TR 2

Check Your Understanding

A. Write **T** for **true statements** and **F** for **false statements**.

1. _____ A thermometer and a yardstick are both used for measuring things.

2. _____ A thermometer measures the temperature of something.

3. _____ A yardstick measures the weight of something.

4. _____ A thermometer can be used to measure a person's temperature.

B. Underline the correct word to complete each sentence.

1. Daniel looked at the (**thermometer / yardstick**) to find out the temperature.

2. Rachel used a (**thermometer / yardstick**) to measure the height of the table.

3. The chef used a (**thermometer / yardstick**) to check if the turkey was cooked.

4. We measured the height of the plant every week with a (**thermometer / yardstick**).

Challenge Words

Check (✔) the words you already know.

☐ compass   ☐ gauge   ☐ measurement   ☐ scale   ☐ speedometer

2. Relationship Markers (Concurrent Action)

Check (✔) the words you already know. Then, listen and repeat.

Tracks 1–9

☐ **when**
TR 1

When my mom is making dinner, I set the table.

I like to work out **at** 3 o'clock.

☐ **at**
TR 2

☐ **together**
TR 3

Sean and Kyle like to ride bikes **together**.

I like to listen to music **while** I paint.

☐ **while**
TR 4

☐ **as**
TR 5

He read a book as he ate his lunch.

Check Your Understanding

A. Underline the correct word to complete each sentence.

1. The party was going to be on Saturday, but (**now / when**) it is on Friday.

2. We left early so that we would be (**at / as**) school by the time the first bell rang.

3. I wake up (**when / at**) the birds start singing.

4. Karen tapped her fingers on the table (**during / while**) she waited for Sarah to finish her lunch.

5. Lisa sat down just (**as / together**) the food was being served.

6. My little brother fell asleep (**during / as**) the movie.

7. Pablo wakes up at a quarter (**during / of**) seven.

8. Rick has a job interview (**on / at**) Wednesday morning.

9. Phillip and Casey walk to school (**when / together**).

B. Circle the correct word for each description.

1. used to talk about the time before the hour
   a. during   b. of   c. when

2. between the beginning and the end of a period of time
   a. during   b. as   c. on

3. happens at the same time
   a. when   b. of   c. as

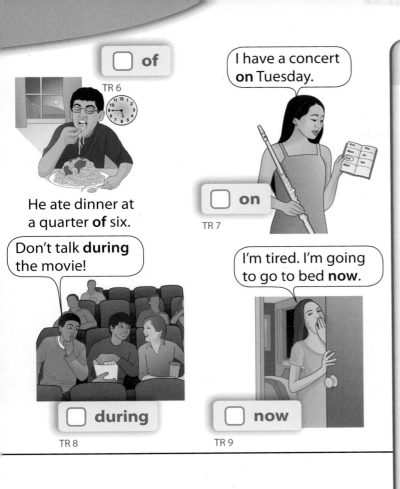

He ate dinner at a quarter **of** six.

☐ **of**
TR 6

I have a concert **on** Tuesday.

☐ **on**
TR 7

Don't talk **during** the movie!

☐ **during**
TR 8

I'm tired. I'm going to go to bed **now**.

☐ **now**
TR 9

Definitions

If one thing happens **as** something else happens, it happens at the same time.

You use **at** to state the time something happens.

If something happens **during** a period of time, it happens between the beginning and the end of that period.

You use **now** to talk about the present time.

You use **of** to indicate the time before the hour.

If something happens **on** a particular day or date, that is when it happens.

If people do something **together**, they do it with each other at the same time.

You use **when** to introduce the part of the sentence where you mention the time at which something happens.

If one thing happens **while** another thing is happening, the two things are happening at the same time.

4. the present time

   a. while   b. now   c. at

5. with each other at the same time

   a. as   b. during   c. together

6. the time at which something happens

   a. together   b. when   c. on

7. two things happening at the same time

   a. while   b. together   c. of

8. the time something happens

   a. at   b. while   c. of

9. a particular day or date when something happens

   a. while   b. at   c. on

Challenge Words

Check (✔) the words you already know.

☐ at the same time   ☐ concurrently   ☐ meanwhile   ☐ simultaneously

☐ at this point   ☐ in the meantime   ☐ nowadays

16. Relationship Markers

Check (✔) the words you already know. Then, listen and repeat.

 Tracks 1–9

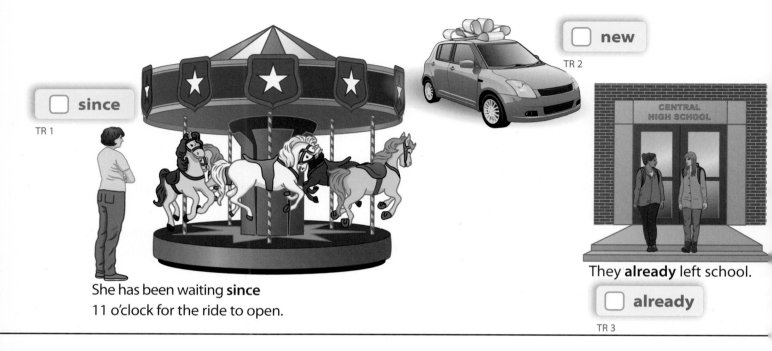

☐ **new**
TR 2

☐ **since**
TR 1

She has been waiting **since** 11 o'clock for the ride to open.

They **already** left school.

☐ **already**
TR 3

Check Your Understanding

A. Underline the correct word to complete each sentence.

1. Marta could remember the movie well because it was still (**fresh / young**) in her mind.

2. I have seen a lot of people riding bicycles in the city (**lately / since**).

3. Ivan graduated from high school two years (**since / ago**), and now he is in college.

4. Ray always gets to work ten minutes (**early / already**) to show his boss that he is responsible.

5. After practicing for two weeks, Amber is now (**ready / fresh**) to perform in the talent show.

6. The (**young / early**) ducklings swam in a row behind their mother.

7. Alfredo offered his extra pen to Paula, but she (**already / ready**) had one.

8. Luis has not been to Florida (**ago / since**) he was eleven years old.

9. Petra is trying on the (**young / new**) boots her mother just bought for her.

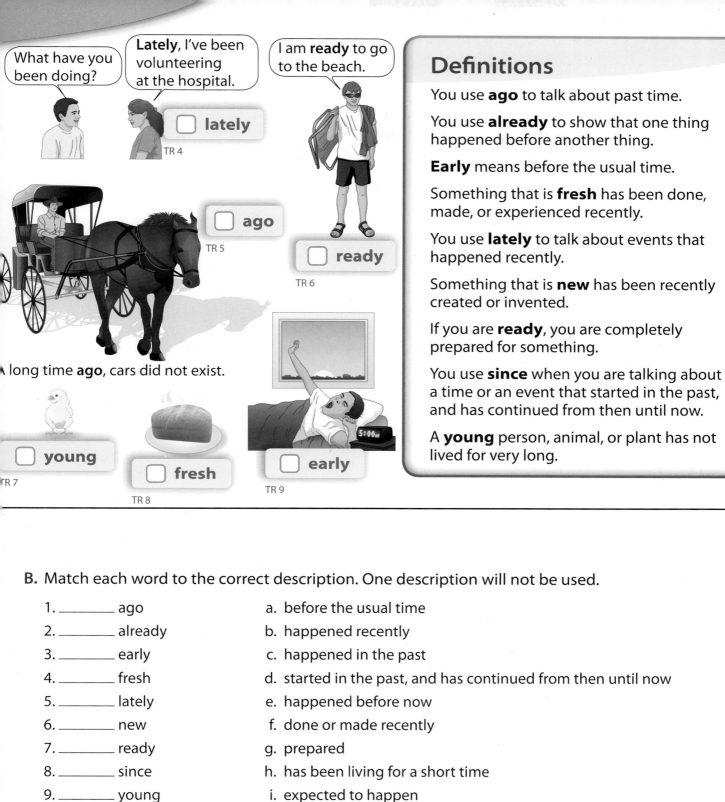

What have you been doing?

Lately, I've been volunteering at the hospital.

I am **ready** to go to the beach.

☐ **lately**
TR 4

☐ **ago**
TR 5

☐ **ready**
TR 6

A long time **ago**, cars did not exist.

☐ **young**
TR 7

☐ **fresh**
TR 8

☐ **early**
TR 9

Definitions

You use **ago** to talk about past time.

You use **already** to show that one thing happened before another thing.

Early means before the usual time.

Something that is **fresh** has been done, made, or experienced recently.

You use **lately** to talk about events that happened recently.

Something that is **new** has been recently created or invented.

If you are **ready**, you are completely prepared for something.

You use **since** when you are talking about a time or an event that started in the past, and has continued from then until now.

A **young** person, animal, or plant has not lived for very long.

B. Match each word to the correct description. One description will not be used.

1. _____ ago
2. _____ already
3. _____ early
4. _____ fresh
5. _____ lately
6. _____ new
7. _____ ready
8. _____ since
9. _____ young

a. before the usual time
b. happened recently
c. happened in the past
d. started in the past, and has continued from then until now
e. happened before now
f. done or made recently
g. prepared
h. has been living for a short time
i. expected to happen
j. recently created or invented

Challenge Words

Check (✔) the words you already know.

☐ as yet
☐ at first
☐ before now
☐ before that
☐ current
☐ due
☐ former
☐ initial
☐ modern
☐ now that

6 TIME

24. Relationship Markers (Subsequent Action)

Check (✔) the words you already know. Then, listen and repeat.

Tracks 1–10

Check Your Understanding

A. Match each word to the correct description. One description will not be used.

1. _____ later
2. _____ before
3. _____ latter
4. _____ late
5. _____ next
6. _____ until
7. _____ soon
8. _____ afterward / afterwards
9. _____ then

a. after a long time

b. happens after a particular time that has been mentioned

c. what happened at a particular time in the past or what will happen in the future

d. happens before a particular time and then stops at that time

e. arrives after the time it should have

f. happening at the end of a unit of time

g. comes immediately after a previous thing

h. happens in the near future

i. happens after a unit of time

j. happened earlier than a particular time

84

☐ **before**

TR 4

☐ **afterward**
☐ **afterwards**

TR 5 and TR 6

☐ **soon**

TR 10

Definitions

If something happens **afterward** or **afterwards**, it happens after a particular time that you have already mentioned.

If something happened **before** a particular time, it happened at an earlier time.

If something is **late**, it arrives after the time it was expected at.

You use **later** to talk about something happening after a specific time.

Latter means coming or happening at the end of a unit of time.

The **next** thing is the one that comes immediately after the thing before it.

If something happens **soon**, it happens in the near future.

Then means what happened at a particular time in the past or what will happen in the future.

If something happens **until** a particular time, it happens before that time and stops at that time.

B. Underline the correct word to complete each sentence.

1. Jeremy studied (**until / afterward**) 8 o'clock, but then he stopped and watched TV.

2. Ms. Gerald is busy right now, but she can speak with you (**latter / later**).

3. Elaine will be fifteen years old (**soon / next**) Friday.

4. Jody turned in her homework (**late / then**), so Mr. Roberts was upset.

5. We will go shopping, and then visit Jeff (**afterwards / before**).

6. Andrew is going on a camping trip in the (**next / latter**) half of the month.

7. Sarah and Jillian hiked the mountain, and (**until / then**) watched the sunset.

8. Jerry said he would pick us up (**soon / before**), so we should get ready to go now.

9. Please make sure the iron is unplugged (**then / before**) you leave the house.

10. Lauren and Vanessa ate dinner, and had dessert (**latter / afterward**).

Challenge Words

Check (✔) the words you already know.

☐ after that   ☐ henceforth   ☐ in the end

☐ eventual   ☐ hereafter   ☐ tardy

29. Days and Months

Check (✔) the words you already know. Then, listen and repeat.

Tracks 1–19

☐ January
TR 1

S	M	T	W	T	F	S
		1	2	3	4	5
6	7	8	9	10	11	12
13	14	15	16	17	18	19
20	21	22	23	24	25	26
27	28	29	30	31		

☐ February
TR 2

S	M	T	W	T	F	S
					1	2
3	4	5	6	7	8	9
10	11	12	13	14	15	16
17	18	19	20	21	22	23
24	25	26	27	28		

☐ March
TR 3

S	M	T	W	T	F	S
					1	2
3	4	5	6	7	8	9
10	11	12	13	14	15	16
17	18	19	20	21	22	23
24	25	26	27	28	29	30
31						

☐ April
TR 4

S	M	T	W	T	F	S
	1	2	3	4	5	6
7	8	9	10	11	12	13
14	15	16	17	18	19	20
21	22	23	24	25	26	27
28	29	30				

☐ May
TR 5

S	M	T	W	T	F	S
			1	2	3	4
5	6	7	8	9	10	11
12	13	14	15	16	17	18
19	20	21	22	23	24	25
26	27	28	29	30	31	

☐ June
TR 6

S	M	T	W	T	F	S
						1
2	3	4	5	6	7	8
9	10	11	12	13	14	15
16	17	18	19	20	21	22
23	24	25	26	27	28	29
30						

☐ July
TR 7

S	M	T	W	T	F	S
	1	2	3	4	5	6
7	8	9	10	11	12	13
14	15	16	17	18	19	20
21	22	23	24	25	26	27
28	29	30	31			

☐ August
TR 8

S	M	T	W	T	F	S
				1	2	3
4	5	6	7	8	9	10
11	12	13	14	15	16	17
18	19	20	21	22	23	24
25	26	27	28	29	30	31

☐ September
TR 9

S	M	T	W	T	F	S
1	2	3	4	5	6	7
8	9	10	11	12	13	14
15	16	17	18	19	20	21
22	23	24	25	26	27	28
29	30					

☐ October
TR 10

S	M	T	W	T	F	S
		1	2	3	4	5
6	7	8	9	10	11	12
13	14	15	16	17	18	19
20	21	22	23	24	25	26
27	28	29	30	31		

☐ November
TR 11

S	M	T	W	T	F	S
					1	2
3	4	5	6	7	8	9
10	11	12	13	14	15	16
17	18	19	20	21	22	23
24	25	26	27	28	29	30

☐ December
TR 12

S	M	T	W	T	F	S
1	2	3	4	5	6	7
8	9	10	11	12	13	14
15	16	17	18	19	20	21
22	23	24	25	26	27	28
29	30	31				

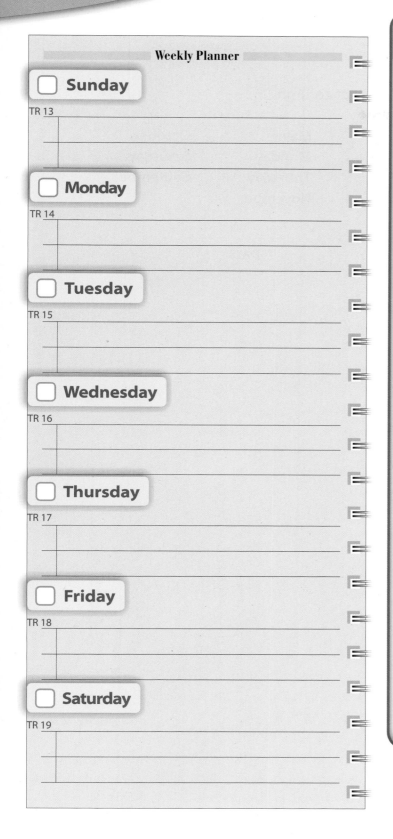

Definitions

April is the fourth month of the year.

August is the eighth month of the year.

December is the twelfth and last month of the year.

February is the second month of the year.

Friday is the day after Thursday and before Saturday.

January is the first month of the year.

July is the seventh month of the year.

June is the sixth month of the year.

March is the third month of the year.

May is the fifth month of the year.

Monday is the day after Sunday and before Tuesday.

November is the eleventh month of the year.

October is the tenth month of the year.

Saturday is the day after Friday and before Sunday.

September is the ninth month of the year.

Sunday is the day after Saturday and before Monday.

Thursday is the day after Wednesday and before Friday.

Tuesday is the day after Monday and before Wednesday.

Wednesday is the day after Tuesday and before Thursday.

Check Your Understanding

A. Write the words from the word bank in the correct column.

April	January	July	May	October
Friday	February	June	Monday	Saturday
August	December	March	Thursday	September
Sunday	Wednesday	Tuesday	November	

MONTHS	DAYS

B. Match each day or month with the day or month that follows it.

1. _____ January   a. Saturday

2. _____ May   b. December

3. _____ Sunday   c. Friday

4. _____ March   d. Monday

5. _____ Thursday   e. June

6. _____ June   f. April

7. _____ November   g. July

8. _____ Tuesday   h. Wednesday

9. _____ October   i. February

10. _____ August   j. November

11. _____ Friday   k. September

52. Periods of Time

Check (✔) the words you already know. Then, listen and repeat.

Tracks 1–14

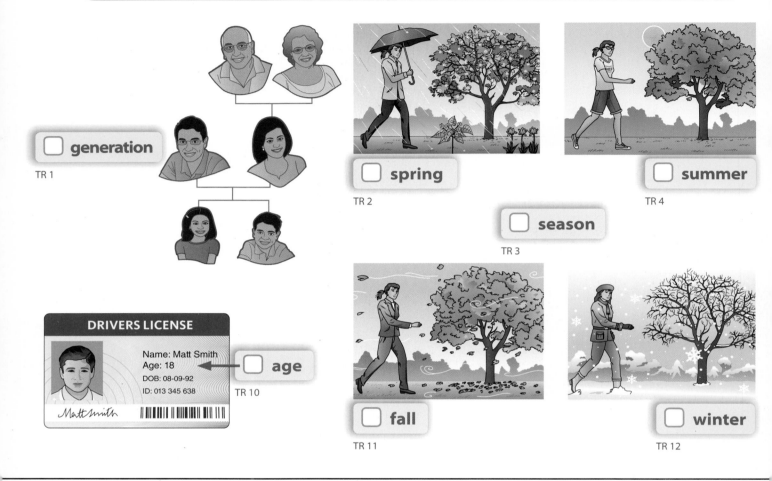

generation
TR 1

spring
TR 2

summer
TR 4

season
TR 3

DRIVERS LICENSE
Name: Matt Smith
Age: 18
DOB: 08-09-92
ID: 013 345 638
Matt Smith

age
TR 10

fall
TR 11

winter
TR 12

Check Your Understanding

A. Write **T** for **true statements** and **F** for **false statements**.

1. _____ Summer is usually a very hot season.

2. _____ Your age is the number of years you have lived.

3. _____ There are eight years in a decade.

4. _____ A generation is a group of people who are around the same age.

5. _____ January, February, and March are all months.

6. _____ Fall comes after summer.

7. _____ Saturday and Sunday are weekdays.

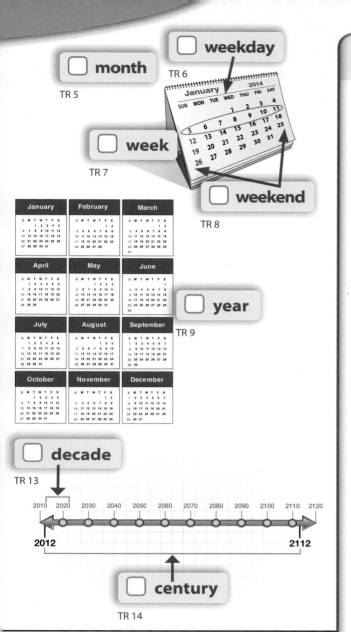

□ month
TR 5

□ weekday
TR 6

□ week
TR 7

□ weekend
TR 8

□ year
TR 9

□ decade
TR 13

2010 2020 2030 2040 2050 2060 2070 2080 2090 2100 2110 2120

2012 — **2112**

□ century
TR 14

Definitions

Your **age** is the number of years that you have lived.

A **century** is one hundred years.

A **decade** is a period of ten years.

Fall is the season between summer and winter when the leaves start to fall off the trees.

A **generation** is all the people in a group or country who are of a similar age.

A **month** is one of the twelve parts that a year is divided into.

A **season** is one of the four parts of a year that has its own typical weather conditions.

Spring is the season between winter and summer when the weather becomes warmer and plants start to grow again.

Summer is the season between spring and fall. In the summer, the weather is usually warm or hot.

A **week** is a period of seven days.

A **weekday** is any of the days of the week except Saturday and Sunday.

The **weekend** is Saturday and Sunday.

Winter is the season between fall and spring. In the winter, the weather is usually cold.

A **year** is a period of twelve months, beginning on the first of January and ending on the thirty-first of December.

8. _____ Monday and Tuesday are weekend days.

9. _____ The weather is usually cold during the winter.

10. _____ There are twelve months in a year.

11. _____ Plants start to grow again in the spring.

12. _____ Winter, spring, summer, and fall are all seasons.

13. _____ There are two hundred years in a century.

14. _____ There are five days in a week.

B. Circle the correct word to complete each sentence.

1. On hot _____ days, Michelle and her friends go swimming at the lake.

   a. winter   b. summer   c. fall

2. During the _____, the leaves change color and fall from the trees.

   a. fall   b. spring   c. winter

3. It's been a _____, or ten years, since I've been to New York.

   a. year   b. century   c. decade

4. The first month of the _____ is January.

   a. week   b. month   c. year

5. Lana's favorite _____ is fall.

   a. season   b. decade   c. weekday

6. There are seven days in a _____.

   a. year   b. week   c. decade

7. Joanne likes when the weather becomes warmer in the _____.

   a. spring   b. fall   c. winter

8. Jerry is taking an art class that is one _____ long.

   a. generation   b. century   c. month

9. Carrie works all week, but then she rests on the _____.

   a. weekday   b. weekend   c. week

10. Will enjoys building snowmen in the _____.

    a. fall   b. winter   c. summer

11. Last _____, televisions did not exist.

    a. century   b. generation   c. month

12. I'm busy this weekend, but I could get together with you on a _____.

    a. weekday   b. week   c. month

13. My grandparents' _____ did not have computers or MP3 players.

    a. decade   b. century   c. generation

14. Caitlin got her driver's license at the _____ of seventeen.

    a. year   b. generation   c. age

Challenge Words

Check (✔) the words you already know.

☐ autumn   ☐ duration   ☐ millennium   ☐ period   ☐ term

☐ cycle   ☐ interval   ☐ perennial   ☐ semester

59. Speed

Check (✔) the words you already know. Then, listen and repeat.

 Tracks 1–10

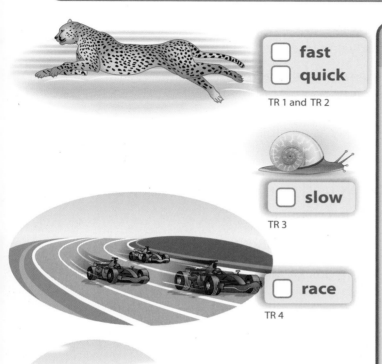

☐ fast
☐ quick

TR 1 and TR 2

☐ slow

TR 3

☐ race

TR 4

☐ rush
☐ hurry

TR 5 and TR 6

☐ speed

TR 7

Definitions

If you **dash** somewhere, you go there quickly and suddenly.

Fast means happening, moving, or doing something at great speed.

If you **hurry**, you move or do something as quickly as you can.

Someone or something that is **quick** moves or does things with great speed.

A **race** is a competition to see who is the fastest.

If you **rush** somewhere, you go there quickly.

If something is **slow**, it does not move or happen quickly.

A **slowdown** is a reduction in speed or activity.

The **speed** of something is how fast it moves or is done.

Sudden means happening quickly and unexpectedly.

☐ sudden

TR 8

☐ dash

TR 9

☐ slowdown

TR 10

Check Your Understanding

A. Match each word to the correct description. One description will not be used.

1. _____ fast
2. _____ race
3. _____ slow
4. _____ speed
5. _____ sudden
6. _____ hurry
7. _____ dash
8. _____ slowdown
9. _____ quick
10. _____ rush

a. to not move fast
b. the rate at which something moves
c. to occur quickly and unexpectedly
d. a contest to see who is the fastest
e. to move at a great speed
f. to move as quickly as possible
g. to change from a fast speed to a slower speed
h. to go somewhere quickly and suddenly
i. lasts for only a short time
j. to move at a great speed; another word for fast
k. to go somewhere quickly; another word for hurry

B. Underline the correct word to complete each sentence.

1. All of a (**sudden** / **fast**), the sky became very dark.

2. If we don't (**hurry** / **quick**), we are going to be late for our appointment.

3. Fred took a (**quick** / **slow**) drive along the coast because he wasn't in a hurry.

4. The (**race** / **speed**) limit is 35 miles per hour on this street.

5. Kim and Danny had a (**race** / **rush**) to see who could get to the lake first.

6. We have to be (**quick** / **slow**) inside the store because we don't have much time.

7. There has been a big (**slowdown** / **hurry**) on the highway, and all the cars are driving very slowly.

8. Let's check to see if cars are coming, and then (**dash** / **fast**) across the street.

9. If you (**rush** / **quick**) out the door, you might forget something.

10. My brother is a (**fast** / **slow**) runner, and he wins a lot of races.

Challenge Words

Check (✔) the words you already know.

☐ abrupt   ☐ automatically   ☐ brisk   ☐ charge   ☐ fuss

☐ automatic   ☐ brief   ☐ bustle   ☐ decelerate   ☐ gradual

6 TIME

79. Parts of a Day

Check (✔) the words you already know. Then, listen and repeat.

Tracks 1–15

☐ **second**
TR 1

☐ **minute**
TR 2

☐ **hour**
TR 3

☐ **sunrise**
TR 4

☐ **morning**
TR 5

☐ **noon**
TR 6

☐ **afternoon**
R 7

☐ **sunset**
☐ **sundown**
TR 8 and TR 9

☐ **evening**
TR 10

☐ **night**
TR 11

☐ **midnight**
TR 12

☐ **day**
TR 13

☐ **tonight**
TR 14

7 PM   Midnight   7 AM

☐ **overnight**
TR 15

Definitions

The **afternoon** is the part of each day that begins at lunchtime and ends at about six o'clock.

A **day** is one period of twenty-four hours. There are seven days in a week.

The **evening** is the part of each day between the end of the afternoon and the time you go to bed.

An **hour** is a period of sixty minutes.

Midnight is twelve o'clock in the middle of the night.

A **minute** is a period of sixty seconds.

The **morning** is the part of each day between the time that people usually wake up and noon.

The **night** is the part of each period of twenty-four hours when the sun has set and it is dark outside.

Noon is twelve o'clock in the middle of the day.

Something that happens **overnight** happens through the whole night or at some point during the night.

A **second** is one of the sixty parts that a minute is divided into.

Sundown, or **sunset**, is the time in the evening when the sun goes down.

Sunrise is the time in the morning when the sun first appears in the sky.

Tonight is the evening of today.

Check Your Understanding

A. Match each word to the correct description. One description will not be used.

1. _____ morning
2. _____ noon
3. _____ hour
4. _____ tonight
5. _____ sundown
6. _____ day
7. _____ midnight
8. _____ evening
9. _____ afternoon
10. _____ overnight
11. _____ minute
12. _____ sunrise
13. _____ night
14. _____ sunset
15. _____ second

a. the time when the sun sets; also known as sunset

b. a period of twenty-four hours

c. the part of each day between the time that people usually wake up and noon

d. through the whole night or at some point during the night

e. a period of sixty seconds

f. twelve o'clock in the middle of the day

g. a period of sixty minutes

h. twelve o'clock in the middle of the night

i. the time in the evening when the sun goes down; also known as sundown

j. the part of each day between the end of the afternoon and the time you go to bed

k. a few seconds

l. one of the sixty parts that a minute is divided into

m. the part of each day that begins at lunchtime and ends around six o'clock

n. the time in the morning when the sun first appears in the sky

o. the part of each day when the sun has set and it is dark outside

p. the evening of today

B. Circle the correct answer.

1. How many seconds are in a minute?
   a. 7   b. 24   c. 60
2. How many minutes are in an hour?
   a. 30   b. 60   c. 10
3. How many hours are in a day?
   a. 24   b. 12   c. 6
4. How many days are in a week?
   a. 1   b. 7   c. 24
5. Which happens earliest?
   a. morning   b. night   c. noon

6. Which happens latest?

    a. noon   b. night   c. morning

7. Which happens second?

    a. morning   b. afternoon   c. evening

8. Which happens last?

    a. evening   b. morning   c. afternoon

9. Which refers to the evening of today?

    a. evening   b. night   c. tonight

10. Which happens during the day?

    a. overnight   b. midnight   c. noon

11. Which happens during the night?

    a. morning   b. midnight   c. noon

12. Which happens in the morning?

    a. sunrise   b. sunset   c. sundown

13. Which happens throughout the night?

    a. sunrise   b. overnight   c. day

14. Which happens in the evening?

    a. noon   b. sunrise   c. sundown

15. Which two words mean the same thing?

    a. sundown and sunrise   b. sundown and sunset   c. sunrise and sunset

Challenge Words

Check (✔) the words you already know.

☐ dawn   ☐ dusk   ☐ midday   ☐ nightfall   ☐ twilight

☐ daybreak   ☐ instant   ☐ moment   ☐ noontime   ☐ workday

83. Time (Relative)

Check (✔) the words you already know. Then, listen and repeat.

Tracks 1–10

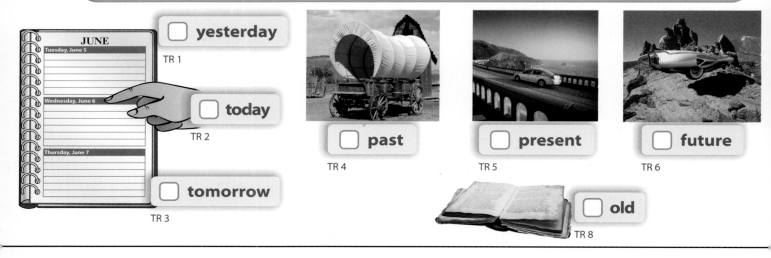

☐ yesterday
TR 1

☐ today
TR 2

☐ tomorrow
TR 3

☐ past
TR 4

☐ present
TR 5

☐ future
TR 6

☐ old
TR 8

Check Your Understanding

A. Circle the correct word to complete each sentence.

1. The television in our attic is very _____ and does not work anymore.

   a. old   b. past   c. history

2. We learned about the _____ civilizations in Greece.

   a. today   b. history   c. ancient

3. Paul has to get up early _____ , so he is going to sleep early tonight.

   a. yesterday   b. tomorrow   c. someday

4. The Civil War is an important part of the _____ of the United States.

   a. ancient   b. future   c. history

5. Helena and George gave a presentation _____ .

   a. yesterday   b. someday   c. past

6. Erica has an appointment at the dentist _____ .

   a. present   b. today   c. yesterday

7. Cell phones did not exist in the _____ .

   a. old   b. ancient   c. past

8. _____ I hope to become a doctor.

   a. Today   b. Someday   c. Future

9. I plan to go to college in the _____ .

   a. future   b. present   c. past

10. At the _____ time, Jackie has two dogs and one cat.

   a. someday   b. past   c. present

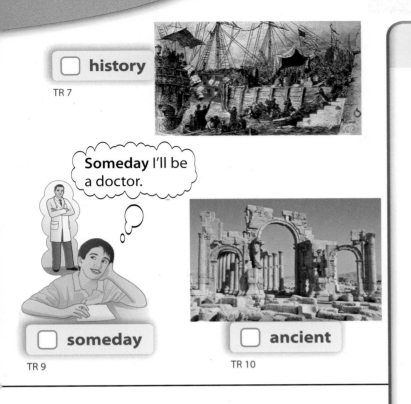

history

TR 7

Someday I'll be a doctor.

someday

TR 9

ancient

TR 10

Definitions

Ancient means very old, or from a long time ago.

The **future** is the time that will come after now.

History is events that happened in the past.

Something that is **old** has existed for many years and is not new.

The **past** is the time before the present, and the things that happened then.

You use **present** to talk about things and people that exist now.

Someday means at a date in the future that you do not yet know.

You use **today** when you are talking about the actual day on which you are speaking or writing.

Tomorrow is the day after today.

Yesterday is the day before today.

B. Write **T** for **true sentences** and **F** for **false statements**.

1. _____ Today is this present day.

2. _____ The past is the things that happened before the present.

3. _____ Yesterday is the day after today.

4. _____ Events in the future have not happened yet.

5. _____ Someday is a specific date in the future.

6. _____ History is past events.

7. _____ Ancient things are from a very long time ago.

8. _____ Things and people that exist right now are in the present.

9. _____ An old object is very new.

10. _____ Tomorrow is the day before today.

Challenge Words

Check (✔) the words you already know.

- antique
- childhood
- eternity
- heirloom
- historic
- medieval
- primitive
- puberty
- relic
- youth

126. Frequency and Duration

Check (✔) the words you already know. Then, listen and repeat.

Tracks 1–20

[ ] **never**
TR 1

She **never** misses the bus.

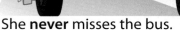
[ ] **sometimes**
TR 2

She **sometimes** studies with friends.

[ ] **always**
TR 3

She **always** eats breakfast.

 [ ] **once**
TR 5

 [ ] **weekly**
TR 6

 [ ] **regular**
TR 7

[ ] **awhile**
TR 8

It will be just **awhile** longer.

[ ] **seldom**
[ ] **rare**
TR 11 and TR 12

Lunar eclipses are **rare**.
They **seldom** happen.

[ ] **long**
TR 13

Have you **ever** been there?

[ ] **ever**
TR 14

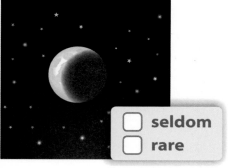
[ ] **repeat**
TR 17

[ ] **often**
TR 18

She waters the plant **often**.

[ ] **daily**
TR 19

☐ **twice**
TR 4

The sweater doesn't fit **anymore**.

☐ **anymore**
TR 9

I'll see you at the **usual** time.

Ok.

☐ **usual**
TR 10

☐ **hourly**
R 15

The clock rings **hourly**.

111 Bus Schedule

TIMES:
05:00 AM
05:10 AM
05:15 AM
05:20 AM
05:25 AM
05:30 AM
05:35 AM
05:40 AM
05:45 AM
05:50 AM
05:55 AM
06:00 AM
06:10 AM
06:15 AM
06:20 AM
06:25 AM
06:30 AM
06:35 AM
06:40 AM
06:45 AM
06:50 AM
06:55 AM

Bus Route

MORE ▶

☐ **frequent**
TR 16

☐ **forever**
TR 20

Definitions

If you **always** do a particular thing, you do it all the time.

If something does not happen or is not true **anymore**, it has stopped happening or is no longer true in the present period of time.

Awhile means for a short time.

Something that happens **daily** happens every day.

Ever means at any time. It is usually used in questions and negative sentences.

Something that will continue **forever** will always continue.

If something is **frequent**, it happens often.

An **hourly** event happens once every hour.

Long means a lot of time.

Never means at no time in the past, the present, or the future.

If something **often** happens, it happens many times or much of the time.

If something happens **once**, it happens one time only.

Something that is **rare** does not happen very often.

Regular events have equal amounts of time between them, so that they happen, for example, at the same time each day or each week.

If you **repeat** something, you say, do, or write it again.

If something **seldom** happens, it does not happen very often.

Sometimes means on some occasions rather than all the time.

If something happens **twice**, it happens two times.

Usual describes what happens most often.

A **weekly** event happens once a week or every week.

Check Your Understanding

A. Write **T** for **true statements** and **F** for **false statements**.

1. _____ If you always do something, you do it all the time.
2. _____ Something that happens daily occurs once every day.
3. _____ A frequent event rarely happens.
4. _____ A clock that rings hourly rings every five minutes.
5. _____ If something never happened, it happened only a few times.
6. _____ If something happened once, it happened only one time.
7. _____ If you repeat an action, you do the same action again.
8. _____ If you seldom do something, you hardly ever do it.
9. _____ If you do something twice, you do it three times.
10. _____ If a newspaper is delivered weekly, it is delivered once every week.
11. _____ Usual events are the things that happen most often.
12. _____ Forever is a limited amount of time.
13. _____ If something is not true anymore, it is no longer true.
14. _____ If something happens often, it happens a lot of the time.
15. _____ If something is rare, it usually happens.
16. _____ If something happens at a regular time, it usually happens at the same time every time.
17. _____ If you can stay somewhere for awhile, you can stay for a long time.
18. _____ If an event is long, it is over quickly.
19. _____ If an event happens sometimes, it does not happen all the time.
20. _____ If your friends ask you if you have ever done something, they want to know if you have done it at least once.

B. Underline the correct word to complete each sentence.

1. I'm sure Eric will arrive at the (**usual** / **weekly**) time.
2. Donny and Michael had to wait a (**awhile** / **long**) time to ride the roller coaster.
3. My family eats dinner together (**often** / **rare**), so we usually get a chance to talk.
4. It is (**never** / **rare**) for Adam to have a day off because he is so busy at work.
5. Sandra asked Hannah if she had (**ever** / **repeat**) gone canoeing before.
6. Because Fred has a vegetable garden, he (**seldom** / **often**) buys vegetables from the grocery store.

7. Cindy played with her dog for (**awhile** / **long**) and then went to soccer practice.

8. Jennifer asked Paul to (**frequent** / **repeat**) himself because she did not hear him the first time.

9. We (**always** / **sometimes**) walk to the beach, but not often.

10. My mom drives me to school in the morning, so I do not ride the bus (**anymore** / **once**).

11. When Tina and Chris got married, they promised to love each other (**forever** / **sometimes**).

12. Bella calls her mother (**twice** / **weekly**) a week.

13. The doctor told me to get (**seldom** / **regular**) exercise in order to stay healthy.

14. My dad listens to the (**hourly** / **repeat**) traffic report on the radio.

15. We make (**never** / **frequent**) trips to the city because we enjoy visiting the museums there.

16. Cedric has (**weekly** / **hourly**) trumpet lessons.

17. Becky (**seldom** / **always**) has a book with her because she loves to read.

18. Brenda has (**always** / **never**) gone swimming because she is afraid of the water.

19. Jill only met Dennis (**once** / **hourly**), so she does not know him very well.

20. The newspaper is delivered to our house (**daily** / **hourly**).

Challenge Words

Check (✔) the words you already know.

- [ ] annual
- [ ] common
- [ ] constant
- [ ] continue
- [ ] continuous
- [ ] customary
- [ ] general
- [ ] habitual
- [ ] infrequent
- [ ] irregular

144. Time Measurement Devices

Check (✔) the words you already know. Then, listen and repeat.

Tracks 1–5

2013						August
M	T	W	T	F	S	S
			1	2	3	4
5	6	7	8	9	10	⑪
12	13	14	15	16	17	18
19	20	21	22	23	24	25
26	27	28	29	30	31	

☐ date
TR 2

☐ calendar
TR 1

Check Your Understanding

A. Match each word to the correct description. One description will not be used.

1. _____ clock
2. _____ date
3. _____ o'clock
4. _____ watch
5. _____ calendar

a. a device that shows what time it is

b. used after numbers one through twelve to say what time it is

c. a chart that shows the days, weeks, and months in a year

d. a small clock you wear on your wrist

e. a specific day and month, or year

f. a watch that can be stopped instantly to time events

B. Underline the word that best completes each sentence.

Derek: Do you know what time it is? I don't think my (1) (**watch / date**) says the right time.

Ron: The (2) (**calendar / clock**) says it's 4:30.

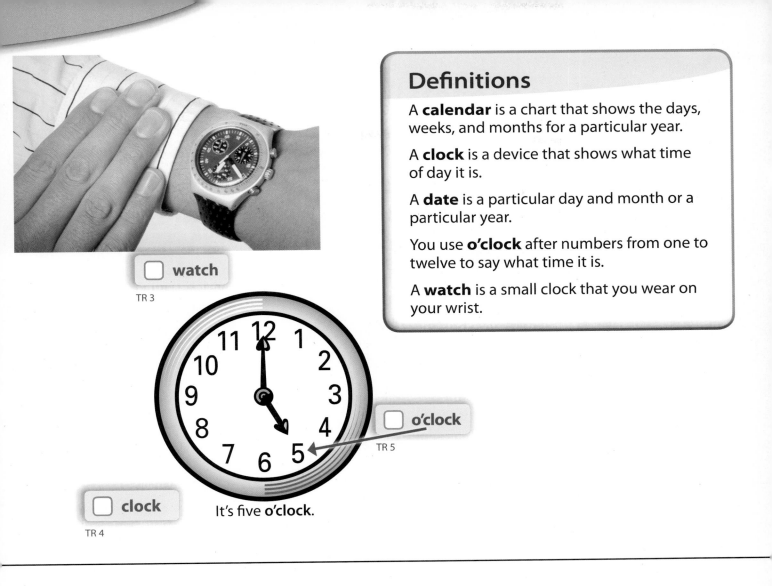

Definitions

A **calendar** is a chart that shows the days, weeks, and months for a particular year.

A **clock** is a device that shows what time of day it is.

A **date** is a particular day and month or a particular year.

You use **o'clock** after numbers from one to twelve to say what time it is.

A **watch** is a small clock that you wear on your wrist.

☐ watch

TR 3

☐ o'clock

TR 5

☐ clock

TR 4

It's five **o'clock**.

Derek: Oh, really? I have to meet Lily at five (3) (**date / o'clock**). We're going to study together.

Ron: What are you studying for?

Derek: We're in the same math class. We have a test.

Ron: We do? What is the (4) (**watch / date**) of the test?

Derek: I wrote it on my (5) (**calendar / clock**). It is on November 16.

Ron: Okay. Thanks! I should study also.

Challenge Words

Check (✔) the words you already know.

☐ hourglass   ☐ stopwatch   ☐ sundial   ☐ wristwatch

105

233. Time (General)

Check (✔) the words you already know. Then, listen and repeat.

Tracks 1–5

☐ **lunchtime**

TR 1

☐ **dinnertime**

TR 2

☐ **bedtime**

TR 3

Check Your Understanding

A. Match each word to the correct description. One description will not be used.

1. _____ bedtime
2. _____ time
3. _____ daytime
4. _____ dinnertime
5. _____ lunchtime

  a. when you go to bed

  b. when you eat dinner

  c. when you eat breakfast

  d. part of the day when there is light outside

  e. when you eat lunch

  f. stated in minutes, hours, days, and years

B. Write **T** for **true statements** and **F** for **false statements**.

1. _____ It is dark outside when it is daytime.

2. _____ People eat breakfast at lunchtime.

☐ **daytime**

TR 4

☐ **time**

TR 5

Definitions

Your **bedtime** is the time when you usually go to bed.

The **daytime** is the part of a day between the time when it gets light and the time when it gets dark.

Dinnertime is the time of the day when people have their dinner.

Lunchtime is the time of the day when people have their lunch.

Time is what we measure in minutes, hours, days, and years.

3. _____ Bedtime is usually when it is dark outside.

4. _____ Time is shown on clocks.

5. _____ Dinnertime is early in the morning.

Challenge Words

Check (✔) the words you already know.

☐ lifetime   ☐ springtime   ☐ suppertime   ☐ wintertime

☐ mealtime   ☐ summertime   ☐ wartime

5. Relationship Markers (Addition)

Check (✔) the words you already know. Then, listen and repeat.

Tracks 1–4

She is a friend **of** mine.

$44.95 ☐ **and**

TR 2

$34.29

I bought a new dress **and** a new hat.

☐ **of**

TR 1

Check Your Understanding

A. Write the correct word from the word bank to complete each sentence.

and	of	too	with

1. Kim is buying a coat and a hat, _____.

2. Denise went to the mall _____ her mother.

3. We enjoyed walking to the park _____ playing at the playground.

4. The governor _____ California was on TV last night.

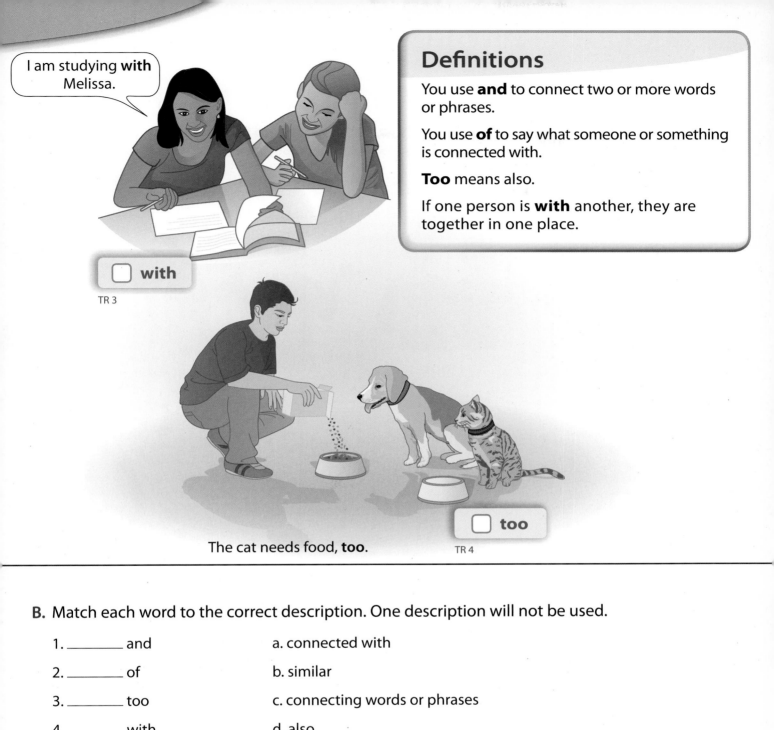

I am studying **with** Melissa.

with

TR 3

The cat needs food, **too**.

TR 4

Definitions

You use **and** to connect two or more words or phrases.

You use **of** to say what someone or something is connected with.

Too means also.

If one person is **with** another, they are together in one place.

too

B. Match each word to the correct description. One description will not be used.

1. _____ and
2. _____ of
3. _____ too
4. _____ with

a. connected with
b. similar
c. connecting words or phrases
d. also
e. together

Challenge Words

Check (✔) the words you already know.

☐ as well
☐ as well as
☐ further
☐ in addition
☐ moreover
☐ namely
☐ likewise

27. Relationship Markers (Contrast)

Check (✔) the words you already know. Then, listen and repeat.

 Tracks 1–16

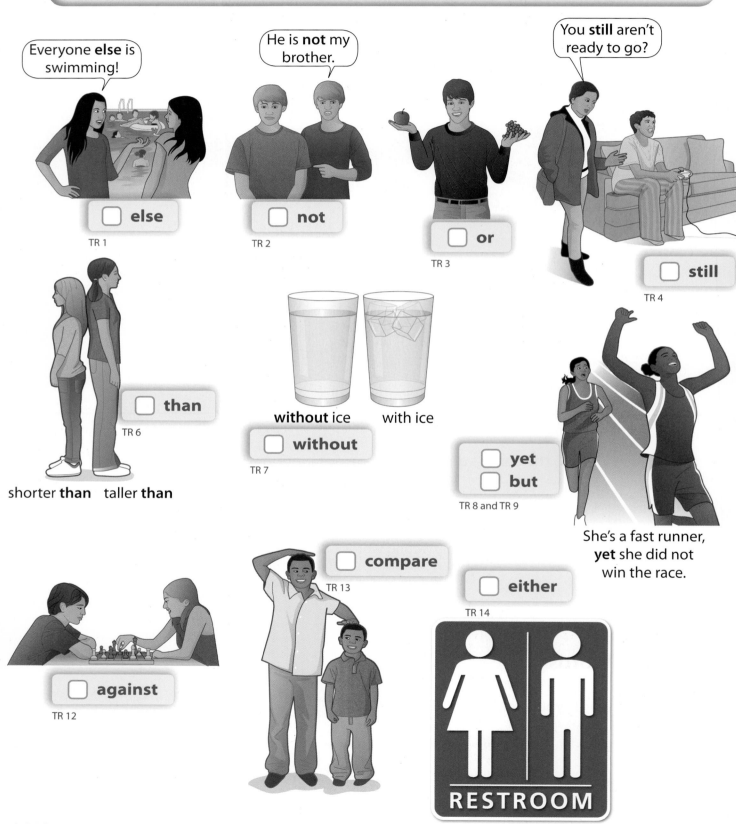

Everyone **else** is swimming!

☐ **else**
TR 1

He is **not** my brother.

☐ **not**
TR 2

☐ **or**
TR 3

You **still** aren't ready to go?

☐ **still**
TR 4

☐ **than**
TR 6

shorter **than**   taller **than**

without ice   with ice

☐ **without**
TR 7

☐ **yet**
☐ **but**
TR 8 and TR 9

She's a fast runner, **yet** she did not win the race.

☐ **compare**
TR 13

☐ **either**
TR 14

☐ **against**
TR 12

RESTROOM

☐ **except**

TR 5

I can't go to the party **unless** I finish my chores.

☐ **unless**

TR 10

☐ **neither**

TR 11

You have two weeks to decide **whether** you want to buy the house.

☐ **whether**

TR 15

☐ **instead**

TR 16

Definitions

If you compete **against** someone, you try to beat that person.

You use **but** to introduce something that is different than what you have just said.

When you **compare** things, you consider how they are different and how they are similar.

You use **either** to show that there are two possibilities to choose from.

You use **else** after words such as *someone*, and *everyone*, and after question words like *what* to talk about another person, place, or thing.

You use **except** to show that you are not including a particular thing or person.

If you do or choose one thing **instead** of another, you do or choose one thing over another.

Neither means not one or the other of two things or people.

You use **not** to form negative sentences.

You use **or** to show choices or possibilities.

If a situation that existed in the past **still** exists, it has continued and exists now.

You use **than** when you are comparing two people or things.

You use **unless** to introduce what will happen, be done, or be true if something else does not happen, is not done, or is not true.

You use **whether** when you are talking about a choice between two or more things.

You use **without** to show that someone or something does not have or use the thing mentioned.

You use **yet** to give additional and different information about something you just said.

Check Your Understanding

A. Match each word to the correct description. One description will not be used.

1. _____ but
2. _____ compare
3. _____ except
4. _____ neither
5. _____ not
6. _____ or
7. _____ unless
8. _____ whether
9. _____ without
10. _____ yet
11. _____ else
12. _____ still
13. _____ than
14. _____ against
15. _____ either
16. _____ instead

a. introduces what will happen or what will be done if something else does not happen or is not done

b. gives additional and different information about something just said

c. introduces something that is different than what you have just said

d. used to show choices or possibilities

e. consider how things are different and similar

f. to not have or use the thing mentioned

g. used to make a negative statement

h. used to show you are not including a person or thing

i. not one and not the other of two things or people

j. a choice between two or more things

k. to try to beat someone at something

l. used to say the result if a situation were true

m. used to compare two people or things

n. something that has existed in the past and still does now

o. shows that there are two possibilities to choose from

p. to do or choose one thing over another

q. used after certain words to talk about another person, place, or thing

B. Circle the correct answer.

1. This sweater is not mine. It belongs to someone _____.

   a. instead   b. except   c. else

2. We are playing _____ a very strong team.

   a. against   b. compare   c. but

3. We should clean the living room _____ of just sitting here.

   a. without   b. yet   c. instead

4. Erin _____ has to tell Mr. Brown that she will be late to class on Friday.

   a. whether   b. still   c. either

5. Michael is shorter _____ his brother.

   a. than   b. compare   c. instead

6. I am _____ going to the gym or to the library after school.

   a. still   b. either   c. unless

7. Erika is wearing a coat, _____ she is not wearing a hat.

   a. or   b. still   c. but

8. James does not know _____ or not he can go to the library tonight.

   a. whether   b. unless   c. than

9. _____ we leave now, we will not make it to the show on time.

   a. Except   b. Either   c. Unless

10. This is Andrew's cell phone. It's _____ mine.

    a. not   b. but   c. than

11. Sam will drink apple, orange, _____ cranberry juice.

    a. compare   b. yet   c. or

12. My mother likes to _____ prices to see which item is less expensive.

    a. against   b. except   c. compare

13. _____ Allie nor Casey wants to go shopping today.

    a. Neither   b. Whether   c. Unless

14. Lance can't ride his bicycle _____ because he still has a flat tire.

    a. but   b. or   c. yet

15. Stacy has read all the books in the series _____ the last one.

    a. except   b. either   c. else

16. Melissa wants a sandwich _____ onions.

    a. without   b. instead   c. except

Challenge Words

Check (✔) the words you already know.

☐ although   ☐ despite   ☐ nonetheless   ☐ otherwise   ☐ though

☐ anyway   ☐ however   ☐ on the other hand ☐ regardless of   ☐ versus

252. Similarity

Check (✔) the words you already know. Then, listen and repeat.

Tracks 1–9

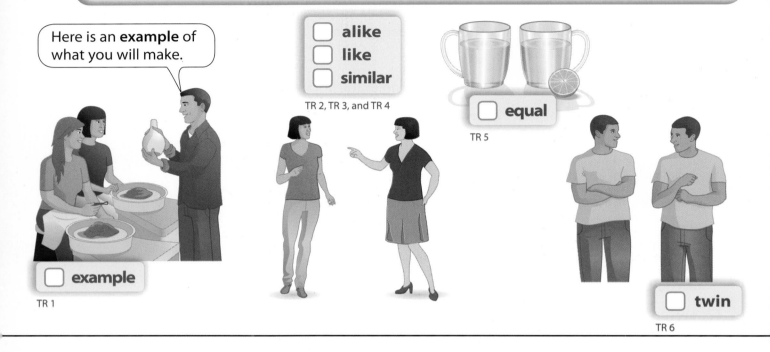

Here is an **example** of what you will make.

☐ example
TR 1

☐ alike
☐ like
☐ similar

TR 2, TR 3, and TR 4

☐ equal
TR 5

☐ twin
TR 6

Check Your Understanding

A. Write **T** for **true statements** and **F** for **false statements**.

1. _____ When you say two things are similar, you are saying that they are the same in some ways.

2. _____ An example shows you what other things in a particular group are like.

3. _____ If one person is like another, they are similar to each other.

4. _____ If two things are alike, they are completely different from each other.

5. _____ If two things are even in length, it means they have different lengths.

6. _____ A copy of something looks exactly like the original thing.

7. _____ Twins are two people who were born two years apart from the same mother.

8. _____ If two things are equal in size, it means they are different sizes.

9. _____ If two things are the same, they are very similar.

B. Circle the correct word to complete each sentence.

1. Ms. Tanner showed the class an _____ of a question that would be on the test.   a. alike   b. even   c. example

2. Christy and Hailey have _____ haircuts.   a. same   b. similar   c. copy

same

TR 7

copy

TR 8

even

TR 9

Definitions

If two or more things are **alike**, they are similar in some way.

If you make a **copy** of something, you produce something that looks like the original thing.

If two things are **equal**, they are the same in size, number, or value.

If two things are **even**, they have the same measurement.

An **example** is something that shows what other things in a particular group are like.

If one person or thing is **like** another, it is similar to that person or thing.

If two or more things are the **same**, they are very similar to each other.

If one thing is **similar** to another, or if two things are **similar**, they are the same in some ways but not in every way.

A **twin** is one of two people who were born at the same time from the same mother.

3. William made a _____ of the baseball practice schedule.   a. copy   b. twin   c. similar

4. Julia poured _____ amounts of water into two cups.   a. like   b. alike   c. equal

5. Sue cut two _____ pieces of string.   a. same   b. even   c. alike

6. All of the puppies look _____ to me.   a. alike   b. even   c. same

7. Robbie and John are wearing the _____ shirt today.   a. same   b. similar   c. twin

8. Mr. Edwards told me that I look just _____ my father.   a. copy   b. like   c. similar

9. Emma and her _____ sister Jenna both have blue eyes and brown hair.   a. same   b. twin   c. copy

Challenge Words

Check (✔) the words you already know.

- agreement
- approximate
- comparison
- consistent
- exact
- identical
- imitate
- match
- resemble
- substitute

299. Dissimilarity

Check (✔) the words you already know. Then, listen and repeat.

Tracks 1–6

☐ **change**

TR 2

☐ **opposite**

TR 1

Check Your Understanding

A. Write **T** for **true statements** and **F** for **false statements**.

1. _____ If two things are unlike each other, they are exactly the same.

2. _____ If two things are different, they are not the same.

3. _____ If something changes, it becomes different.

4. _____ Two things that are completely different in a particular way are the opposite of each other.

5. _____ The difference between two things is the way that they are similar.

6. _____ If two amounts of something are unequal, they are different.

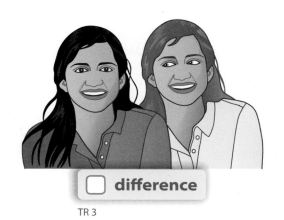

Definitions

When something **changes** or when you **change** it, it becomes different.

The **difference** between two people or things is the way in which they are different from each other.

If two people or things are **different**, they are not like each other.

Opposite describes people or things that are completely different in a particular way.

If one thing is **unequal** to another, it is different in amount, quantity, size, or time.

If one thing is **unlike** another thing, the two things are different.

☐ **difference**

TR 3

☐ **unequal**

TR 4

☐ **different**
☐ **unlike**

TR 5 and TR 6

B. Underline the correct word to complete each sentence.

1. My brother is the complete (**opposite** / **different**) of me.

2. You gave Matt and Nate (**unequal** / **unlike**) amounts of supplies.

3. Sharon and Gloria's eyes are (**change** / **different**) colors.

4. Derek (**changed** / **difference**) his clothes after he got home from school.

5. I cannot see any (**difference** / **different**) between the twin sisters.

6. Jordan is (**unequal** / **unlike**) her sister.

Challenge Words

Check (✔) the words you already know.

- ☐ adapt
- ☐ develop
- ☐ differ
- ☐ discriminate
- ☐ reform
- ☐ separate
- ☐ transform
- ☐ transition
- ☐ variety
- ☐ various

8 COLOR

57. Color

Check (✔) the words you already know. Then, listen and repeat.

Tracks 1–16

- ☐ color
  TR 1
- ☐ colorful
  TR 2
- ☐ silver
  TR 3
- ☐ white
  TR 4
- ☐ pink
  TR 5
- ☐ brown
  TR 6
- ☐ blue
  TR 7
- ☐ black
  TR 8
- ☐ yellow
  TR 9
- ☐ purple
  TR 10
- ☐ orange
  TR 11
- ☐ gray
  TR 12
- ☐ red
  TR 13
- ☐ gold
  TR 14
- ☐ green
  TR 15
- ☐ blonde
  TR 16

Definitions

Something that is **black** is the color of the sky at night.

Someone who has **blonde** hair has yellow or very light brown-colored hair.

Something that is **blue** is the color of the sky on a sunny day.

Something that is **brown** is the color of earth or wood.

The **color** of something is the way it looks in the light. Red, blue, and green are colors.

Something that is **colorful** has bright colors or a lot of different colors.

Something that is **gold** is bright yellow in color and is often shiny.

Something that is **gray** is a mixture of black and white, like the color of clouds on a rainy day.

Something that is **green** is the color of grass or leaves.

Something that is **orange** is of a color between red and yellow.

Something that is **pink** is of a color between red and white.

Something that is **purple** is a red-blue color.

Something that is **red** is the color of blood or of a tomato.

Something that is **silver** is shiny and pale gray in color.

Something that is **white** is the color of snow or milk.

Something that is **yellow** is the color of lemons or butter.

Check Your Understanding

A. Match each word to the correct object. One object will not be used.

1. _____ black	a. dirt
2. _____ blue	b. a pumpkin
3. _____ brown	c. a sunflower
4. _____ gold	d. ocean
5. _____ gray	e. grass
6. _____ green	f. a tomato
7. _____ orange	g. a tire
8. _____ purple	h. a ring
9. _____ red	i. a plum
10. _____ white	j. an elephant
11. _____ yellow	k. milk
12. _____ blonde	l. a spoon
13. _____ colorful	m. light hair
14. _____ silver	n. a parrot
15. _____ pink	o. dark hair
	p. a pig

B. Answer the questions.

1. What is your favorite color?

_____

2. What colors are you wearing today?

_____

3. What color is your hair?

_____

4. What colors do you see outside your classroom window?

_____

5. What colors do you see inside your classroom?

_____

Challenge Words

Check (✔) the words you already know.

☐ brunette   ☐ hazel   ☐ iridescent   ☐ tangerine   ☐ tawny

☐ crimson   ☐ indigo   ☐ maroon   ☐ taupe

415. Paint

Check (✔) the words you already know. Then, listen and repeat.

 Track 1

☐ paint

TR 1

Definition

Paint is a colored material that you put onto a surface with a brush.

Check Your Understanding

A. Choose the sentence that correctly uses the underlined word.

1. a. Every year, Tina buys new <u>paint</u> for the walls of her room.

   b. The boys mixed the <u>paint</u> for their bread.

2. a. The woman wanted to eat red <u>paint</u>.

   b. After 20 years, the <u>paint</u> on the house began to peel.

3. a. Steve brought his <u>paint</u> and paintbrushes to art class.

   b. Jenny was in a lot of <u>paint</u> after she fell down the stairs.

B. Write **T** for **true statements** and **F** for **false statements**.

1. _____ Paint is used to make beautiful pictures.

2. _____ Paint is used to make food.

3. _____ There are many different colors of paint.

Challenge Words

Check (✔) the words you already know.

☐ dye   ☐ enamel   ☐ lacquer   ☐ stain   ☐ tint

14. Exclamations

Check (✔) the words you already know. Then, listen and repeat.

Tracks 1–18

Ah! Now I understand!

2x+4=10
2x=6
(x=3)

☐ **ah**
TR 1

Gee, that hurt.

☐ **gee**
TR 2

Hi!

☐ **hi**
TR 3

Oh! It stopped raining.

☐ **oh**
TR 8

Are you going on the ski trip?

I don't know. Maybe.

☐ **maybe**
TR 9

OK, I'll talk to you later. Good-bye.

☐ **good-bye**
TR 10

Good night.

☐ **good night**
TR 13

Hello.

☐ **hello**
TR 14

Wow!

Hey!

☐ **hey**
TR 15

Ha!

☐ **ha**
TR 16

☐ **wow**
TR 17

123

Definitions

People say "**ah**" to show that they understand something, or that they are surprised or pleased.

People say "**aha**" to show that they are satisfied or surprised.

Bye is an informal way of saying goodbye.

People sometimes say "**gee**" to make a comment stronger.

You say "**good-bye**" to people when you or they are leaving a place, or at the end of a telephone conversation.

You say "**good night**" to someone late in the evening before you go home or go to bed.

People say "**ha**" to show that they are surprised, annoyed, or pleased.

You say "**hello**" when you meet someone.

In informal situations, you say or shout "**hey**" to attract someone's attention.

In informal situations, you say "**hi**" to greet someone.

You use **maybe** when you are uncertain about something.

You use **no** to give a negative response to a question.

You use **oh** to express a feeling such as surprise, pain, annoyance, or happiness.

You can say "**OK**" or "**okay**" to show that you agree to something.

People say "**ooh**" when they are surprised or excited, or when they think something is pleasant or unpleasant.

You can say "**wow**" when you think something is very good or surprising.

You use **yes** to give a positive answer to a question.

Check Your Understanding

A. Circle the word in each group that does not belong.

1. aha	ha	okay
2. no	gee	wow
3. hey	oh	ooh
4. hello	okay	hi
5. bye	gee	good-bye
6. OK	yes	maybe
7. aha	good night	ah

B. Underline the word that best completes each sentence.

Jason: (1) (**Hi / Good night**), Lauren!

Lauren: (2) (**Gee / Hello**), Jason!

Jason: Are you going to Devon's birthday party on Sunday?

Lauren: (3) (**No / Yes**), I can't go. I have to finish an art project that is due on Monday.

Jason: (4) (**Maybe / Oh**), that's too bad! Is that your art project in your bag?

Lauren: (5) (**Aha / Yes**), it is.

Jason: (6) (**Ah / Hello**), can I see it?

Lauren: (7) (**Okay / Gee**), here it is.

Jason: (8) (**Wow / Maybe**), that's amazing! I didn't know you could draw!

Lauren: Thanks! (9) (**Hey / Ha**), I have an idea. (10) (**Yes / Maybe**) I can finish this project tonight. Then I'll be able to go to the party on Sunday!

Jason: (11) (**Good-bye / Ooh**), that's a great idea! I hope you finish. See you later!

Lauren: (12) (**Bye / Ha**)!

Challenge Words

Check (✔) the words you already know.

- [ ] alas
- [ ] beware
- [ ] bravo
- [ ] farewell
- [ ] howdy
- [ ] hurrah
- [ ] ugh

61. Communication (Presentation of Information)

Check (✔) the words you already know. Then, listen and repeat.

Tracks 1–10

Shall I compare thee to a summer's day?

☐ **recite**
TR 1

I'm so good at spelling. Of course I won the spelling bee!

☐ **brag**
TR 2

Tonight I want to begin by. . .

☐ **state**
TR 3

☐ **present**
TR 4

You have a quiz tomorrow.

I have to leave at 3:30.

☐ **mention**
TR 7

☐ **tell**
☐ **say**
TR 5 and TR 6

The town meeting is tomorrow at 7:00.

☐ **inform**
TR 8

When you eat food, it travels down your esophagus . . .

☐ **explain**
TR 9

Definitions

If you **brag**, you talk proudly about yourself and your successes or achievements to others.

If you **describe** something, you say what it is like.

If you **explain** something, you describe it so that others can understand it.

If you **inform** someone of something, you give information to that person.

If you **mention** something, you say something about it without giving much information.

If you **present** something, you formally show it to a group of people.

If you **recite** a poem or other piece of writing, you say it aloud after you have learned it.

When you **say** something, you speak words.

If you **state** something, you say it or write it in a formal or definite way.

If you **tell** someone something, you say something to that person.

This outfit is perfect for the spring. It is light and comfortable.

☐ **describe**
TR 10

Check Your Understanding

A. Match each word to the correct description. One description will not be used.

1. _____ brag
2. _____ present
3. _____ describe
4. _____ explain
5. _____ inform
6. _____ mention
7. _____ recite
8. _____ state
9. _____ tell
10. _____ say

a. to give someone information about something
b. to say something to someone without giving much information about it
c. to say or write something in a formal way
d. to show how something works
e. to speak words
f. to proudly talk about something you have done
g. to say something to someone
h. to formally show something to a group of people
i. to say what something is like
j. to say something aloud after it has been learned
k. to describe something so that it is easy to understand

B. Underline the correct word to complete each sentence.

1. Ted is nervous because he has to (**recite / inform**) a poem in front of the class today.
2. The president will (**inform / state**) her reasons for leaving the company at a meeting this afternoon.
3. Please (**mention / tell**) me what time the concert starts.
4. If you ask Nick to help you, he will probably (**mention / say**) yes.
5. Everyone is annoyed with Kevin because he (**describes / brags**) too much about himself.
6. Carla (**presented / bragged**) her project at the science fair today.
7. James (**informed / presented**) his manager that he was getting a new job.
8. Andrew (**mentioned / recited**) that he had to go somewhere this afternoon, but he did not say where.
9. Mrs. Crane (**recited / explained**) the math problem to me so that I could understand it.
10. Alexa (**bragged / described**) the camping trip as fun and exciting.

Challenge Words

Check (✔) the words you already know.

☐ announce   ☐ claim   ☐ demonstrate   ☐ notify   ☐ specify
☐ boast   ☐ clarify   ☐ express   ☐ refer   ☐ utter

100. Communication (Positive Information)

Check (✔) the words you already know. Then, listen and repeat.

Tracks 1–10

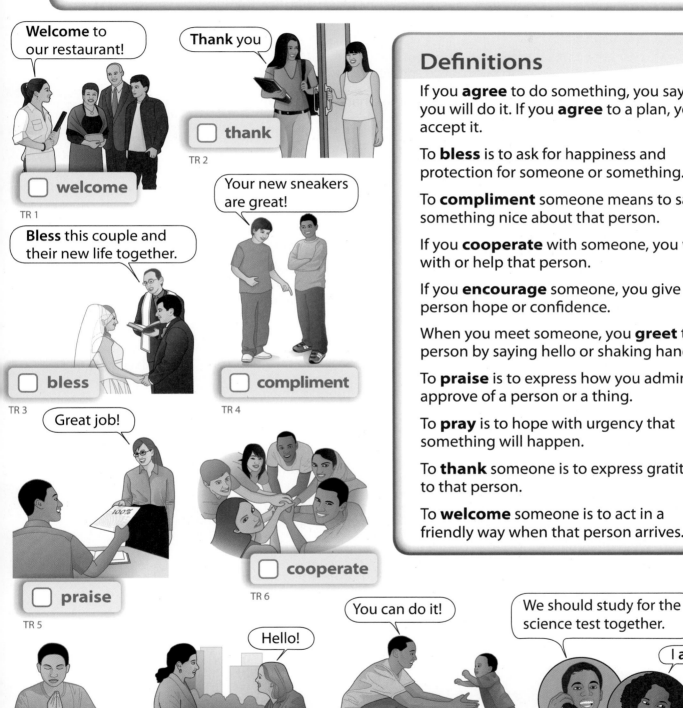

Welcome to our restaurant!

☐ welcome
TR 1

Thank you

☐ thank
TR 2

Bless this couple and their new life together.

☐ bless
TR 3

Your new sneakers are great!

☐ compliment
TR 4

Great job!

☐ praise
TR 5

☐ cooperate
TR 6

Definitions

If you **agree** to do something, you say that you will do it. If you **agree** to a plan, you accept it.

To **bless** is to ask for happiness and protection for someone or something.

To **compliment** someone means to say something nice about that person.

If you **cooperate** with someone, you work with or help that person.

If you **encourage** someone, you give that person hope or confidence.

When you meet someone, you **greet** that person by saying hello or shaking hands.

To **praise** is to express how you admire or approve of a person or a thing.

To **pray** is to hope with urgency that something will happen.

To **thank** someone is to express gratitude to that person.

To **welcome** someone is to act in a friendly way when that person arrives.

☐ pray
TR 7

Hello!

☐ greet
TR 8

You can do it!

☐ encourage
TR 9

We should study for the science test together.

I agree.

☐ agree
TR 10

Check Your Understanding

A. Write each word in the word bank next to the correct definition.

agree	thank	bless	pray	praise
greet	compliment	encourage	welcome	cooperate

1. _____ to say that you admire or approve of someone

2. _____ to say "hello" or shake hands with someone you meet

3. _____ to say something nice about someone

4. _____ to accept a plan

5. _____ to work with or help someone

6. _____ to ask for protection and happiness for someone or something

7. _____ to act friendly when someone arrives

8. _____ to give someone hope or confidence

9. _____ to say that you are grateful to someone

10. _____ to hope with urgency that something will happen

B. Underline the correct word to complete each sentence.

1. I (**agreed / encouraged**) to pick up Gary from his friend's house at 8 o'clock.

2. Everyone at the wedding hoped that the new couple would be (**prayed / blessed**) in their new life together.

3. The hostess (**praised / greeted**) the guests as they entered the restaurant.

4. Joe (**prayed / thanked**) for his sick mother to get better.

5. Mark (**agreed / thanked**) Drew for showing him how to get to the cafeteria.

6. Charlie (**welcomed / cooperated**) his grandmother when she arrived at his house.

7. Laura (**complimented / blessed**) Olivia on her new outfit.

8. We need to (**cooperate / welcome**) with each other in order to finish this project.

9. The coach (**encouraged / thanked**) the last runner to finish the race.

10. The firefighter was (**agreed / praised**) for saving the family from the burning house.

Challenge Words

Check (✔) the words you already know.

- [ ] acknowledge
- [ ] assure
- [ ] congratulations
- [ ] participate
- [ ] teamwork
- [ ] apology
- [ ] blessing
- [ ] credit
- [ ] prayer
- [ ] worship

105. Communication (General)

Check (✔) the words you already know. Then, listen and repeat.

Tracks 1–6

☐ **speech**

TR 1

Definitions

When people **chat**, they talk in an informal, friendly way.

If people **discuss** something, they talk about it.

When you **speak**, you use your voice in order to say something.

A **speech** is a formal talk that someone gives to a group of people.

A **statement** is something that you say or write that gives information in a formal way.

If you **talk**, you say words or speak to someone about your thoughts, ideas, or feelings.

The math test was really hard.

☐ **talk**
☐ **speak**

TR 2 and TR 3

☐ **statement**

TR 4

I would like to read my client's **statement**.

Let's **discuss** when we are going to go camping.

OK. I think we can go next weekend.

Hi, how are you?

I'm great! How are you?

☐ **discuss**

TR 5

☐ **chat**

TR 6

Check Your Understanding

A. Match each word to the correct description. One description will not be used.

1. _____ chat

2. _____ discuss

3. _____ speak

4. _____ speech

5. _____ statement

6. _____ talk

a. to use your voice to say something

b. information said or written in a formal way

c. to talk in an informal, friendly way

d. to say words, or speak about your ideas

e. to talk about something

f. a formal talk that is given to a group of people

g. a talk someone gives in order to teach people about something

B. Write the words from the word bank in the correct column.

| chat | speak | talk |
| discuss | speech | statement |

VERBS	NOUNS

Challenge Words

Check (✔) the words you already know.

- ☐ brainstorm
- ☐ comment
- ☐ communicate
- ☐ dialogue
- ☐ discussion
- ☐ lecture
- ☐ negotiate
- ☐ proclamation
- ☐ proposal
- ☐ talkative

177. Questioning

Check (✔) the words you already know. Then, listen and repeat.

Tracks 1–9

Who was the first president of the United States?

George Washington.

☐ **test**

TR 1

Do we have homework tonight?

☐ **ask**

TR 2

☐ **offer**

TR 3

Here kitty, kitty!

☐ **call**

TR 4

Check Your Understanding

A. Circle the correct word for each definition.

1. to say an answer

   a. test   b. question   c. reply

2. to react to something by doing or saying something

   a. call   b. respond   c. request

3. to ask a lot of questions about something

   a. question   b. answer   c. reply

4. to ask questions to find out how much someone knows

   a. ask   b. test   c. question

5. to say something in a loud voice

   a. offer   b. reply   c. call

6. to say something back in response to a question

   a. answer   b. offer   c. request

7. to say something in the form of a question

   a. reply   b. test   c. ask

8. to ask a person if he or she would like to accept something

   a. question   b. answer   c. offer

9. to ask for something politely

   a. call   b. reply   c. request

I'd like to **request** a song, please.

☐ **request**
TR 5

What time are you coming over?

☐ **question**
TR 6

8 PM.

☐ **answer**
☐ **reply**
☐ **respond**
TR 7, TR 8, and TR 9

Definitions

When you **answer**, you say something back in response to a question.

If you **ask**, you say something in the form of a question.

If you **call** something, you say it in a loud voice.

If you **offer**, you ask someone if he or she would like to accept something you are willing to give or do.

If you **question** someone, you ask a lot of questions about something.

When you **reply** to something that someone says to you, you say an answer to that person.

If you **request** something, you ask for it politely or formally.

When you **respond** to something that someone does or says, you react to it by doing or saying something.

If you **test** someone, you ask questions in order to find out how much that person knows about something.

B. Underline the correct words to complete the story.

The day before the exam on U.S. presidents, Ms. Martinez decided to play a question and answer game with her students. She (1) (**requested** / **replied**) that everyone listen carefully to her questions. Then, Ms. Martinez began to (2) (**test** / **ask**) their knowledge. She soon realized that none of the students were raising their hands. She (3) (**asked** / **answered**) her students, "Do you know the answers to my questions? Did any of you study?" She (4) (**offered** / **questioned**), "Are you prepared for the exam tomorrow?" The classroom was silent and no one (5) (**replied** / **called**).

Because no one (6) (**requested** / **answered**) Ms. Martinez, she (7) (**called** / **questioned**) on Tim. "Did you study, Tim?" she asked. Tim (8) (**asked** / **responded**) that he did study, but that he could not remember anything. Ms. Martinez realized that her students needed more practice. She (9) (**offered** / **tested**) them extra help and stayed after school to help them study.

Challenge Words

Check (✔) the words you already know.

☐ beckon ☐ confer ☐ inquire ☐ invite ☐ propose
☐ bid ☐ consult ☐ interview ☐ poll ☐ quiz

135

198. Communication (Confrontation / Negative Information)

Check (✔) the words you already know. Then, listen and repeat.

Tracks 1–13

☐ **blame**
TR 1

☐ **cheat**
TR 2

Did you eat the cookies?

No, I didn't.

☐ **lie**
TR 3

You stole the diamond necklace.

☐ **accuse**
TR 8

No, I didn't.

Yes, you did!

☐ **argue**
☐ **quarrel**
TR 9 and TR 10

This does not taste very good.

☐ **complain**
TR 11

Check Your Understanding

A. Underline the correct word to complete each sentence.

1. Annie always tells the truth because she cannot (**disobey / lie**).

2. Valerie (**argues / complains**) about her homework because she thinks it is too difficult.

3. Andy tried to (**cheat / tease**) on his test by copying his friend's answers.

4. Carl (**disobeyed / scolded**) his son for coming home late.

5. Sam (**dared / teased**) his sister about her new haircut.

6. Linda (**disagreed /warned**) with Ken when he said that basketball was the best sport.

I dare you to hold it.

I think you should wear these.

No, I think I will wear these.

dare
TR 4

disagree
TR 5

disobey
TR 6

scold
TR 7

tease
TR 12

Be careful! There's a mean dog in there!

warn
TR 13

Definitions

If you **accuse** someone **of** something, you say that person did something wrong or dishonest.

If you **argue** with someone, you disagree or fight with that person using angry words.

If you **blame** someone or something for something bad, you say that person or thing caused it.

If someone **cheats**, that person does not obey the rules in a game or exam.

If you **complain**, you say that you are not satisfied with someone or something.

If you **dare** someone to do something, you ask that person to do it in order to see if he or she is brave enough.

If you **disagree** with someone, you have a different opinion from that person.

When someone **disobeys**, that person does not do what he or she has been told to do.

If you **lie**, you say something you know is not true.

When two or more people **quarrel**, they have an angry argument.

To **scold** is to speak in an angry way to a person or animal that has done something wrong.

To **tease** is to laugh at or makes jokes about someone in order to embarrass or annoy that person.

If you **warn** someone about a possible danger, you tell that person about it.

7. The sign (**complained / warned**) drivers that the road was under construction.

8. Angela's friends (**argued / dared**) her to ask Sam out on a date.

9. Evan apologized to his friend for (**quarreling / daring**) with him earlier.

10. Mrs. Hanson (**disagreed / accused**) a student of cheating.

11. Christa (**lied / blamed**) Edward for missing the bus.

12. Ben (**argued / teased**) with Henry because he disagreed with him.

13. Jack always listens to what his father tells him and never (**disobeys / warns**) him.

B. Match each word to the correct description. One description will not be used.

1. _____ disagree

2. _____ lie

3. _____ argue

4. _____ cheat

5. _____ quarrel

6. _____ complain

7. _____ scold

8. _____ tease

9. _____ disobey

10. _____ accuse

11. _____ warn

12. _____ blame

13. _____ dare

a. to say that someone did something wrong or dishonest

b. to say that you are not happy with someone or something

c. to disagree or fight with someone using angry words

d. to have a different opinion from someone else

e. to say something that is not true

f. to ask someone to do something to see if they are brave enough

g. to politely refuse something

h. to laugh or make jokes about someone

i. to not follow the rules in a game or exam

j. to speak in an angry way to someone who did something wrong

k. to tell someone about possible danger

l. to tell someone that he or she has caused something bad

m. to not do what someone told you to do

n. to have an angry argument

Challenge Words

Check (✔) the words you already know.

☐ annoy ☐ decline ☐ exaggerate ☐ threaten ☐ warning

☐ criticism ☐ embarrass ☐ rumor ☐ trial

207. Communication (Supervision / Commands)

Check (✔) the words you already know. Then, listen and repeat.

Tracks 1–17

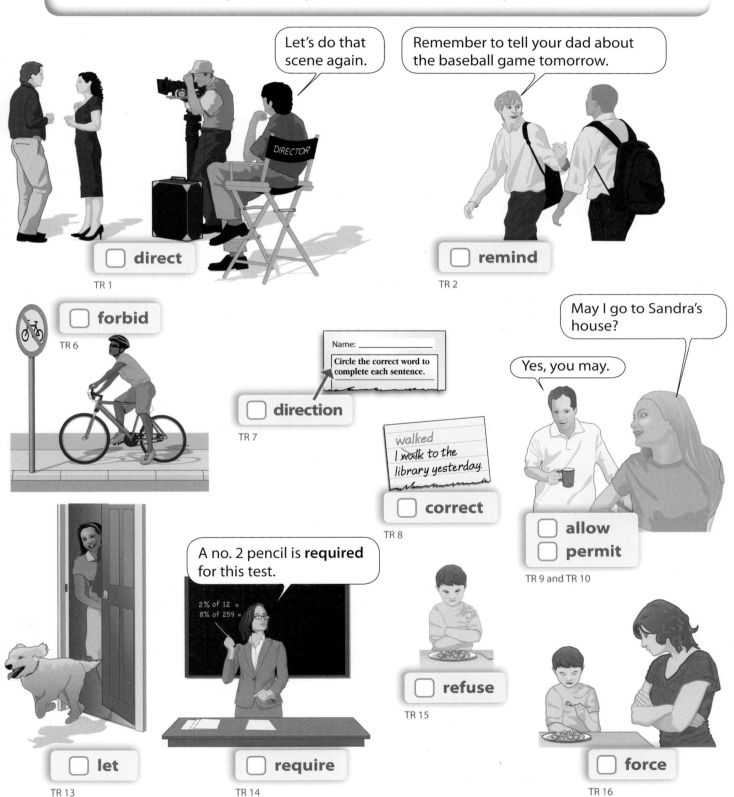

Let's do that scene again.

Remember to tell your dad about the baseball game tomorrow.

☐ **direct**

TR 1

☐ **remind**

TR 2

☐ **forbid**

TR 6

Name: _____
Circle the correct word to complete each sentence.

☐ **direction**

TR 7

May I go to Sandra's house?

Yes, you may.

walked
I walk to the library yesterday.

☐ **correct**

TR 8

☐ **allow**
☐ **permit**

TR 9 and TR 10

A no. 2 pencil is **required** for this test.

2% of 12 =
8% of 259 =

☐ **refuse**

TR 15

☐ **let**

TR 13

☐ **require**

TR 14

☐ **force**

TR 16

139

Where were you at 10 PM yesterday?

☐ **demand**

TR 3

Sit!

☐ **command**

TR 4

Continue
Yes   No

☐ **control**

TR 5

Here's my **advice**: tell her that you're sorry.

☐ **advice**

TR 11

That's OK.

Oh, I'm sorry!

☐ **excuse**

TR 12

Load the dishwasher before you watch TV.

☐ **obey**

TR 17

Definitions

If you give someone **advice**, you tell that person what you think he or she should do.

If you **allow** something, you give permission to do it, have it, or use it.

If you **command** someone to do something, you tell that person that he or she must do it.

If you **control** something, you have the power to make all the important decisions about it.

If you **correct** a problem or a mistake, you make it right.

If you **demand** information or action, you ask for it in a very firm way.

When you **direct** a project or a group of people, you are responsible for organizing it or them.

A **direction** is an instruction that tells you what to do, how to do something, or how to get somewhere.

If you **excuse** someone for doing something, you forgive that person for it.

If you **forbid** someone to do something, you tell that person not to do it.

If you **force** someone to do something, you make that person do it.

If you **let** something happen, you do not try to stop it.

If you **obey** a person or a command, you do what you are told to do.

If you **permit** someone to do something, you allow that person to do it.

If you **refuse** to do something, you say strongly that you will not do it.

If you **remind** someone to do a certain thing, you say something that makes that person remember to do it.

If you **require** something, you need it.

Check Your Understanding

A. Write **T** for **true statements** and **F** for **false statements**.

1. _____ If someone commands you to do something, that person is telling you that you must do it.

2. _____ If a person directs a project, he or she is in charge of organizing it.

3. _____ If you demand information from someone, you ask for it in a very firm way.

4. _____ If you allow a person to do something, you give that person permission to do it.

5. _____ A direction is an instruction that tells you how to do something.

6. _____ If you control something, you are not in charge of making decisions about it.

7. _____ If you excuse someone for doing something wrong, you forgive that person for doing it.

8. _____ If a person forces you to do something, that person makes you do it.

9. _____ If you give advice to a person, you tell that person what you think he or she should do.

10. _____ If you correct a mistake, you make it right.

11. _____ If something is permitted, it is not allowed.

12. _____ Something that is required is needed.

13. _____ If you refuse to do something, you agree to do it.

14. _____ If you obey a person, you do what that person has told you to do.

15. _____ If you remind someone to do something, you tell that person not to do it.

16. _____ If someone forbids you to do something, that person tells you that you must not do it.

17. _____ If you let someone do something, you allow that person to do it.

B. Circle the word in each group that does not belong.

1. command   advice   direct

2. force   require   forbid

3. correct   let   allow

4. direction   obey   advice

5. excuse   demand   require

6. control   direct   refuse

Challenge Words

Check (✔) the words you already know.

- ☐ administer
- ☐ authority
- ☐ ban
- ☐ compel
- ☐ compromise
- ☐ deny
- ☐ instruction
- ☐ leadership
- ☐ regulate
- ☐ submit

255. Persuasion / Advice

Check (✔) the words you already know. Then, listen and repeat.

 Tracks 1–8

☐ **beg**
TR 1

Please?

Your next line is, "What a beautiful day!"

☐ **cue**
TR 2

*I **suggest** you wear a coat today. It's cold outside.*

☐ **suggest**
TR 3

*I **advise** you to save that money for college.*

☐ **advise**
TR 4

Definitions

If you **advise** someone to do something, you tell that person what you think he or she should do.

If you **appeal** to someone, you make a serious or urgent request to that person.

To **beg** is to ask someone to do something in a way that shows you very much want it done.

To **convince** someone is to persuade that person to do or believe something.

A **cue** is an action or a statement that tells someone to do something.

To **persuade** is to talk someone into doing something.

To **recommend** is to suggest that a person or thing is good or useful.

To **suggest** is to put forward a plan or idea for someone to think about.

*I **recommend** this book. You should read it.*

☐ **recommend**
TR 5

*She **convinced** me. I'm voting for Smith.*

Vote **Smith**

☐ **convince**
☐ **persuade**
TR 6 and TR 7

I really need your help.

☐ **appeal**
TR 8

Check Your Understanding

A. Match each word to the correct description. One description will not be used.

1. _____ suggest
2. _____ beg
3. _____ convince
4. _____ appeal
5. _____ cue
6. _____ recommend
7. _____ persuade
8. _____ advise

a. to make a serious or urgent request
b. to suggest a good or useful thing to someone else
c. to tell someone a plan or idea for them to think about
d. to talk someone into doing something
e. to persuade someone to do something
f. to tell someone what you think they should do
g. an action that tells someone to do something
h. to offer a person money to persuade them to do something
i. to ask for something in a way that shows that you really want it

B. Choose the sentence that correctly uses the underlined word.

1. a. I <u>advised</u> a new band to my sister.
   b. Scott's mother <u>advises</u> him on relationships.
2. a. My friend <u>appealed</u> the movie to me.
   b. His parents <u>appealed</u> to Adam to spend more time on his homework.
3. a. Erica and Ellen <u>begged</u> their mother to take them on a vacation.
   b. Maya <u>begged</u> this book to me because she thinks I will enjoy it.
4. a. The painting does not <u>convince</u> Mark, because he thinks it is ugly.
   b. It was not difficult to <u>convince</u> Heather to go swimming today.
5. a. When Sylvia heard her <u>cue</u>, she walked onstage and began to sing.
   b. Andrew talked with his son and <u>cued</u> him to save money to buy a car.
6. a. Michael <u>persuaded</u> some videos at the store.
   b. Leah <u>persuaded</u> her brother to go for a walk with her.
7. a. Wendy tried to <u>recommend</u> Alex to say yes.
   b. Iliana <u>recommended</u> the Italian restaurant to all of her friends.
8. a. Mrs. Smith <u>suggested</u> that we study our notes.
   b. The new coffee shop <u>suggests</u> to a lot of customers.

Challenge Words

Check (✔) the words you already know.

☐ bait   ☐ corrupt   ☐ petition
☐ bias   ☐ hint   ☐ tempt
☐ bribe   ☐ influence   ☐ urge

144

345. Communication (Information Previously Withheld)

Check (✔) the words you already know. Then, listen and repeat.

Tracks 1–2

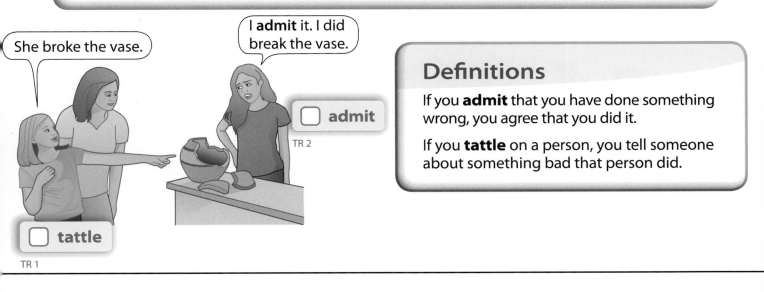

She broke the vase.

I **admit** it. I did break the vase.

☐ **admit**

TR 2

☐ **tattle**

TR 1

Definitions

If you **admit** that you have done something wrong, you agree that you did it.

If you **tattle** on a person, you tell someone about something bad that person did.

Check Your Understanding

A. Write **T** for **true statements** and **F** for **false statements**.

1. _____ When you admit that you did something, you are saying that you did not do it.

2. _____ When you admit something, you are telling the truth about something you did.

3. _____ When you tattle on a person, you tell about something bad that person did.

4. _____ If you tattle on a person, that person is usually happy with you.

B. Underline the correct word to complete each sentence.

1. I (**admit** / **tattle**) that I borrowed your necklace without asking.

2. I am going to (**admit** / **tattle**) on you for stealing my book.

3. Josh (**admitted** / **tattled**) that he broke his brother's bicycle.

4. Anita (**admitted** / **tattled**) on Jeremy for taking her sandwich.

Challenge Words

Check (✔) the words you already know.

☐ confess   ☐ confide   ☐ divulge   ☐ expose   ☐ reveal

346. Recording / Translating Information

Check (✔) the words you already know. Then, listen and repeat.

 Tracks 1–3

☐ **record**

TR 1

☐ **recording**

TR 2

Check Your Understanding

A. Match each word to the correct description. One description will not be used.

1. _____ record
2. _____ video
3. _____ recording

   a. a file or disk that stores moving pictures and sounds
   b. to write down or photograph an event
   c. a file of graphics or a piece of text
   d. a recorded event

B. Underline the correct word to complete each sentence.

1. Pete is watching a (**record** / **recording**) of his favorite show.

2. My mother is going to (**video** / **record**) my graduation by taking many pictures.

3. We are watching a (**record** / **video**) of my baby brother taking his first steps.

4. I will e-mail you the (**recording** / **record**) of our band practicing for the concert.

Definitions

If you **record** a piece of information or an event, you write it down or photograph it so that in the future people can read or look at it.

A **recording** of moving pictures and sounds is a computer file or a disk on which the images and sounds are stored.

A **video** is a recording of an event or a movie.

 video

TR 3

Challenge Words

Check (✔) the words you already know.

☐ cassette ☐ decode ☐ interpret ☐ score ☐ translate

383. Promises

Check (✔) the word you already know. Then, listen and repeat.

I **promise** to tell the truth.

Definition

If you **promise** that you will do something, you say that you will certainly do it.

☐ promise

TR 1

Check Your Understanding

A. Write **T** for **true statements** and **F** for **false statements**.

1. _____ If you promise to do something, you are saying that you will do it.

2. _____ If you promise not to do something, you are saying that you will not do it.

3. _____ If you promise to do something, it means you are lying.

B. Choose the sentence that correctly uses the underlined word.

1. a. Simon <u>promised</u> the dog early in the morning.

   b. Ben <u>promised</u> to take the dog for a walk.

2. a. Andrew <u>promised</u> to be home by 10:00.

   b. Janice <u>promised</u> early in the morning.

3. a. Sarah <u>promised</u> not to be late again.

   b. Stephanie didn't agree with me and we <u>promised</u> for hours.

Challenge Words

Check (✔) the words you already know.

☐ guarantee   ☐ pact   ☐ plea   ☐ pledge   ☐ vow

32. Birds

Check (✔) the words you already know. Then, listen and repeat.

Tracks 1–14

☐ chicken
TR 1

☐ rooster
TR 2

☐ hen
TR 3

☐ fowl
TR 4

☐ parrot
TR 5

☐ turkey
TR 6

☐ eagle
TR 7

☐ robin
TR 8

☐ goose
TR 9

☐ bird
TR 10

☐ crow
TR 11

☐ jay
TR 12

☐ duck
TR 13

☐ owl
TR 14

Definitions

A **bird** is a creature with feathers and wings.

A **chicken** is a bird that is raised on a farm for its eggs and for its meat.

A **crow** is a large, black bird that makes a loud noise.

A **duck** is a bird that lives near water.

An **eagle** is a large bird that eats small animals.

Fowl are birds that can be eaten as food, such as chickens.

A **goose** is a large bird that has a long neck.

A **hen** is a female chicken.

A **jay** is a noisy bird with blue or gray feathers.

An **owl** is a bird with large eyes that is active at night.

A **parrot** is a tropical bird with a curved beak and either very bright or gray feathers.

A **robin** is a brown bird with a red chest.

A **rooster** is an adult male chicken.

A **turkey** is a large bird that is raised on a farm for its meat.

Check Your Understanding

A. Write each bird in the correct column.

jay	crow	robin	goose	turkey
owl	duck	eagle	parrot	chicken

LIVES ON A FARM	LIVES IN THE TREES	LIVES BY WATER

B. Circle the correct answer.

1. What is a creature with feathers and wings called?

   a. a bird   b. a fish   c. a cat

2. Which bird is awake at night?

   a. fowl   b. a jay   c. an owl

3. Which bird is all black?

   a. a crow   b. a turkey   c. a duck

4. Which bird is a female chicken?

   a. a goose   b. a hen   c. a rooster

5. Which bird can be very bright and colorful?

   a. a parrot   b. an eagle   c. a robin

6. Which bird eats small animals?

   a. a duck   b. a turkey   c. an eagle

7. Which bird is raised for its meat?

    a. a turkey   b. a crow   c. a robin

8. Which bird has a red chest?

    a. a hen   b. a robin   c. a crow

9. Which bird is a male chicken?

    a. a chicken   b. a rooster   c. a hen

10. What are birds that can be eaten called?

    a. parrots   b. fowl   c. food

11. Which bird lives by water?

    a. an owl   b. an eagle   c. a duck

12. Which bird has a long neck?

    a. a goose   b. a turkey   c. a jay

13. Which bird's eggs do people eat?

    a. a robin's   b. a crow's   c. a chicken's

14. Which bird is very noisy?

    a. a duck   b. a jay   c. a hen

Challenge Words

Check (✔) the words you already know.

☐ bluebird	☐ dove	☐ hummingbird	☐ penguin	☐ seagull
☐ canary	☐ heron	☐ ostrich	☐ pigeon	☐ swan

35. Baby Animals

Check (✔) the words you already know. Then, listen and repeat.

 Tracks 1–7

☐ **calf**
TR 1

☐ **bunny**
TR 2

☐ **cub**
TR 3

Check Your Understanding

A. Match the adult name of the animal to the baby name. One adult name will not be used.

1. _____ bunny   a. cow

2. _____ tadpole   b. frog

3. _____ pup / puppy   c. rabbit

4. _____ calf   d. hen

5. _____ kitten   e. cat

6. _____ cub   f. dog

                          g. bear

B. Write where each animal lives.

1. tadpole _____

2. bunny _____

3. kitten _____

Definitions

Bunny is a child's word for a rabbit.

A **calf** is a young cow.

A **cub** is a young wild animal, such as a bear.

A **kitten** is a young cat.

A **puppy** or **pup** is a young dog.

A **tadpole** is a very small water creature that looks like a fish and that develops into a frog or a toad.

☐ **puppy**
☐ **pup**

TR 4 and TR 5

☐ **kitten**

TR 6

☐ **tadpole**

TR 7

4. pup / puppy _____

5. calf _____

6. cub _____

Challenge Words

Check (✔) the words you already know.

☐ chick   ☐ colt   ☐ fawn

64. Cats/Dogs

Check (✔) the words you already know. Then, listen and repeat.

☐ cat
TR 1

☐ lion
TR 2

☐ fox
TR 3

☐ bulldog
TR 6

☐ dog
☐ doggie
TR 7 and TR 8

Check Your Understanding

A. Write **T** for **true statements** and **F** for **false statements**.

1. _____ Cats are never kept as pets.

2. _____ Foxes have black fur.

3. _____ Tigers have black stripes.

4. _____ *Doggie* is another word for dog.

5. _____ A wolf is part of the dog family.

6. _____ Bulldogs have large, square heads.

7. _____ Collies have short hair.

8. _____ Lions come from Africa.

9. _____ People often have dogs as pets.

Definitions

A **bulldog** is a short dog with a large, square head.

A **cat** is a small animal covered with fur that people often keep as a pet.

A **collie** or a **collie dog** is a dog with long hair and a long, narrow nose.

A **dog** is an animal that is often kept by people as a pet.

Doggie is a child's word for a dog.

A **fox** is a wild animal that looks like a dog. It has red fur and a thick tail.

A **lion** is a large, wild cat that mainly lives in Africa. Lions have yellow fur, and male lions have long hair on their head and neck.

A **tiger** is a large, wild animal of the cat family. Tigers are orange with black stripes.

A **wolf** is a wild animal that looks like a large dog.

collie
TR 4

wolf
TR 5

tiger
TR 9

B. Write each animal in the correct column.

| fox | lion | collie | bulldog |
| wolf | tiger | doggie | |

CAT FAMILY	DOG FAMILY

Challenge Words

Check (✔) the words you already know.

- beagle
- coyote
- hyena
- leopard
- pug
- cougar
- greyhound
- Labrador
- panther
- puma

65. Land Animals (General)

Check (✔) the words you already know. Then, listen and repeat.

Tracks 1–20

☐ bear
TR 1

☐ cow
TR 2

☐ horse
TR 3

☐ deer
TR 5

☐ donkey
TR 6

☐ lamb
TR 7

☐ elephant
TR 11

☐ giraffe
TR 12

☐ pony
TR 13

☐ pig
TR 16

☐ rabbit
TR 17

☐ bat
TR 18

☐ sheep
TR 19

bull
TR 4

raccoon
TR 9

kangaroo
TR 8

skunk
TR 10

moose
TR 14

reindeer
TR 15

zebra
TR 20

Definitions

A **bat** is a small flying animal that looks like a mouse with wings. Bats hang upside down when they sleep during the day, and come out to fly at night.

A **bear** is a large, strong, wild animal with thick fur and sharp claws.

A **bull** is a male animal of the cow family.

A **cow** is a large female animal that is raised on farms for its milk.

A **deer** is a large wild animal that eats grass and leaves. A male deer usually has large horns that look like branches.

A **donkey** is an animal like a small horse with long ears.

An **elephant** is a very large animal with a long nose called a trunk.

A **giraffe** is a large animal with a very long neck, long legs, and dark spots on its body.

A **horse** is a large animal that people can ride.

A **kangaroo** is a large Australian animal. Female kangaroos carry their babies in a pocket on their stomach.

A **lamb** is a young sheep.

A **moose** is the largest member of the deer family.

A **pig** is a farm animal with a fat body and short legs. It is raised for its meat.

A **pony** is a small horse.

A **rabbit** is a small animal that has long ears and lives in a hole in the ground.

A **raccoon** is a small animal from North and Central America that has dark fur with white stripes on its face and on its long tail.

A **reindeer** is a big animal with large horns that lives in northern areas of Europe, Asia, and North America.

A **sheep** is a farm animal with thick hair called wool. Farmers raise sheep for their wool or for their meat.

A **skunk** is a small, black and white animal from North America that can give off an unpleasant smell.

A **zebra** is a wild horse with black and white stripes that lives in Africa.

Check Your Understanding

A. Circle the correct answer.

1. _____ have black and white stripes.

   a. Skunks   b. Zebras   c. Cows

2. _____ have very thick hair called wool.

   a. Sheep   b. Rabbits   c. Giraffes

3. A _____ has a fat body and short legs.

   a. elephant   b. bull   c. pig

4. A _____ is very tall and has dark spots on its body.

   a. rabbit   b. reindeer   c. giraffe

5. A _____ can make a very unpleasant smell.

   a. zebra   b. skunk   c. bear

6. _____ provide milk for people to drink.

   a. Raccoons   b. Cows   c. Bulls

7. Baby _____ are carried in a pocket on their mother's stomach.

   a. bats   b. lambs   c. kangaroos

8. _____ have very long noses called trunks.

   a. Elephants   b. Giraffes   c. Reindeer

9. Male _____ have large horns that look like branches.

   a. bulls   b. sheep   c. deer

10. _____ have long ears and live in holes in the ground.

    a. Cows   b. Rabbits   c. Pigs

11. People often ride _____.

    a. pigs   b. raccoons   c. horses

12. A _____ has thick fur and sharp claws.

    a. lamb   b. moose   c. bear

13. _____ hang upside down when they sleep.

    a. Sheep   b. Bats   c. Raccoons

14. _____ have white stripes on their long tails.

    a. Raccoons   b. Rabbits   c. Lambs

15. A _____ is a male animal.

    a. bull   b. raccoon   c. donkey

16. A small horse is called a _____ .

    a. deer   b. pony   c. lamb

17. A _____ is the largest member of the deer family.

    a. moose   b. reindeer   c. deer

18. A _____ is like a horse with long ears.

    a. horse   b. pony   c. donkey

19. A young sheep is called a _____ .

    a. lamb   b. pony   c. bat

20. A _____ is a big animal with large horns.

    a. giraffe   b. rabbit   c. reindeer

B. Circle the animal that is larger.

1. bear   pig

2. skunk   donkey

3. raccoon   reindeer

4. cow   rabbit

5. deer   moose

6. pony   horse

7. bat   bull

8. giraffe   zebra

9. kangaroo   elephant

10. sheep   lamb

Challenge Words

Check (✔) the words you already know.

☐ antelope   ☐ camel   ☐ hedgehog   ☐ llama   ☐ ram

☐ buffalo   ☐ ferret   ☐ hippopotamus   ☐ mole   ☐ rhinoceros

70. Sea Animals

Check (✔) the words you already know. Then, listen and repeat.

☐ **shark**

TR 1

☐ **whale**

TR 3

☐ **tuna**

TR 2

Check Your Understanding

A. Write each sea animal in the correct column.

seal	shark	salmon
tuna	whale	

FISH	MAMMAL

seal
TR 4

salmon
TR 5

fish
TR 6

Definitions

A **fish** is a creature that lives and swims in water. People eat many kinds of fish.

A **salmon** is a large fish with silver skin.

A **seal** is a large mammal with a rounded body and short fur that eats fish and lives near the ocean.

A **shark** is a very large fish. Some sharks have very sharp teeth and may attack people.

A **tuna** or a **tuna fish** is a large fish that lives in warm seas.

A **whale** is a very large mammal that lives in the ocean.

B. Write **T** for **true statements** and F for **false statements**.

1. _____ Some people eat fish.

2. _____ Seals do not eat fish.

3. _____ Tuna live in cold waters.

4. _____ Some sharks have very sharp teeth.

5. _____ Whales are very small mammals.

6. _____ Salmon are fish.

Challenge Words

Check (✔) the words you already know.

☐ catfish   ☐ dolphin   ☐ herring   ☐ sardine   ☐ trout
☐ cod   ☐ hammerhead ☐ porpoise ☐ swordfish ☐ walrus

82. Reptiles / Mythical Animals

Check (✔) the words you already know. Then, listen and repeat.

Tracks 1–9

☐ frog

TR 2

☐ alligator

TR 1

☐ toad

TR 5

☐ turtle

TR 4

☐ snake

TR 6

☐ dinosaur

TR 7

Check Your Understanding

A. Use the words from the word bank to fill in the blanks. One word will not be used.

dragon	frog	toad	turtle
alligator	monster	snake	
dinosaurs	mermaid	unicorn	

1. A _____ has wings and breathes fire.

2. A woman with a fish's tail is called a _____ .

3. A _____ does not have legs.

4. A long creature with short legs and rough skin is called an _____ .

5. A _____ is big and scary.

6. A _____ has a thick shell around its body.

7. A _____ has big eyes, smooth skin, and long back legs.

8. Like a frog, a _____ has long legs.

9. There are no _____ alive today.

dragon
TR 3

monster
TR 8

mermaid
TR 9

Definitions

An **alligator** is a long animal with rough skin, big teeth, and short legs.

A **dinosaur** was a large creature that lived millions of years ago.

In stories, a **dragon** is an animal with rough skin that has wings and breathes fire.

A **frog** is a small creature with smooth skin, big eyes, and long back legs that it uses for jumping and swimming. It lives in water.

In stories, a **mermaid** is a woman who has a fish's tail and lives in the ocean.

In stories, a **monster** is a big, ugly, frightening creature.

A **snake** is a long, thin creature with no legs that slides along the ground.

A **toad** is a small, brown or green creature with bumps on its skin. Adult toads live on land.

A **turtle** is a creature that has a thick shell around its body, and it may live on land or in water.

B. Write each word in the correct column.

dragon	frog	toad
alligator	monster	snake
dinosaur	mermaid	turtle

REAL CREATURES	FAKE CREATURES

Challenge Words

Check (✔) the words you already know.

☐ cobra   ☐ lizard   ☐ rattlesnake   ☐ serpent   ☐ unicorn

☐ crocodile   ☐ nymph   ☐ reptile   ☐ tortoise

95. Insects

Check (✔) the words you already know. Then, listen and repeat.

Tracks 1–18

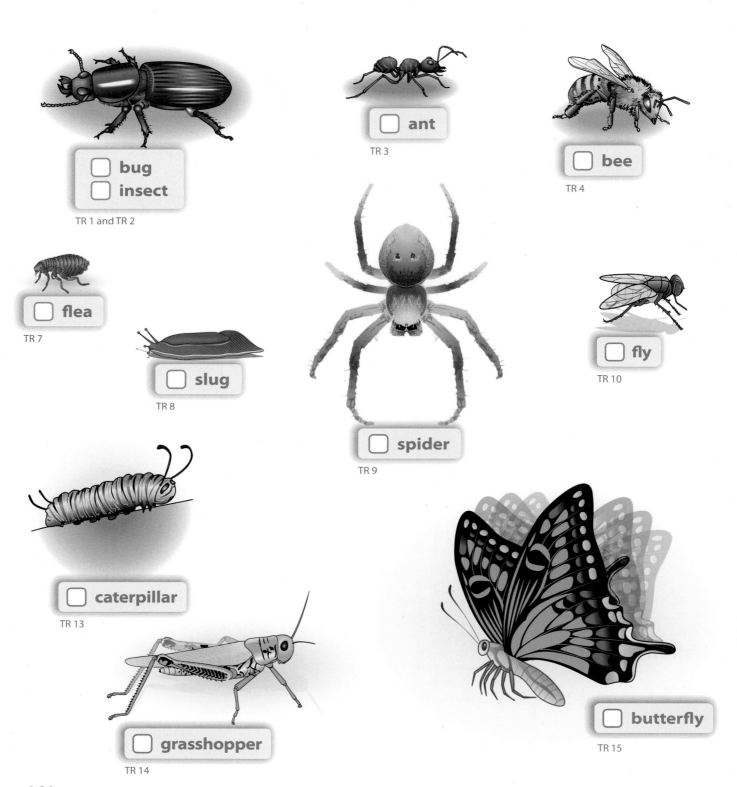

- [ ] **bug**
- [ ] **insect**

TR 1 and TR 2

- [ ] **ant**

TR 3

- [ ] **bee**

TR 4

- [ ] **flea**

TR 7

- [ ] **slug**

TR 8

- [ ] **spider**

TR 9

- [ ] **fly**

TR 10

- [ ] **caterpillar**

TR 13

- [ ] **grasshopper**

TR 14

- [ ] **butterfly**

TR 15

164

mosquito

TR 5

cockroach

TR 6

wasp

TR 11

bumblebee

TR 12

moth

TR 16

ladybug

TR 17

worm

TR 18

Definitions

An **ant** is a small insect that lives in large groups.

A **bee** is a flying insect with a yellow-and-black striped body. Bees make a sweet food (honey), and they can sting you.

A **bug** is an insect.

A **bumblebee** is a large bee.

A **butterfly** is an insect with large colored wings.

A **caterpillar** is a small animal with a long body that develops into a butterfly.

A **cockroach** is a large, brown insect that likes to live in places where food is kept.

A **flea** is a very small insect that jumps. Fleas live on the bodies of humans or animals, and drink their blood as food.

A **fly** is a small insect with two wings.

A **grasshopper** is an insect that jumps high into the air and makes a sound with its long back legs.

An **insect** is a very small creature that has six legs. Most insects have wings.

A **ladybug** is a small, round insect that is red or yellow with black spots.

A **mosquito** is a small flying insect that bites people and animals.

A **moth** is an insect that has large wings and is attracted by lights at night.

A **slug** is a small creature with a long, soft body and no legs that moves very slowly.

A **spider** is a small creature with eight legs.

A **wasp** is an insect with wings and yellow and black stripes across its slender body. Wasps can sting people.

A **worm** is a small creature with a long, thin body, no bones, and no legs.

Check Your Understanding

A. Match each word to the correct description. One description will not be used.

1. _____ mosquito
2. _____ cockroach
3. _____ slug
4. _____ ladybug
5. _____ fly
6. _____ wasp
7. _____ butterfly
8. _____ ant
9. _____ bug
10. _____ moth
11. _____ insect
12. _____ bumblebee
13. _____ bee
14. _____ worm
15. _____ caterpillar
16. _____ grasshopper
17. _____ spider
18. _____ flea

a. a flying insect with black and yellow stripes on its slender body that stings people

b. a flying insect with black and yellow stripes on its body that makes honey

c. a small creature with a long, thin body

d. a large bee

e. a very small creature with six legs which usually has wings

f. an insect that uses its long legs to jump high and to make a sound

g. a small insect that lives on animals and humans

h. a small creature that turns into a butterfly

i. an insect that is large and brown and likes to live near food

j. a small creature with eight legs

k. a small, round insect that is red or yellow, with black spots

l. a small insect that lives in large groups

m. a small insect with two wings

n. an insect that is attracted to light at night

o. an insect with large, colorful wings

p. a small flying insect that bites people and animals

q. another word for insect

r. a brightly colored insect with a long body and two sets of wings

s. a small creature with a long, soft body that moves very slowly

B. Circle the word in each group that does not belong.

1. ladybug   slug   worm

2. bumblebee   grasshopper   bee

3. insect   bug   spider

4. ant   butterfly   moth

5. wasp   caterpillar   fly

6. mosquito   flea   cockroach

Challenge Words

Check (✔) the words you already know.

☐ beetle   ☐ cricket   ☐ firefly   ☐ lice   ☐ termite

☐ centipede   ☐ dragonfly   ☐ hornet   ☐ mite   ☐ yellow jacket

117. Actions Related to Animals

Check (✔) the words you already know. Then, listen and repeat.

Tracks 1–8

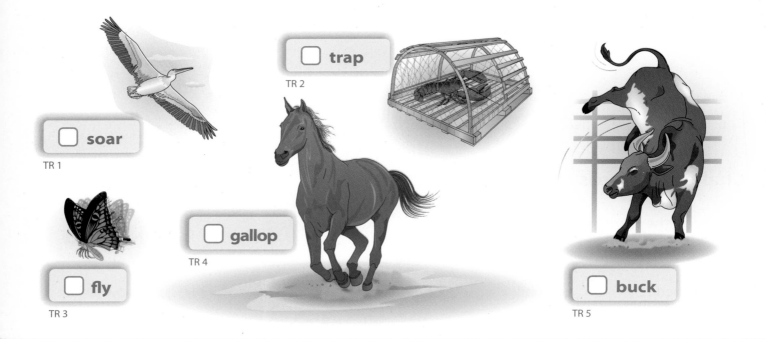

☐ **soar**
TR 1

☐ **trap**
TR 2

☐ **fly**
TR 3

☐ **gallop**
TR 4

☐ **buck**
TR 5

Check Your Understanding

A. Write **T** for **true statements** and **F** for **false statements**.

1. _____ It feels nice when a bee stings you.

2. _____ Cows often soar in the sky.

3. _____ Lions hunt other animals for food.

4. _____ If an animal has wings, it can usually fly.

5. _____ The pony passed by quickly as it galloped along the dirt trail.

6. _____ Sarah knew her horse was tired because it was bucking wildly.

7. _____ Mike catches lobsters by trapping them in the ocean.

8. _____ The bear had to fish in the lake to find food.

☐ fish
TR 6

☐ sting
TR 7

☐ hunt
TR 8

Definitions

If an animal **bucks**, it kicks both of its back legs into the air, or jumps into the air with all four feet off the ground.

If you **fish**, you try to catch fish.

When things **fly**, they move through the air.

When horses **gallop**, they run very fast.

When people or animals **hunt**, they chase and kill wild animals for food or as a sport.

If birds or aircraft **soar** into the air, they go quickly upward.

If an animal or an insect **stings** you, it cuts into your skin and causes you to feel pain.

To **trap** animals means to catch them using traps.

B. Match each word to the correct description. One description will not be used.

1. _____ buck
2. _____ fish
3. _____ fly
4. _____ gallop
5. _____ hunt
6. _____ soar
7. _____ sting
8. _____ trap

a. to move through the air
b. to chase and kill an animal for food
c. to kick or jump into the air
d. to catch an animal using a trap
e. to go quickly upward while flying
f. to try to catch fish
g. to run very fast
h. to push a pointed part into skin and cause pain
i. to feed on grass

Challenge Words

Check (✔) the words you already know.

☐ bareback
☐ graze

☐ horseback
☐ snare

☐ stampede
☐ swarm

155. Parts of Animals

Check (✔) the words you already know. Then, listen and repeat.

Tracks 1–13

☐ hide
TR 1

☐ flipper
TR 2

☐ fur
TR 8

☐ claw
TR 11

☐ whisker
TR 7

☐ tail
TR 10

☐ paw
TR 9

Check Your Understanding

A. Circle the correct word to complete each sentence.

1. A cat's feet are called _____.

    a. feathers   b. flippers   c. paws

2. A _____ is the hard and pointed part at the end of an animal's foot.

    a. claw   b. paw   c. beak

3. _____ are like wings and they help fish swim.

    a. Fins   b. Tails   c. Claws

bill
beak

TR 3 and TR 4

feather

TR 5

fin

TR 6

snout

TR 12

hoof

TR 13

Definitions

A bird's **beak** is the hard, pointed part of its mouth.

A **bill** is a bird's beak.

The **claw** of a bird or animal is the thin, hard, pointed part at the end of its feet.

A **feathe**r is a light, soft thing that covers the body of a bird.

A fish's **fin** is the flat part like a wing that helps it to swim.

A **flipper** is a flat limb used for swimming.

Fur is the thick hair that grows on the bodies of many animals.

A **hide** is the skin of a large animal that can be used for making leather.

A **hoof** is the hard part of the feet of horses, cows, and some other animals.

The **paw** of an animal, such as a cat, dog, or bear, is its foot.

The **snout** of an animal, such as a pig, is its long nose.

The **tail** of an animal is the long, thin part at the end of its body.

A **whisker** of an animal, such as a cat or mouse, is a long, stiff hair that grows near its mouth.

4. The skin of a large animal is called its _____.

   a. fur   b. hide   c. whisker

5. A _____ is the long, thin part at the end of an animal's body.

   a. feather   b. snout   c. tail

6. The long nose of an animal, such as a pig, is called a _____.

   a. snout   b. bill   c. hoof

7. _____ are the long, stiff hairs that grow by a cat's mouth.

   a. Tails   b. Whiskers   c. Claws

8. Many animals are covered with thick hair called _____.

   a. hide   b. fur   c. paw

9. The hard, pointed part of a bird's mouth is called a _____.

   a. hoof   b. beak   c. claw

10. A flat limb used for swimming is called a _____.

    a. tail   b. bill   c. flipper

11. A _____ is the hard part of a cow's foot.

    a. paw   b. claw   c. hoof

12. A _____ is a bird's beak.

    a. bill   b. hide   c. snout

13. A bird's body is covered with _____, or light, soft things.

    a. feathers   b. fur   c. bills

B. Write each word in the correct column. Some words may be used in more than one column.

fin	paw	claw	snout	whisker
fur	tail	beak	flipper	
bill	hide	hoof	feather	

LOCATED ON THE FACE	LOCATED ON THE BODY	LOCATED ON THE LEGS

Challenge Words

Check (✔) the words you already know.

☐ antenna   ☐ fleece   ☐ ivory   ☐ pouch   ☐ talon

☐ antler   ☐ gill   ☐ mane   ☐ quill   ☐ tusk

188. Rodents

Check (✔) the words you already know. Then, listen and repeat.

Tracks 1–6

☐ **mouse**
TR 1

☐ **squirrel**
TR 2

☐ **rat**
TR 3

☐ **beaver**
TR 4

☐ **hamster**
TR 5

☐ **groundhog**
TR 6

Definitions

A **beaver** is an animal with thick fur, a big, flat tail, and large teeth.

A **groundhog** is a small animal with red or brown fur that is found in North America.

A **hamster** is a small animal similar to a mouse and is often kept as a pet.

A **mouse** is a small animal with a long tail.

A **rat** is an animal that has a long tail and looks like a large mouse.

A **squirrel** is a small animal with a long, thick tail. Squirrels live mainly in trees.

Check Your Understanding

A. Fill in the blanks with words from the word bank.

rat	beaver	squirrel
mouse	hamster	groundhog

Most people know what a (1) _____ looks like. Once they see that small animal with its long tail, they usually scream and stand on a chair. A similar, larger animal is called a (2) _____. Another similar animal is the (3) _____. People often keep them as pets.

An animal that you often see outside is called a (4) _____. This animal has a long, thick tail. It lives in the trees. Another bigger animal is a (5) _____. This animal has red or brown fur and likes to dig.

An animal that you can find living by water is called a (6) _____. This animal has thick fur. It also has large teeth and a big, flat tail.

B. Write **T** for **true statements** and **F** for **false statements**.

1. _____ Beavers do not have tails.
2. _____ Hamsters are never kept as pets.
3. _____ Groundhogs can have red or brown fur.
4. _____ A mouse is smaller than a rat.
5. _____ Rats have large, flat tails.
6. _____ Squirrels mostly live in trees.

Challenge Words

Check (✔) the words you already know.

- ☐ chipmunk
- ☐ muskrat
- ☐ otter
- ☐ porcupine
- ☐ rodent
- ☐ woodchuck

189. Dwellings for Animals

Check (✔) the words you already know. Then, listen and repeat.

Tracks 1–7

☐ **zoo**

TR 1

Definitions

An **aquarium** is a building where fish and ocean animals live. An **aquarium** is also a glass box filled with water in which people keep fish.

A **beehive** is a container for bees to live in.

A **birdhouse** is a box placed in a tree or other high place that birds can build a nest in.

A **cocoon** is a case that some insects make around themselves before they grow into adults.

A **hive** is a structure in which bees live.

A **nest** is the place where a bird, a small animal, or an insect keeps its eggs or its babies.

A **zoo** is a park where animals are kept and people can go to look at them.

☐ **cocoon**

TR 2

☐ **birdhouse**

TR 3

☐ **nest**

TR 4

☐ **beehive**
☐ **hive**

TR 5 and TR 6

☐ **aquarium**

TR 7

Check Your Understanding

A. Circle the correct answer.

1. What can you find at the zoo?

   a. animals   b. sea animals   c. bees

2. What can you find at the aquarium?

   a. sea animals   b. insects   c. animals

3. What is inside a nest?

   a. bees and eggs   b. birds and eggs   c. fish and eggs

4. What is inside a cocoon?

   a. a bird   b. a fish   c. an insect

5. What is inside a beehive or hive?

   a. fish   b. bees   c. birds

6. What is inside a birdhouse?

   a. birds and a nest   b. bees and a hive   c. fish and an aquarium

B. Choose the sentence that correctly uses the underlined word.

1. a. The <u>aquarium</u> had monkeys from all over the world.

   b. We visited the <u>aquarium</u> and saw sea turtles.

2. a. The bird kept her eggs in the <u>nest</u>.

   b. The sharks swim into the <u>nest</u>.

3. a. The bees are flying to the <u>beehive</u>.

   b. The <u>beehive</u> was full of elephants.

4. a. The birds lived in a <u>cocoon</u> for the winter.

   b. The caterpillar made a <u>cocoon</u> so it could turn into a butterfly.

5. a. The <u>zoo</u> had animals from Africa, Asia, and North America.

   b. We walked to the <u>zoo</u> to buy food.

6. a. George made a <u>birdhouse</u> to hang in the tree.

   b. There was a colorful <u>birdhouse</u> sleeping in the tree.

7. a. We went to the <u>hive</u> to see sharks and jellyfish.

   b. The bees in that <u>hive</u> are making honey.

Challenge Words

Check (✔) the words you already know.

☐ perch   ☐ roost   ☐ stable   ☐ stall

194. Animals (General)

Check (✔) the words you already know. Then, listen and repeat.

Tracks 1–3

☐ **pet**

TR 1

Definitions

An **animal** is a creature such as a dog, a cat, a bear, or a tiger, but not a bird, a fish, an insect, or a human.

A **pet** is an animal or creature that you keep in your home.

You can use **wildlife** to talk about the animals and other living things that live in nature.

☐ **wildlife**

TR 2

☐ **animal**

TR 3

Check Your Understanding

A. Match each word to the correct description. One description will not be used.

1. _____ animal
2. _____ pet
3. _____ wildlife

   a. an animal you keep in your home

   b. an animal living in nature

   c. a creature that is not a bird, fish, or human

   d. an animal eaten by another animal

B. Write each animal in the correct column. Some animals can go in both columns.

cat	lion	snake	parrot
dog	deer	mouse	elephant

PETS	WILDLIFE

Challenge Words

Check (✔) the words you already know.

- [ ] amphibian
- [ ] beast
- [ ] carnivorous
- [ ] creature
- [ ] fossil
- [ ] mammal
- [ ] mascot
- [ ] prey

309. Shellfish (and Others)

Check (✔) the words you already know. Then, listen and repeat.

Tracks 1–5

☐ **starfish**

TR 1

Definitions

A **lobster** is an ocean animal that has a hard shell and eight legs.

A **shell** is the hard, outer part of small sea creatures. Shells are often found on beaches.

Shrimp are small, pink or gray sea animals, with long tails and many legs, that you can eat.

A **snail** is a small animal with a long, soft body, no legs, and a round shell on its back.

A **starfish** is a flat creature in the shape of a star that lives in the ocean.

☐ **shell**

TR 2

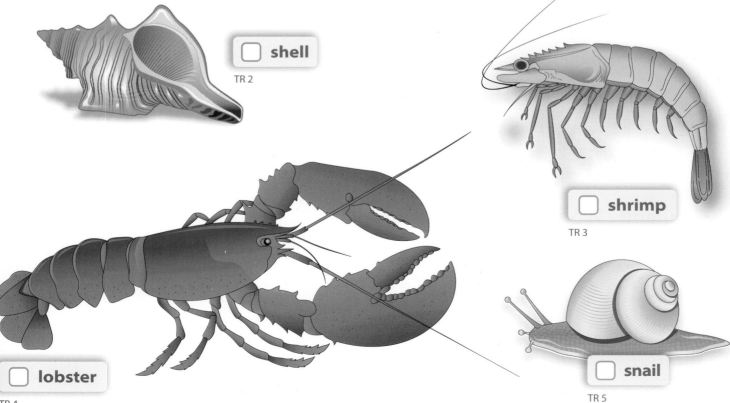

☐ **shrimp**

TR 3

☐ **lobster**

TR 4

☐ **snail**

TR 5

Check Your Understanding

A. Write each word in the correct column.

starfish	lobster	shrimp	snail

SHELL	NO SHELL

B. Underline the correct word to complete each sentence.

1. (**Snails / Starfish**) have no legs, a soft body, and a shell.

2. (**Shells / Shrimp**) have long tails and many legs.

3. A (**shrimp / lobster**) has a hard shell and eight legs.

4. The hard, outer parts of small sea creatures are called (**shells / snails**).

5. A (**lobster / starfish**) lives in the ocean and has the shape of a star.

Challenge Words

Check (✔) the words you already know.

☐ clam   ☐ crab   ☐ eel   ☐ octopus   ☐ squid
☐ coral   ☐ crayfish   ☐ jellyfish ☐ oyster   ☐ stingray

310. Equipment Used with Animals

Check (✔) the words you already know. Then, listen and repeat.

Tracks 1–4

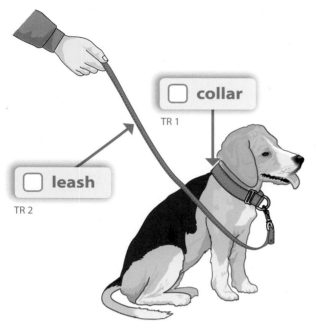

☐ **collar**

TR 1

☐ **leash**

TR 2

Definitions

A **collar** is a band of leather or plastic that you put around the neck of a dog or cat.

A **horseshoe** is a piece of metal in the shape of a U that is fixed to a horse's foot.

A **leash** is a long, thin piece of leather or a chain that you use to control a dog.

A **saddle** is a leather seat that you put on the back of an animal.

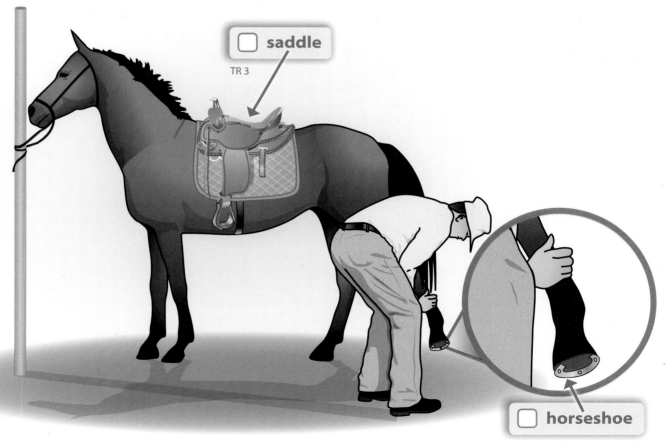

☐ **saddle**

TR 3

☐ **horseshoe**

TR 4

Check Your Understanding

A. Match each word with the correct body part. One body part will be used twice.

1. _____ collar   a. back

2. _____ horseshoe   b. foot

3. _____ leash   c. neck

4. _____ saddle

B. Write each word in the correct column.

leash	collar	saddle	horseshoe

DOG	HORSE

Challenge Words

Check (✔) the words you already know.

- [ ] bridle
- [ ] chaps
- [ ] halter
- [ ] harness
- [ ] muzzle
- [ ] rein
- [ ] stirrup
- [ ] yoke

341. Primates

Check (✔) the words you already know. Then, listen and repeat.

 Tracks 1–2

☐ **monkey**

TR 1

☐ **gorilla**

TR 2

Definitions

A **gorilla** is a very large animal with long arms, black fur, and a black face.

A **monkey** is an animal that has a long tail and can climb trees.

Check Your Understanding

A. Write **T** for **true statements** and **F** for **false statements**.

1. _____ Monkeys are bigger than gorillas.

2. _____ Gorillas have short arms.

3. _____ Monkeys have long tails.

4. _____ Gorillas have black faces.

5. _____ Monkeys can't climb trees.

B. Complete the sentences.

1. Monkeys and gorillas are alike because _____

   _____.

2. Monkeys and gorillas are different because _____

   _____.

Challenge Words

Check (✔) the words you already know.

☐ ape   ☐ baboon   ☐ chimpanzee

58. Importance and Value

Check (✔) the words you already know. Then, listen and repeat.

Tracks 1–10

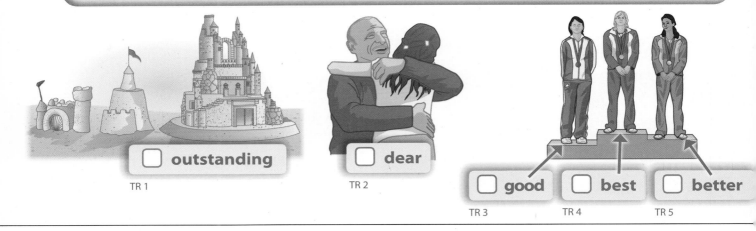

☐ **outstanding**

TR 1

☐ **dear**

TR 2

☐ **good**   ☐ **best**   ☐ **better**

TR 3   TR 4   TR 5

Check Your Understanding

A. Circle the correct word to complete each sentence.

1. Something that is _____ is much better than other similar things.
   a. useful   b. outstanding   c. dear

2. Something that is _____ is of a high quality or level.
   a. dear   b. important   c. good

3. Something that is _____ than something else is more enjoyable or attractive.
   a. better   b. best   c. good

4. Something that is larger or better than others is _____.
   a. good   b. important   c. super

5. Something that is the _____ is better than all the others.
   a. super   b. best   c. fine

6. Someone that is _____ to you is loved by you.
   a. better   b. dear   c. fine

7. Something that is _____ is as good as it could possibly be.
   a. perfect   b. fine   c. better

8. Something that is _____ is very good.
   a. perfect   b. useful   c. fine

9. Something that is _____ helps you out in some way.
   a. useful   b. perfect   c. best

10. Something that is _____ is very significant or highly valued.
    a. better   b. important   c. good

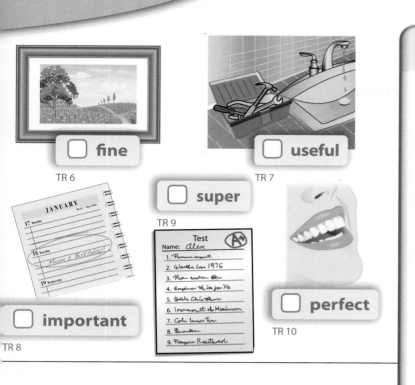

fine — TR 6

useful — TR 7

super — TR 9

important — TR 8

perfect — TR 10

JANUARY
Mom's Birthday!

Test — Name: Alex — A+

B. Underline the correct word to complete each sentence.

1. Anita said it was the (**best / super**) meal she ever had.

2. This book was (**best / better**) than the last one I read.

3. I love my (**better / dear**) cousin as if he were my brother.

4. Janet enjoys buying (**dear / fine**) jewelry for herself.

5. Marie was a (**good / useful**) swimmer and could swim for a long distance.

6. The principal is going to make an (**important / fine**) announcement in the auditorium.

7. Ethan answered all the questions correctly on the exam, and received a (**perfect / dear**) score.

8. Michael is an (**important / outstanding**) swimmer and usually wins all the competitions that he is in.

9. Aaron is (**super / perfect**) strong and can lift up to two hundred pounds.

10. A GPS device would have been (**useful / important**) when we were lost.

Challenge Words

Check (✔) the words you already know.

absolute	crucial	excellent	main	necessary
basic	essential	impressive	major	value

72. Right and Wrong

Check (✔) the words you already know. Then, listen and repeat.

Tracks 1–13

true
TR 1

false
TR 2

Did you drop this?

honest
TR 3

fair
just
TR 5 and TR 6

There is a ranebow in the sky.

mistake
error
TR 7 and TR 8

right
TR 9

Check Your Understanding

A. Circle the word in each group that does not belong.

1. correct   right   false

2. just   fair   honest

□ real

TR 4

□ correct

TR 10

$$1+1=2$$
$$1+1=3$$

□ wrong

TR 11

I promise to tell the **truth**.

□ truth

TR 12

It's not my **fault**.

□ fault

TR 13

Definitions

Something is **correct** when it is right or true.

An **error** is a mistake.

Something or someone that is **fair** treats everyone in the same way.

If something is **false**, it is wrong or not true.

If something bad is your **fault**, you made it happen.

An **honest** person always tells the truth and does not steal or cheat.

A situation that is **just** is fair or right.

If you make a **mistake**, you do something which you did not intend to do, or which produces a result that you do not want.

Something that is **real** actually exists.

If something is **right**, it is correct, or it is morally a good thing to do.

If something is **true**, it is based on facts and is not invented or imagined.

The **truth** about something is the facts about it, rather than things that are imagined or invented.

If something is **wrong**, it is not correct.

3. real	fault	true
4. true	error	mistake
5. honest	wrong	truth

B. Match each word to the correct description. One description will not be used.

1. _____ true   a. something that is not true

2. _____ right   b. something that is fair or right

3. _____ error   c. something you did not mean to do, or that gives you a result you did not want

4. _____ real   d. something that is correct

5. _____ wrong   e. something that is based on facts

6. _____ fair   f. something that the law says is not allowed

7. _____ false   g. a mistake

8. _____ correct   h. to treat everyone the same way

9. _____ fault   i. something that actually exists

10. _____ truth   j. something that is not correct

11. _____ honest   k. something that is right or true

12. _____ mistake   l. when you cause something bad to happen

13. _____ just   m. all the facts about something

                          n. someone who always tells the truth

Challenge Words

Check (✔) the words you already know.

☐ acceptable   ☐ appropriate   ☐ honesty   ☐ justice   ☐ realistic

☐ accurate   ☐ crime   ☐ illegal   ☐ legal   ☐ relevant

243. Lack of Value

Check (✔) the words you already know. Then, listen and repeat.

 Tracks 1–7

☐ terrible
☐ awful

TR 1 and TR 2

Definitions

Something that is **awful** is very bad.

Something that is **bad** is low in quality.

An act or a person that is **evil** is morally very bad.

If something is **terrible**, it is extremely bad.

Someone or something that is **wicked** is morally very bad.

Something that is **worse** is lower in quality.

Something that is the **worst** is lowest in quality.

☐ evil
☐ wicked

TR 3 and TR 4

☐ bad

TR 5

☐ worse

TR 6

☐ worst

TR 7

Check Your Understanding

A. Underline the correct word to complete each sentence.

1. Marta felt (**awful / wicked**) when her friend got sick from the food she made.

2. Tonight's performance was (**evil / worse**) than last night's performance.

3. Jenna is home today because she has a (**bad / worst**) cold.

4. Steven's dad was in a (**terrible / wicked**) accident, but he did not get hurt.

5. Destroying someone's favorite things would be an (**evil / worst**) thing to do.

6. The (**terrible / worst**) day of my life was when I realized that I failed math class.

7. Criminals who hurt people on purpose are (**wicked / worse**).

B. Complete the sentences.

1. It was awful when _____.

2. Something that is evil is _____.

3. Something that is wicked is _____.

4. It was terrible when _____.

5. Something that is bad is _____.

6. Something that is worse is _____.

7. The worst thing is _____.

Challenge Words

Check (✔) the words you already know.

☐ corrupt   ☐ negative   ☐ sinister   ☐ worthless

☐ horrible   ☐ petty   ☐ useless

368. Failure and Success

Check (✔) the words you already know. Then, listen and repeat.

Tracks 1–2

Definitions

If you **fail** at doing something, you do not get the result you wanted.

If you **succeed**, you get the result that you wanted; you achieve your goal.

☐ **fail**

TR 1

☐ **succeed**

TR 2

Check Your Understanding

A. Write **S** for **actions that succeed** and **F** for **actions that fail**.

1. _____ Richard did not pass his driver's test.

2. _____ Annie's pie did not win first prize in the baking contest.

3. _____ Jeff won an essay contest.

4. _____ Karen graduated from high school.

B. Underline the correct word to complete each sentence.

1. The new company is (**failing / succeeding**) by making a lot of money.

2. Amy (**failed / succeeded**) to tell me that my dad called, so I didn't call him back.

3. Kim is afraid she will (**fail / succeed**) the exam.

4. Carlos (**failed / succeeded**) in making a delicious meal that everyone loved.

Challenge Words

Check (✔) the words you already know.

☐ bumble   ☐ deserve   ☐ muff

☐ bungle   ☐ merit   ☐ qualify

75. Limbs

Check (✔) the words you already know. Then, listen and repeat.

Tracks 1–7

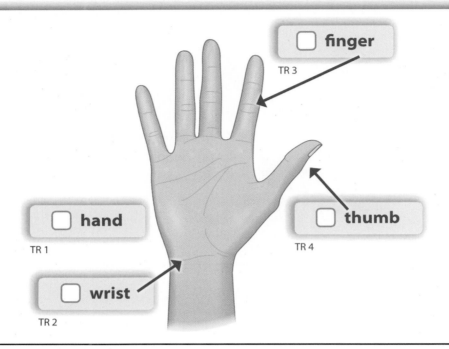

☐ **finger**

TR 3

☐ **hand**

TR 1

☐ **thumb**

TR 4

☐ **wrist**

TR 2

Check Your Understanding

A. Match each word to the correct description. One description will not be used.

1. _____ arm
2. _____ elbow
3. _____ finger
4. _____ hand
5. _____ shoulders
6. _____ thumb
7. _____ wrist

a. located between your neck and the tops of your arms
b. short thick finger
c. used for holding things
d. long and thin part at the end of your hand
e. the inside part of your hand, between your fingers and wrist
f. part of your arm that bends
g. between your shoulders and your hand
h. bends when you move your hand

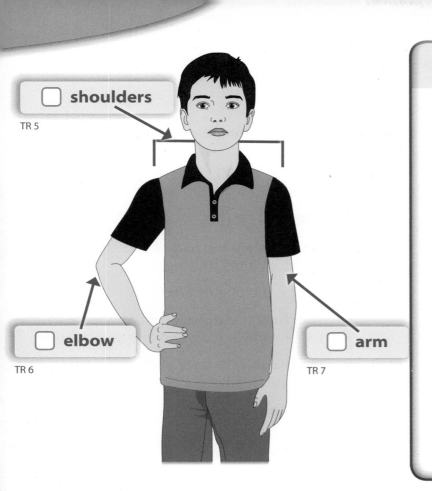

☐ **shoulders**
TR 5

☐ **elbow**
TR 6

☐ **arm**
TR 7

Definitions

Your **arm** is the part of your body between your shoulder and your hand.

Your **elbow** is the part in the middle of your arm where it bends.

Your **finger** is the long, thin part at the end of each hand. You have five fingers on each of your two hands.

Your **hand** is the part of your body at the end of your arm that you use for holding things. You have two hands.

Your **shoulders** are the two parts of your body between your neck and the tops of your arms.

Your **thumb** is the short, thick finger on your hand.

Your **wrist** is the part between your hand and your arm that bends when you move your hand.

B. Underline the correct word to complete each sentence.

1. Luis is carrying a baby in his (**thumbs / arms**).

2. Tom bent his arms and rested his (**wrists / elbows**) on the table.

3. Emily has a beautiful ring on her (**shoulder / finger**).

4. How many apples can you hold in your (**hands / shoulders**)?

5. Aaron held the small rock between his finger and (**arm / thumb**) and looked at it carefully.

6. My backpack is too heavy so the straps are hurting my (**shoulders / fingers**).

7. Sharleen is wearing a watch on her (**wrist / thumb**).

Challenge Words

Check (✔) the words you already know.

☐ armpit
☐ biceps
☐ cuticle
☐ forearm
☐ knuckle
☐ nails
☐ palm

76. Legs and Feet

Check (✔) the words you already know. Then, listen and repeat.

Tracks 1–7

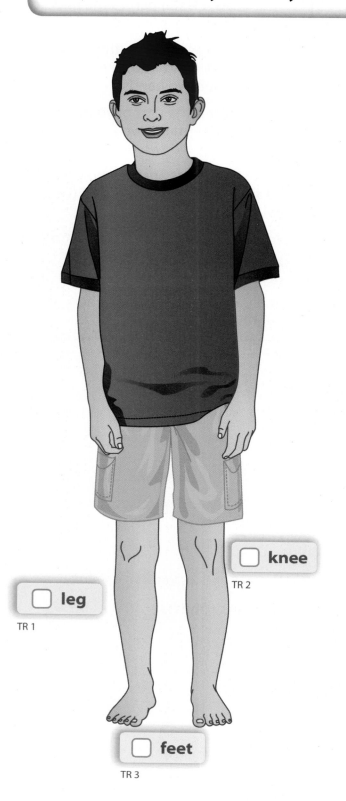

Definitions

Your **ankle** is the part of your body where your foot joins your leg.

Feet is the plural of foot.

Your **foot** is the part of your body that is at the end of your leg, and that you stand on.

Your **heel** is the back part of your foot, just below your ankle.

Your **knee** is the part in the middle of your leg where it bends.

Your **leg** is the long part of your body that is used for walking and standing. People have two legs.

Your **toe** is one of the five parts at the end of your foot.

☐ knee
TR 2

☐ leg
TR 1

☐ feet
TR 3

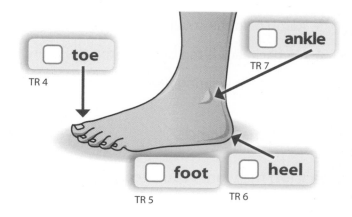

☐ toe
TR 4

☐ ankle
TR 7

☐ foot
TR 5

☐ heel
TR 6

Check Your Understanding

A. Match each word to the correct description. One description will not be used.

1. _____ ankle
2. _____ feet
3. _____ foot
4. _____ heel
5. _____ knee
6. _____ leg
7. _____ toe

a. part of the leg that bends

b. body part used for walking and standing

c. back part of a foot

d. located at the end of the foot

e. body part at the end of the leg

f. more than one foot

g. body part where the foot joins the leg

h. front part of the leg between the knee and the ankle

B. Write **T** for **true statements** and **F** for **false statements**.

1. _____ The ankle connects your toes to your foot.

2. _____ The heel is right below the ankle.

3. _____ Each foot has five toes.

4. _____ People stand on their feet.

5. _____ Legs are shorter than toes.

6. _____ The knee is located in the middle of the heel.

Challenge Words

Check (✔) the words you already know.

☐ arch   ☐ shin   ☐ thigh

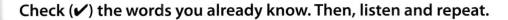

80. Throat and Mouth

Check (✔) the words you already know. Then, listen and repeat.

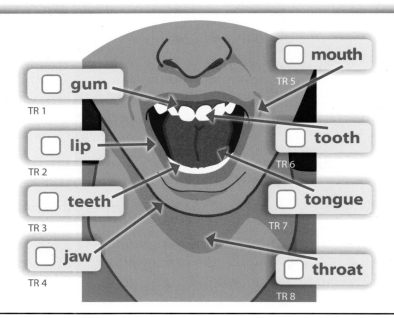

- ☐ gum — TR 1
- ☐ lip — TR 2
- ☐ teeth — TR 3
- ☐ jaw — TR 4
- ☐ mouth — TR 5
- ☐ tooth — TR 6
- ☐ tongue — TR 7
- ☐ throat — TR 8

Check Your Understanding

A. Complete each sentence with words from the word bank. The first letter for each word is provided. One word will not be used.

teeth	jaw	lips	voice	tooth
gums	throat	tongue	molar	mouth

1. Andy's little brother stuck his **t**_____ out at him.

2. After she brushed her teeth, she noticed her **g**_____ were bleeding.

3. Yolanda's **t**_____ felt clean after she brushed them.

4. Jill's throat was sore and she lost her **v**_____ when she got sick.

5. Joseph's **t**_____ hurt from coughing all week.

6. Paula has a gap in the front of her mouth because her **t**_____ fell out.

7. Daniel's **j**_____ hurt from chewing on the sticky caramel.

8. Jonathan opened his **m**_____ wide to take a bite of his taco.

9. She licked her **l**_____ after eating the ice cream cone.

voice

TR 9

Definitions

Your **gum** is the area of firm, pink flesh inside your mouth, where each tooth grows.

Your **jaw** is one of the two bones that form your mouth. You have a top and a bottom jaw.

Your **lip** is one of the two outer parts of the edge of your mouth. You have two lips.

Your **mouth** is the part of your face that you use for eating or speaking.

Teeth is the plural of tooth. You use your teeth for biting and eating.

Your **throat** is the back of your mouth, where you swallow, and at the front of your neck.

Your **tongue** is the soft part inside your mouth that moves when you speak or eat.

Your **tooth** is a hard, white object in your mouth that you use for biting and eating.

Your **voice** is the sound that comes from your mouth when you speak or sing.

B. Write **T** for **true statements** and **F** for **false statements**.

1. _____ Your teeth grow from your gums.

2. _____ Your teeth are inside your mouth.

3. _____ Your throat is at the front of your mouth.

4. _____ You have two lips.

5. _____ Your tongue moves when you speak.

6. _____ Your jaws are the top and bottom bones of your mouth.

7. _____ A tooth is soft and white.

8. _____ You do not use your mouth for eating.

9. _____ Your voice comes from your mouth.

Challenge Words

Check (✔) the words you already know.

☐ bicuspid   ☐ fang   ☐ molar   ☐ oral   ☐ windpipe

115. Head and Face

Check (✔) the words you already know. Then, listen and repeat.

Tracks 1–7

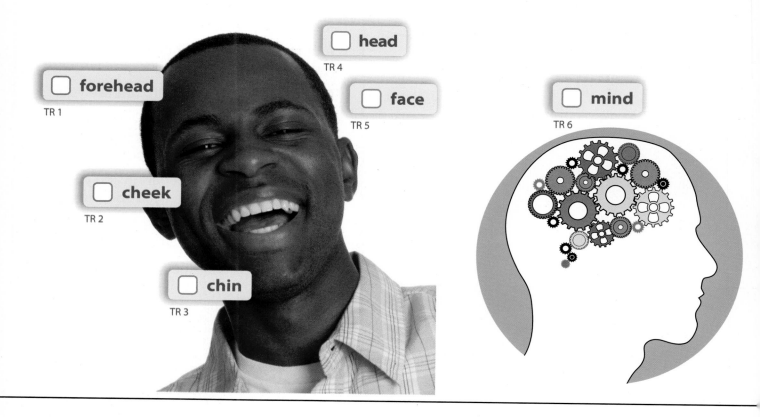

forehead
TR 1

cheek
TR 2

chin
TR 3

head
TR 4

face
TR 5

mind
TR 6

Check Your Understanding

A. Match each word to the correct description. One description will not be used.

1. _____ forehead
2. _____ face
3. _____ brain
4. _____ mind
5. _____ chin
6. _____ cheek
7. _____ head

a. bony part of your head that holds your brain
b. on either side of your face
c. front part of your head
d. top part of your body
e. bottom part of your face
f. controls your body's activities
g. front part of head between eyebrows and hair
h. your ability to think and reason

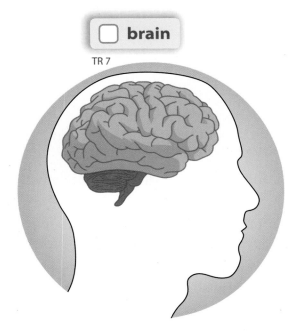

☐ **brain**

TR 7

Definitions

Your **brain** is the organ inside your head that controls your body's activities and allows you to think and to feel things.

You have a **cheek** on each side of your face, from below your eye to your chin. Each person has two cheeks.

Your **chin** is the part of your face that is below your mouth and above your neck.

Your **face** is the front part of your head.

Your **forehead** is the front part of your head between your eyebrows and your hair.

Your **head** is the top part of your body that includes your eyes, mouth, and brain.

Your **mind** is the part of you that reasons, thinks, feels, and remembers.

B. Write the words in the correct column.

brain	chin	cheek
face	mind	forehead

ON THE HEAD	IN THE HEAD

Challenge Words

Check (✔) the words you already know.

☐ ego   ☐ skull

140. Ears, Eyes, and Nose

Check (✔) the words you already know. Then, listen and repeat.

Tracks 1–6

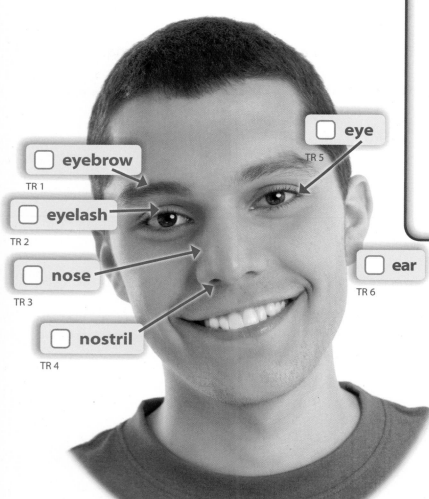

☐ **eye**
TR 5

☐ **eyebrow**
TR 1

☐ **eyelash**
TR 2

☐ **nose**
TR 3

☐ **nostril**
TR 4

☐ **ear**
TR 6

Definitions

Your **ear** is the part of your body on the side of your head used for hearing. You have two ears.

Your **eye** is the part of your body with which you see. You have two eyes.

Your **eyebrow** is the line of hair that grows above each eye. You have two eyebrows.

Your **eyelash** is one of the hairs that grows along the edges of your eye.

Your **nose** is the part of your face that sticks out above your mouth. You use it for smelling and for breathing.

You breathe through each **nostril**, or opening, at the end of your nose. Your nose has two nostrils.

Check Your Understanding

A. Underline the correct word to complete each sentence.

1. You smell with your (**ear / nose**).

2. (**Eyebrows / Nostrils**) are the holes at the end of your nose.

3. You hear with your (**ears / eyes**).

4. You see with your (**eyes / nose**).

5. The lines of hair that grow above your eyes are (**eyelashes / eyebrows**).

6. (**Eyelashes / Nostrils**) are hairs that grow along the edges of your eyes.

B. Fill in the blanks by unscrambling the words in parentheses.

1. Wear sunglasses to protect your _____ (yese) from the sun.

2. Clean your _____ (ntriosls) with a tissue if you are sick.

3. Hold your _____ (enso) when you jump into a pool.

4. During winter, wear a hat to protect your _____ (ares) from the cold.

5. Wash your hands before you try to remove an _____ (eleysha) that has fallen in your eye.

6. Try not to raise your _____ (beywoers) when you do not believe someone.

Challenge Words

Check (✔) the words you already know.

☐ brow ☐ eardrum ☐ lobe ☐ retina

157. Body Coverings and Marks

Check (✔) the words you already know. Then, listen and repeat.

Tracks 1–10

☐ bump
TR 1

☐ hair
TR 2

☐ rash
TR 4

☐ skin
TR 3

☐ beard
TR 7

☐ freckle
TR 8

☐ bruise
TR 9

Check Your Understanding

A. Match each word to the correct description. One description will not be used.

1. _____ bald
2. _____ beard
3. _____ bruise
4. _____ bump
5. _____ freckle
6. _____ hair
7. _____ pigtail
8. _____ rash
9. _____ scar
10. _____ skin

a. a minor injury from something hitting you

b. a temporary dark mark on your skin

c. grows on the head

d. someone with no hair on his or her head

e. a small, light brown spot on skin

f. skin that has been turned an attractive brown color by the sun

g. a mark on your skin where a cut has healed

h. the natural covering on a person

i. red spots on skin

j. hair that is tied together

k. hair on a man's face

scar
TR 5

bald
TR 6

pigtail
TR 10

Definitions

Someone who is **bald** has no hair, or very little hair, on the top of his or her head.

A man's **beard** is the hair that grows on his chin and cheeks.

A **bruise** is an injury that appears as a purple mark on your body.

A **bump** is a minor injury that you get if you knock into something or if something hits you.

Freckles are small, light brown spots on your skin, especially on your face.

Your **hair** is the fine threads that grow on your head.

A **pigtail** is hair that is tied together.

A **rash** is an area of red spots that appears on your skin.

A **scar** is a mark that is left on the skin by an old wound.

Skin is the natural covering of your body.

B. Circle the word in each group that does not belong.

1. beard	pigtail	bruise
2. rash	hair	pigtail
3. skin	freckle	scar
4. bald	bump	bruise

Challenge Words

Check (✔) the words you already know.

- birthmark
- blackhead
- blemish
- hairline
- mustache
- pimple
- pore
- scalp
- suntan
- wart

160. The Body (General)

Check (✔) the words you already know. Then, listen and repeat.

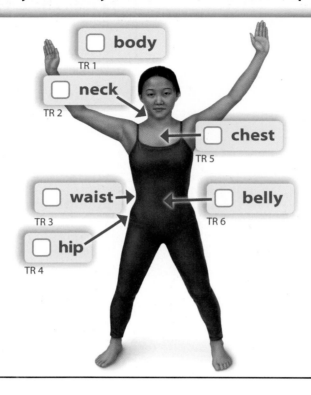

body
TR 1

neck
TR 2

chest
TR 5

waist→
TR 3

belly
TR 6

hip
TR 4

Check Your Understanding

A. Match each word to the correct description. One description will not be used.

1. _____ body
2. _____ belly
3. _____ chest
4. _____ hip
5. _____ lap
6. _____ neck
7. _____ waist

a. another word for stomach
b. middle part of the body
c. top part of the front of the body
d. part of the body that has a particular purpose or function
e. connects the head to the rest of the body
f. a bone at the side of your body near your waist
g. formed by the tops of your legs when you are sitting
h. physical form of a human

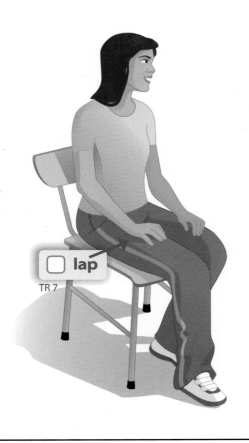

lap

TR 7

Definitions

Your **belly** is your stomach.

Your **body** is all your physical parts.

Your **chest** is the top part of the front of your body.

Your **hip** is the area or bone at each side of your body between the top of your leg and your waist. You have two hips.

Your **lap** is the flat area formed by the tops of your legs when you are sitting down.

Your **neck** is the part of your body which joins your head to the rest of your body.

Your **waist** is the middle part of your body.

B. Choose the correct word from the word bank to complete each sentence.

lap	neck	chest	hips
body	belly	waist	

1. April sat on her grandmother's _____ while she read her a story.

2. Ken put a belt around his _____ because his pants were too big.

3. Richard wrapped a warm scarf around his _____ because it was cold outside.

4. After eating a huge dinner, Kim's _____ was full.

5. I think I'm sick because my whole _____ aches.

6. Ellie put her hands on her _____ as she told the children to behave.

7. Will folded his arms across his _____ because he was angry.

Challenge Words

Check (✔) the words you already know.

☐ limbs ☐ nape ☐ physical ☐ trunk ☐ vertebrate

☐ mental ☐ organ ☐ scruff ☐ udder

205

191. Body Fluids

Check (✔) the words you already know. Then, listen and repeat.

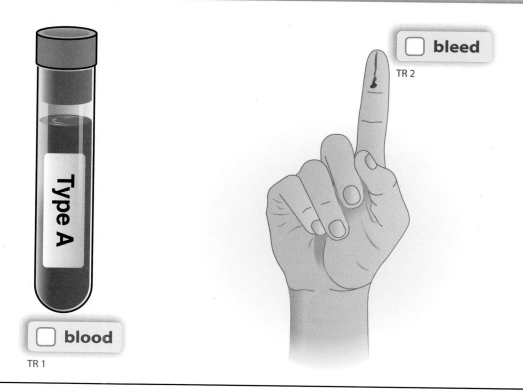

Type A

☐ **blood**

TR 1

☐ **bleed**

TR 2

Check Your Understanding

A. Write **T** for **true statements** and **F** for **false statements**.

1. _____ Blood and sweat are liquids.

2. _____ Sweat is red.

3. _____ Blood is red.

4. _____ If you are bleeding, that means blood is going into your body.

5. _____ If you are sweating, you might be hot, sick, or afraid.

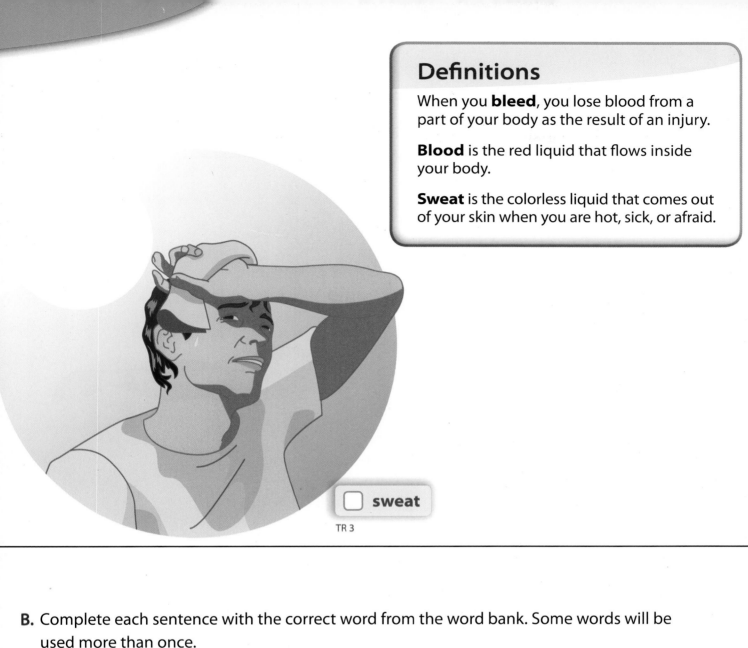

☐ sweat

TR 3

B. Complete each sentence with the correct word from the word bank. Some words will be used more than once.

bleed	blood	sweat

1. The hot sun made Sasha very hot, and _____ dripped down her face.

2. David got a paper cut and his finger started to _____ .

3. The heart pumps _____ through the body.

4. Blood is red, but _____ does not have a color.

5. Andrew fell and scraped his knee, but it did not _____ .

Challenge Words

Check (✔) the words you already know.

☐ artery   ☐ clot   ☐ perspiration   ☐ saliva   ☐ vessel

☐ circulate   ☐ mucus   ☐ pus   ☐ vein

213. Muscles, Bones, and Nerves

Check (✔) the words you already know. Then, listen and repeat.

Tracks 1–4

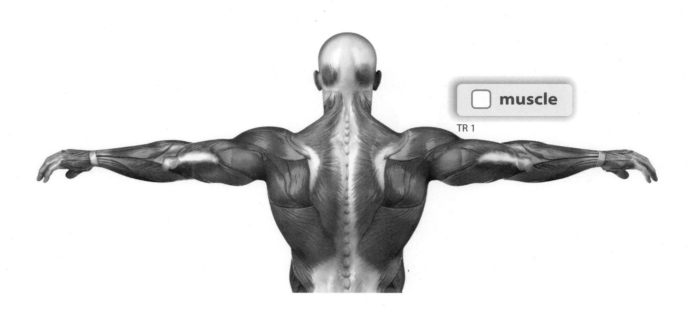

☐ **muscle**

TR 1

Check Your Understanding

A. Circle the correct word to complete each sentence.

1. Alfredo lifted weights to strengthen his _____.

   a. skeletons   b. bones   c. muscles

2. Elbows and knees are examples of _____.

   a. joints   b. bones   c. muscles

3. When Josh fell off his bike, he broke the _____ in his right arm.

   a. bone   b. skeleton   c. muscle

4. _____ are made up of many different types of bones.

   a. Muscles   b. Skeletons   c. Bones

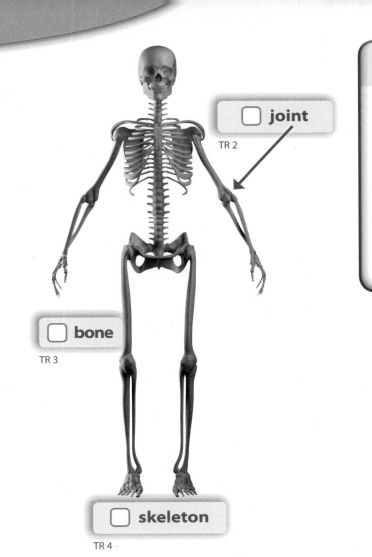

joint
TR 2

bone
TR 3

skeleton
TR 4

B. Match each word to the correct description. One description will not be used.

1. _____ bone

2. _____ joint

3. _____ muscle

4. _____ skeleton

a. where two bones meet and move together

b. twelve pairs of curved bones that surround your chest

c. connected to your bones; helps you move

d. hard part inside your body

e. all the bones in your body

Challenge Words

Check (✔) the words you already know.

- backbone
- ligament
- rib
- tendon
- cartilage
- nerve
- spine

336. Organs

Check (✔) the words you already know. Then, listen and repeat.

Tracks 1–2

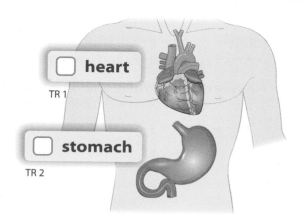

☐ **heart**

TR 1

☐ **stomach**

TR 2

Definitions

Your **heart** is the organ inside your chest that pumps or moves the blood around your body.

Your **stomach** is the organ inside your body where food goes and is broken down after you've eaten it.

Check Your Understanding

A. Write each description in the correct column.

| pumps blood | inside the chest | all people have it |
| food goes here | inside the body | |

STOMACH	BOTH	HEART

B. Fill in the blanks with *stomach* or *heart*.

1. Joe's _____ was full after he ate a big breakfast.

2. Kellie's _____ was beating fast as she finished the race.

3. The _____ moves blood around the body.

4. After you eat food, it goes to your _____.

Challenge Words

Check (✔) the words you already know.

☐ gland   ☐ intestine   ☐ kidney   ☐ liver   ☐ lung

36. Vegetation (General)

Check (✔) the words you already know. Then, listen and repeat.

 Tracks 1–6

Definitions

A **bush** is a large plant with leaves and branches that is smaller than a tree.

A **flower** is the brightly colored part of a plant that grows at the end of a stem.

A **plant** is a living thing that grows in the earth and has a stem, leaves, and roots.

A **tree** is a tall plant that lives for a long time. It has a trunk, branches, and leaves.

Plants, trees, and flowers can be called **vegetation**.

A **weed** is a wild plant that grows in gardens or fields and prevents other plants from growing properly.

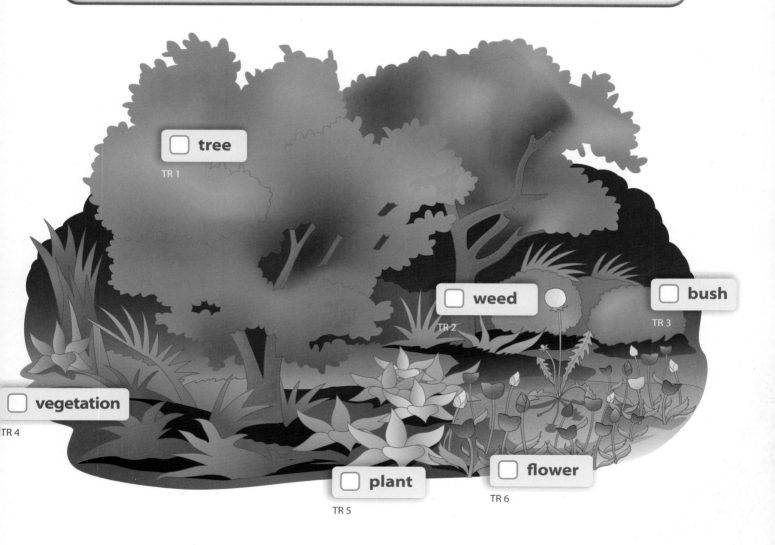

☐ tree
TR 1

☐ weed
TR 2

☐ bush
TR 3

☐ vegetation
TR 4

☐ plant
TR 5

☐ flower
TR 6

Check Your Understanding

A. Match each word to the correct description. One description will not be used.

1. _____ bush
2. _____ flower
3. _____ plant
4. _____ tree
5. _____ vegetation
6. _____ weed

a. large plant with leaves and branches

b. living thing that grows in the earth

c. plant with several woody stems

d. tall plant that lives for a long time

e. plants, trees, and flowers

f. brightly colored part of a plant

g. wild plant that prevents other plants from growing

B. Underline the word that best completes each sentence.

Henry: Wow, look at the amazing plants, trees, and flowers in this park!

Lola: Yes, the (1) (**vegetation / plant**) here is beautiful.

Henry: I am glad we came here. Where should we eat lunch?

Lola: We could eat near those purple and red (2) (**trees / flowers**). They are pretty and smell nice. I do not see any (3) (**weeds / plants**) growing near them.

Henry: Yes, we could. But, it is very sunny today. We might get hot.

Lola: You are right. We can eat our lunch under this tall (4) (**weed / tree**) and sit in the shade.

Henry: That is a great idea!

Lola: After we eat, we can take a walk to see the rest of the (5) (**plants / weeds**) growing here.

Henry: Yes, I saw a (6) (**vegetation / bush**) with interesting leaves that I wanted to look at.

Challenge Words

Check (✔) the words you already know.

☐ arbor

☐ flora

☐ oasis

☐ photosynthesis

☐ shrub

☐ underbrush

108. Trees/Bushes (Parts)

Check (✔) the words you already know. Then, listen and repeat.

Tracks 1–6

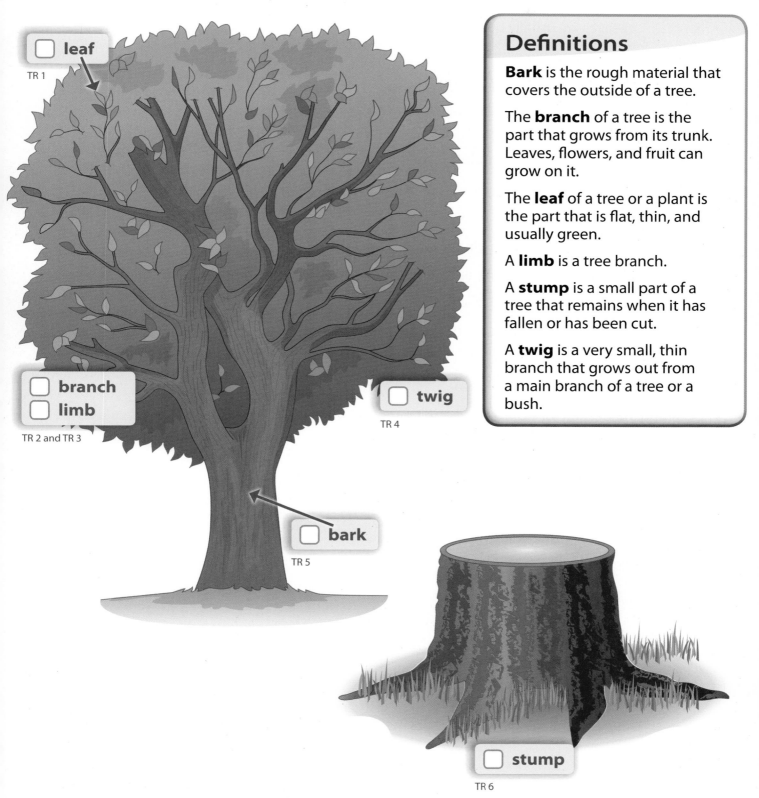

☐ **leaf**

TR 1

☐ **branch**
☐ **limb**

TR 2 and TR 3

☐ **twig**

TR 4

☐ **bark**

TR 5

☐ **stump**

TR 6

Definitions

Bark is the rough material that covers the outside of a tree.

The **branch** of a tree is the part that grows from its trunk. Leaves, flowers, and fruit can grow on it.

The **leaf** of a tree or a plant is the part that is flat, thin, and usually green.

A **limb** is a tree branch.

A **stump** is a small part of a tree that remains when it has fallen or has been cut.

A **twig** is a very small, thin branch that grows out from a main branch of a tree or a bush.

Check Your Understanding

A. Write **T** for **true statements** and **F** for **false statements**.

1. _____ Bark is very smooth.

2. _____ Branches grow from trunks.

3. _____ Leaves are usually purple.

4. _____ *Limb* is another word for stump.

5. _____ A stump is what is left after a tree has been cut.

6. _____ Twigs grow on trees and branches.

B. Circle the correct word to complete each sentence.

1. Jennifer and Maria gathered _____ to make a fire.

   a. trees   b. twigs   c. stumps

2. The tree's _____ are swaying in the wind.

   a. stumps   b. bark   c. branches

3. There is a swing hanging from the tree's strongest _____.

   a. leaf   b. limb   c. twig

4. Annie carved her name in the _____ of the tall tree.

   a. bark   b. leaf   c. twig

5. George made a big pile of _____ and jumped in it.

   a. leaves   b. twigs   c. branches

6. Luke sat on a _____ in the woods and rested.

   a. twig   b. bark   c. stump

Challenge Words

Check (✔) the words you already know.

☐ foliage   ☐ resin   ☐ sap   ☐ sticker   ☐ treetop

☐ latex   ☐ rubber   ☐ stem   ☐ thorn   ☐ wicker

192. Vegetation (Other)

Check (✔) the words you already know. Then, listen and repeat.

 Tracks 1-4

☐ **vine**

TR 1

Definitions

Grass is a common plant made of thin, flat, green leaves that cover the surface of the ground.

A **lawn** is an area of short grass.

The **root** is the part of a plant that grows under the ground and brings food and water into the plant.

A **vine** is a plant that climbs up or around things.

☐ **grass**

TR 2

☐ **root**

TR 3

☐ **lawn**

TR 4

Check Your Understanding

A. Match each word to the correct description. One description will not be used.

1. _____ grass
2. _____ lawn
3. _____ root
4. _____ vine

a. grass which has been cut and dried
b. a climbing plant
c. plant with thin, flat leaves
d. brings food and water to plants
e. area of short grass

B. Underline the correct word to complete each sentence.

1. Yuri is mowing the (**lawn** / **vine**) at his uncle's house.

2. Many (**roots** / **vines**) are growing up that brick wall.

3. Tree (**roots** / **grass**) reach deep into the earth.

4. Emma sat on the (**grass** / **vine**) and watched the clouds float by.

Challenge Words

Check (✔) the words you already know.

- ☐ algae
- ☐ bamboo
- ☐ cattail
- ☐ cob
- ☐ fern
- ☐ fungus
- ☐ hay
- ☐ mushroom
- ☐ straw
- ☐ thatch

269. Plants and Flowers

Check (✔) the words you already know. Then, listen and repeat.

Tracks 1–5

Definitions

A **berry** is a small, round fruit that grows on a bush or a tree.

A **blossom** is the flower that appears on a fruit tree before the fruit grows.

A **dandelion** is a wild plant with yellow flowers.

A **rose** is a flower with a pleasant smell. It has sharp thorns on its stem.

A **seed** is the small, hard part of a plant from which a new plant grows.

☐ **berry**

TR 1

☐ **rose**

TR 3

☐ **seed**

TR 2

☐ **dandelion**

TR 4

☐ **blossom**

TR 5

Check Your Understanding

A. Write **T** for **true statements** and **F** for **false statements**.

1. _____ Berries grow on trees and bushes.

2. _____ Dandelions are red flowers.

3. _____ Plants grow from seeds.

4. _____ Blossoms grow on fruit trees after the fruit.

5. _____ Roses have sharp thorns on their stems.

B. Circle the correct word to complete each sentence.

1. The _____ on the cherry tree bloom in the spring.

   a. blossoms　　　　　　b. dandelions　　　　　　c. seeds

2. After you plant a _____ , you have to water it to make it grow.

   a. berry　　　　　　　b. seed　　　　　　　　c. blossom

3. Strawberries are my favorite type of _____ .

   a. berry　　　　　　　b. seed　　　　　　　　c. blossom

4. There are pink and red _____ growing in the flower garden.

   a. dandelions　　　　　b. berries　　　　　　c. roses

5. Kate enjoys picking _____ because her favorite color is yellow.

   a. seeds　　　　　　　b. blossoms　　　　　　c. dandelions

Challenge Words

Check (✔) the words you already know.

☐ bud　　　　☐ hemp　　　　☐ pollen　　　　☐ tulip

☐ cactus　　　☐ petal　　　　☐ sunflower

41. Ownership/Possession

Check (✔) the words you already know. Then, listen and repeat.

Tracks 1–4

Definitions

If something **belongs** to you, you own it.

You use **have** to say that someone or something owns something.

If you **own** something, it belongs to you.

If you **possess** something, you have it or own it.

☐ **have**

TR 1

☐ **belongs**

TR 2

☐ **own**
☐ **possess**

TR 3 and TR 4

Check Your Understanding

A. Complete the sentences.

1. I have _____.

2. I own _____.

3. That _____ belongs to _____.

4. _____ possesses _____.

B. Underline the correct word to complete each sentence.

1. All of my friends (**belong / own**) MP3 players.

2. I (**have / belong**) a new coat.

3. That book (**owns / belongs**) to Joshua.

4. The farmer (**belongs / possesses**) a lot of land.

Challenge Words

Check (✔) the words you already know.

☐ custody   ☐ maintain   ☐ occupy   ☐ possession

☐ heirloom   ☐ monopoly   ☐ ownership   ☐ property

89. Losing / Winning

Check (✔) the words you already know. Then, listen and repeat.

 Tracks 1–15

| | champion |
| | winner |

TR 1 and TR 2

Definitions

A **champion** is the winner of a competition.

If you **defeat** someone, you beat him or her in a battle, a game, or a competition and that person is defeated, or suffers a loss.

A **loss** is when you do not win after competing in a battle, a fight, or a game.

If you **win** a competition, a fight, or an argument, you do better than everyone else involved.

The **winner** of a prize, a race, or a competition is the one that does the best.

| | loss |

TR 3

| | defeat |

TR 4

SPELLING BEE

| | win |

TR 5

Check Your Understanding

A. Write the words from the word bank in the correct column.

champion	win	defeat	winner	loss

WINNING	LOSING

B. Match each word to the correct description. One description will not be used.

1. _____ win

2. _____ loss

3. _____ champion

4. _____ winner

5. _____ defeat

a. the person that does the best

b. reaching a goal

c. the winner of a competition

d. beat someone in a competition, causing that person to suffer a loss

e. do better in something than everyone else does

f. when you do not win

Challenge Words

Check (✔) the words you already know.

☐ accomplishment   ☐ dominate   ☐ excel   ☐ subdue   ☐ triumphant

☐ conquest   ☐ downfall   ☐ prevail   ☐ success   ☐ victor

148. Receiving/Taking Actions

Check (✔) the words you already know. Then, listen and repeat.

Tracks 1–5

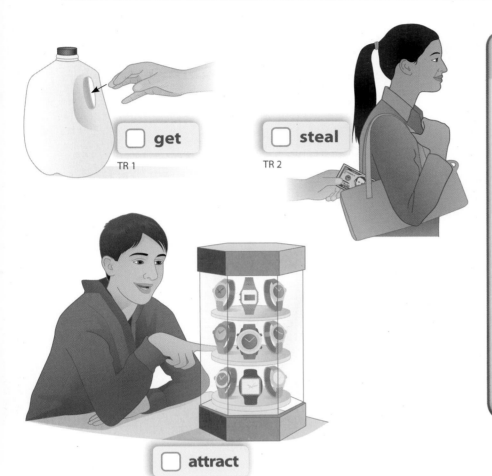

☐ **get**
TR 1

☐ **steal**
TR 2

☐ **attract**
TR 3

Definitions

If you **accept** something that someone offers you, you say yes to it or agree to take it.

If someone or something **attracts** you, you like and are interested in knowing more about that person or thing.

If you **capture** someone or something, you catch, keep, and prevent from leaving, that person or thing.

If you **get** something, you buy it or obtain it.

If you **steal** something from someone, you take it without that person's permission.

☐ **capture**
TR 4

Would you like some water?

Yes, please.

☐ **accept**
TR 5

Check Your Understanding

A. Write **T** for **true statements** and **F** for **false statements**.

1. _____ If you capture something, you let it go free.

2. _____ If you are attracted to something, you do not want to know more about it.

3. _____ If someone steals something from you, that person takes it without your permission.

4. _____ When you accept something, you take what is being given to you.

5. _____ If you get something, you do not have it anymore.

B. Circle the correct word to complete each sentence.

1. Steve _____ some fish in a net.

    a. captured   b. accepted   c. got

2. The large diamond ring in the store's window _____ many customers, attention.

    a. accepted   b. stole   c. attracted

3. John _____ a new job at the company.

    a. stole   b. accepted   c. captured

4. A thief tried to _____ money from the bank, but the police caught him.

    a. steal   b. accept   c. get

5. My dad went to the store to _____ more milk.

    a. capture   b. get   c. attract

Challenge Words

Check (✔) the words you already know.

| ☐ abduct | ☐ arrest | ☐ hijack | ☐ plunder | ☐ rob |
| ☐ achieve | ☐ deprive | ☐ inherit | ☐ ransack | ☐ trespass |

171. Finding / Keeping

Check (✔) the words you already know. Then, listen and repeat.

Tracks 1–5

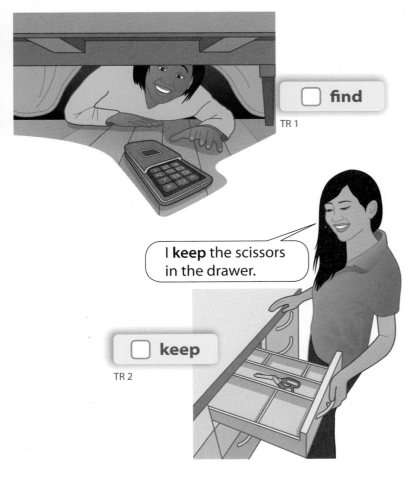

☐ **find**

TR 1

I **keep** the scissors in the drawer.

☐ **keep**

TR 2

Definitions

To **bury** something means to put it into a hole in the ground and cover it up.

If you **find** something, you see it after you have been looking for it.

To **hide** is to put a person or object in a place where the person or object won't be easily seen or found.

If you **keep** something, you continue to have it. If you **keep** it somewhere, you store it there.

If you **spot** something or someone, you notice that thing or person.

☐ **hide**

TR 4

There she is!

☐ **spot**

TR 3

☐ **bury**

TR 5

225

Check Your Understanding

A. Match each word to the correct description. One description will not be used.

1. _____ bury   a. to store something somewhere

2. _____ spot   b. to cover something in a hole in the ground

3. _____ find   c. to put something in a place where it will not be seen

4. _____ hide   d. to make difficult to see with leaves, branches, or paint

5. _____ keep   e. to look for something and locate it

                             f. to notice something or someone

B. Underline the correct word to complete each sentence.

1. Ana (**keeps / spots**) her phone in her backpack at school.

2. My dog likes to dig holes and (**keep / bury**) his bones in the backyard.

3. Roberto is very easy to (**hide / spot**) in a crowd because he is wearing a bright yellow shirt.

4. Linda (**finds / hides**) her journal under her bed so her brother won't read it.

5. Paul's room is very messy, so it is difficult to (**find / bury**) things.

Challenge Words

Check (✔) the words you already know.

☐ camouflage   ☐ conserve   ☐ hoard   ☐ masquerade   ☐ restrict

☐ conceal   ☐ distinguish   ☐ locate   ☐ pinpoint   ☐ tuck

184. Giving Up / Losing

Check (✔) the words you already know. Then, listen and repeat.

Tracks 1–6

☐ **borrow**

TR 1

Definitions

If you **borrow** something that belongs to someone else, you use it for a period of time and then return it.

If you **lose** a game, you do not win it.

The **losers** of a game are the people who do not win.

If you **share** something with another person, you both have it or use it.

If you **show** something, you let others see it.

If you **trade** one thing for another, you give someone that thing and get something else in exchange.

☐ **show**

TR 2

☐ **lose**

TR 3

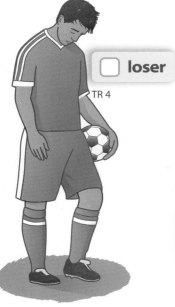

☐ **loser**

TR 4

Let's **trade.**

☐ **trade**

TR 5

I'll **share** with you.

☐ **share**

TR 6

Check Your Understanding

A. Match each word to the correct description. One description will not be used.

1. _____ lose   a. to use and return something that belongs to someone else

2. _____ borrow   b. to have or use something with someone else

3. _____ share   c. to not win a game

4. _____ trade   d. to give something in exchange for something else

5. _____ show   e. to pay to be able to use something

6. _____ loser   f. person who does not win

                                g. to let someone see something

B. Circle the word that means the same thing as the underlined words.

1. Melissa didn't have a pen, so she used Claire's pen and gave it back later.

    a. traded   b. showed   c. borrowed

2. Dave gave his apple to Mike in exchange for an orange.

    a. traded   b. borrowed   c. shared

3. Ken let me see the pictures from his trip to New York City.

    a. showed   b. traded   c. lost

4. Amanda's team did not practice, so they probably will not win the game tonight.

    a. loser   b. lose   c. borrow

5. The people who did not win looked very sad after the hockey game.

    a. losers   b. trades   c. shows

6. I couldn't eat the whole sandwich, so I ate one half and gave the other half to my sister.

    a. showed   b. traded   c. shared

Challenge Words

Check (✔) the words you already know.

☐ abandon	☐ displace	☐ eject	☐ lease	☐ loan
☐ alternate	☐ dispose	☐ exchange	☐ lend	☐ swap

15 PARTS OF DWELLINGS

91. Rooms

Check (✔) the words you already know. Then, listen and repeat.

 Tracks 1–14

☐ **basement**
☐ **cellar**

TR 1 and TR 2

☐ **bathroom**

TR 3

☐ **nursery**

TR 5

☐ **garage**

TR 6

☐ **bedroom**

TR 10

☐ **kitchen**

TR 11

☐ **playroom**

TR 12

229

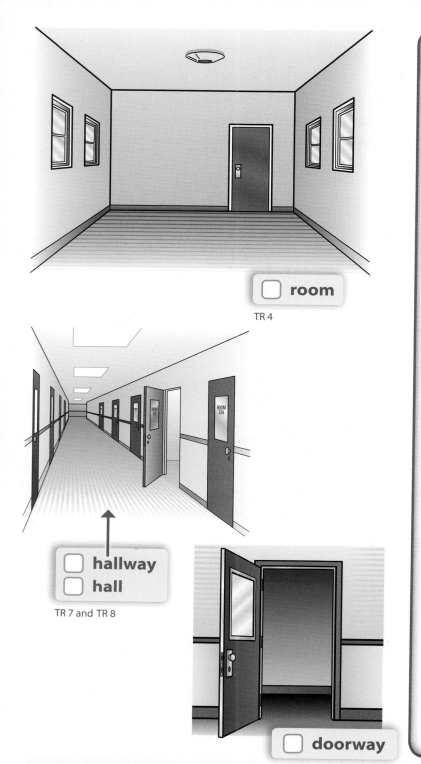

☐ **room**

TR 4

☐ **hallway**
☐ **hall**

TR 7 and TR 8

☐ **doorway**

TR 9

Definitions

The **basement** of a building is a room that is built below ground level.

A **bathroom** is a room in a house that contains a sink, a toilet, and usually a shower or bathtub.

A **bedroom** is a room that is used for sleeping.

A **cellar** is a room under a building.

A **closet** is a very small room for storing things, especially clothes.

A **doorway** is a space in a wall where a door opens and closes.

A **garage** is a building, or a part of a building, where you keep a car.

The **hall** in a house or an apartment is the area that leads from one room to another.

A **hallway** is an area with doors that leads into other rooms.

A **kitchen** is a room that is used for cooking.

A **nursery** is a room in a family home in which the young children of the family sleep or play.

A **playroom** is a room in a house for children to play in.

A **porch** is a raised structure that is built along the outside wall of a house and is often covered with a roof.

A **room** is a separate area inside a building that has its own walls.

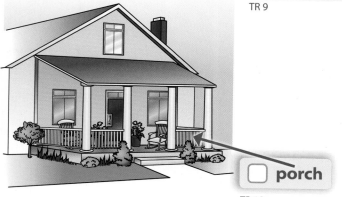

☐ **porch**

TR 13

☐ **closet**

TR 14

Check Your Understanding

A. Match each word to the correct description. One description will not be used.

1. _____ basement   a. room that is below ground level
2. _____ room   b. room that has a bathtub or shower
3. _____ nursery   c. area that leads from one room to another
4. _____ cellar   d. walled area in a building
5. _____ closet   e. young child's room
6. _____ bathroom   f. structure on the outside of a house
7. _____ garage   g. space where a door opens and closes
8. _____ hall   h. area with doors that leads to other rooms
9. _____ kitchen   i. long, narrow gap that people can walk along
10. _____ bedroom   j. room where cooking takes place
11. _____ doorway   k. another word for basement
12. _____ hallway   l. small room to keep clothes in
13. _____ playroom   m. room where people sleep
14. _____ porch   n. room for children to play in
                             o. building where a car is kept

B. Circle the word in each group that does not belong.

1. garage   nursery   playroom
2. cellar   basement   doorway
3. bedroom   porch   bathroom
4. hall   closet   hallway
5. porch   kitchen   room

Challenge Words

Check (✔) the words you already know.

☐ aisle   ☐ balcony   ☐ entrance   ☐ parlor   ☐ washroom
☐ attic   ☐ den   ☐ lobby   ☐ threshold

113. Furniture

Check (✔) the words you already know. Then, listen and repeat.

Tracks 1–16

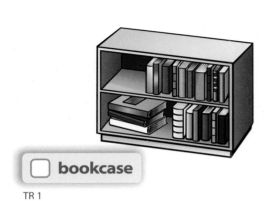

☐ **bookcase**

TR 1

☐ **counter**

TR 2

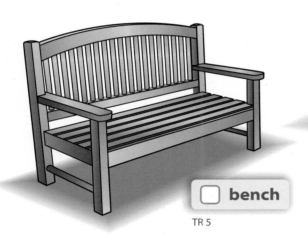

☐ **bench**

TR 5

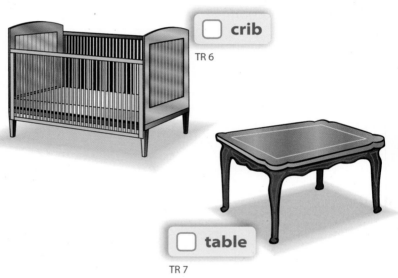

☐ **crib**

TR 6

☐ **table**

TR 7

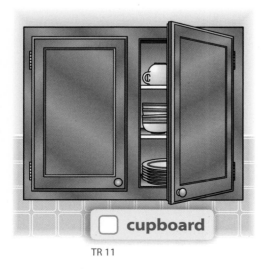

☐ **cupboard**

TR 11

☐ **bed**

TR 12

□ sofa
□ couch

TR 3 and TR 4

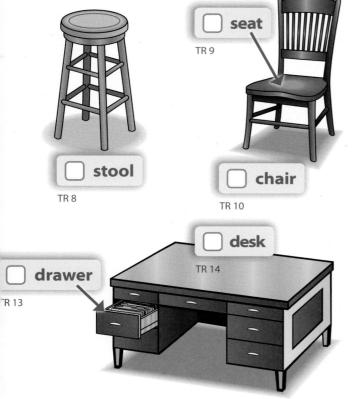

□ stool

TR 8

□ seat

TR 9

□ chair

TR 10

□ drawer

TR 13

□ desk

TR 14

□ playpen

TR 15

□ cradle

TR 16

Definitions

A **bed** is a piece of furniture that you lie on when you sleep.

A **bench** is a long seat made of wood or metal.

A **bookcase** is a piece of furniture with shelves that you keep books on.

A **chair** is a piece of furniture for one person to sit on. It has a back and four legs.

A **couch** is a long, comfortable seat for two or three people.

A **counter** is a long, flat surface.

A **cradle** is a baby's bed that you can rock from side to side.

A **crib** is a bed with high sides for a baby.

A **cupboard** is a piece of furniture with doors, and shelves for storing food or dishes.

A **desk** is a table that you sit at to write or work.

A **drawer** is a part of a piece of furniture, such as a desk, that you can pull out and put things in.

A **playpen** is a small structure with bars or a net around the sides, where young children can play safely.

A **seat** is something that you can sit on.

A **sofa** is a long, comfortable seat with a back, and usually with arms. Two or three people can sit on it.

A **stool** is a seat with legs and no support for your arms or back.

A **table** is a piece of furniture with a flat top that you put things on or sit at.

233

Check Your Understanding

A. Underline the correct word to complete each sentence.

1. Wendy helped Eric put the books back in the (**playpen / bookcase**).

2. Mary is sitting at her (**bed / desk**) and doing her homework.

3. My family sits at the (**table / bed**) and eats dinner together every evening.

4. Rob and Jessie sat on (**tables / stools**) at the kitchen counter.

5. We need an extra (**cradle / chair**) so that Martin can sit down.

6. Franklin put the dishes in the (**cupboard / desk**).

7. We can sit on a (**bench / bookcase**) while we wait.

8. Cecilia found the scissors in the top (**seat / drawer**) of the desk.

9. After I washed the dishes, I let them dry on the (**counter / playpen**).

10. The baby is falling asleep as her mother rocks her (**cradle / seat**).

11. Melanie sat on the (**stool / couch**) with her brother and sister.

12. Claire snuggled on the (**stool / sofa**) with a warm blanket and watched a movie.

13. My little cousin Sean woke up from his nap and stood in his (**counter / crib**).

14. Kate took a (**cupboard / seat**) near the fireplace because she was cold.

15. Nelson was tired so he took a nap in his (**bed / table**).

16. Joseph's little brother is playing with his toys in the (**drawer / playpen**).

B. Circle the word in each group that does not belong.

1. playpen	drawer	cradle	crib
2. table	counter	desk	cupboard
3. chair	bookcase	stool	seat
4. bench	bed	couch	sofa

Challenge Words

Check (✔) the words you already know.

- ☐ armchair
- ☐ bureau
- ☐ cabinet
- ☐ furniture
- ☐ hammock
- ☐ mat
- ☐ mattress
- ☐ tabletop
- ☐ wheelchair

123. Parts of a Home

Check (✔) the words you already know. Then, listen and repeat.

Tracks 1–12

- ☐ roof TR 1
- ☐ chimney TR 2
- ☐ window TR 3
- ☐ door TR 4
- ☐ doorstep TR 5

Check Your Understanding

A. Circle the correct word to complete each sentence.

1. Tom is so tall that he almost hit his head on the _____.

   a. wall   b. ceiling   c. doorstep

2. There was smoke coming out of the _____ so Tina knew she could warm up by the fire.

   a. roof   b. floor   c. chimney

3. Laura knocked on the _____, but no one answered.

   a. door   b. stair   c. doorstep

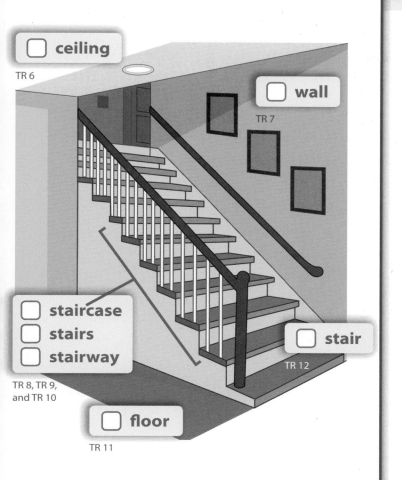

ceiling

TR 6

wall

TR 7

staircase
stairs
stairway

TR 8, TR 9, and TR 10

stair

TR 12

floor

TR 11

Definitions

A **ceiling** is the flat surface that forms the top inside part a room.

A **chimney** is a pipe or hollow brick structure that lets the smoke travel up and away from a fire or a furnace into the open air.

A **door** is a moveable piece of wood, glass, or metal, which allows entrance or exit from a building, room, or closet.

A **doorstep** is a step in front of a door outside a building.

The **floor** of a room is the part of it that you walk on.

The **roof** of a building is the covering that protects the people and things inside from the weather.

A **stair** is one of the steps in a set of stairs.

A **staircase** is a set of stairs inside a building.

Stairs are a set of steps inside a building that go from one level to another.

A **stairway** is a set of steps, inside or outside a building.

A **wall** is one of the sides of a building or a room.

A **window** is a space in the wall of a building that has glass in it. It lets light in and you can see through it.

---

4. Ella stood on the _____ and knocked on the door.

   a. chimney   b. doorstep   c. wall

5. Jeremy took off his muddy shoes before he walked across the _____.

   a. door   b. window   c. floor

6. During the thunderstorm, we all listened to the rain pounding on the _____.

   a. roof   b. stair   c. floor

7. The cat likes to sit on the first _____ and wait for John to come home.

   a. stair   b. wall   c. ceiling

8. Billy climbed the _____ up to his room slowly because he was tired.

   a. wall   b. window   c. stairs

9. The sun is shining in through the _____ .

   a. chimney   b. floor   c. window

10. The _____ behind the house leads up to the balcony.

    a. doorstep   b. stairway   c. roof

11. Caroline is looking at the picture that is hanging on the _____ .

    a. floor   b. wall   c. ceiling

12. There is a large _____ in the center of the room that leads to the second floor.

    a. staircase   b. wall   c. doorstep

B. Circle the word in each group that does not belong.

1. stairway   staircase   floor

2. roof   stairs   chimney

3. chimney   wall   ceiling

4. door   window   roof

5. doorstep   chimney   stair

Challenge Words

Check (✔) the words you already know.

☐ hearth   ☐ mantel   ☐ pane   ☐ vent

134. Linens

Check (✔) the words you already know. Then, listen and repeat.

🎧 Tracks 1–10

☐ **napkin**
TR 1

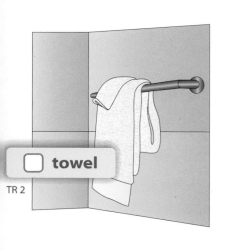

☐ **towel**
TR 2

☐ **blanket**
TR 4

☐ **tablecloth**
TR 3

☐ **pillowcase**
TR 5

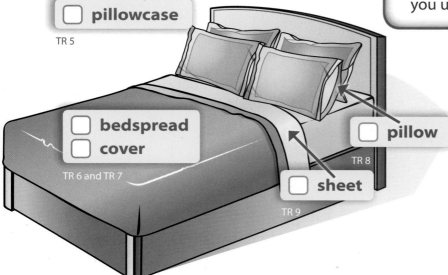

☐ **bedspread**
☐ **cover**
TR 6 and TR 7

☐ **pillow**
TR 8

☐ **sheet**
TR 9

☐ **cushion**
TR 10

Definitions

A **bedspread** is a decorative cover that you put on a bed.

A **blanket** is a large, thick piece of cloth that you put on a bed to keep you warm.

Bed **covers** are sheets, blankets, and comforters.

A **cushion** is a bag of soft material that you put on a seat to make it more comfortable.

A **napkin** is a square of cloth or paper that you use when you are eating to protect your clothes, or to wipe your mouth or hands.

A **pillow** is a soft object that you rest your head on when you are lying down.

A **pillowcase** is a cloth cover for a pillow.

A **sheet** is a large, light piece of cloth that you sleep on or cover yourself with in bed.

A **tablecloth** is a cloth that you use to cover a table.

A **towel** is a piece of thick, soft cloth that you use to dry yourself.

Check Your Understanding

A. Underline the correct word to complete each sentence.

1. The table is covered with a (**pillowcase / tablecloth**).

2. Matt wiped the crumbs off his face with a (**napkin / blanket**).

3. When Glen got out of the pool, he dried off with a (**bedspread / towel**).

4. Ana put her head on the (**sheet / pillow**) and fell asleep.

5. The seat of this chair should have a (**cushion / cover**) on it because it is very hard.

6. Sam covered himself with a (**napkin / blanket**) to keep warm.

7. I want to wash the (**covers / cushions**), so please remove your blankets and sheets from your bed.

8. Please put this (**sheet / pillowcase**) on Jason's pillow.

9. Gary has a blue and white (**tablecloth / bedspread**) on his bed.

10. Sophie covered the mattress with a blue (**sheet / tablecloth**).

B. Circle the word in each group that does not belong.

1. cover	napkin	sheet
2. cushion	pillow	towel
3. bedspread	blanket	tablecloth
4. blanket	napkin	towel
5. cover	napkin	tablecloth

Challenge Words

Check (✔) the words you already know.

☐ doily   ☐ drape   ☐ pad   ☐ quilt

217. Fences and Ledges

Check (✔) the words you already know. Then, listen and repeat.

Tracks 1–4

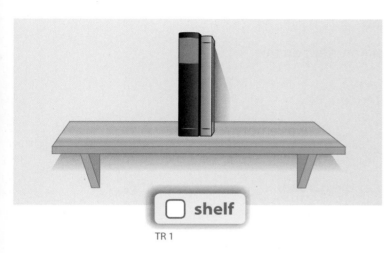

☐ **shelf**

TR 1

Definitions

A **fence** is a wooden or metal wall around a piece of land or area.

A **gate** is a door in a fence.

A **mailbox** is a box outside your home where your mail is delivered.

A **shelf** is a long, flat surface on a wall or in a cabinet that you can keep things on.

☐ **gate**

TR 2

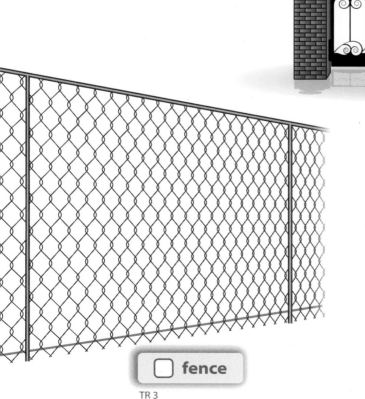

☐ **fence**

TR 3

☐ **mailbox**

TR 4

Check Your Understanding

A. Match each word to the correct description. One description will not be used.

1. _____ shelf   a. a door in a fence

2. _____ gate   b. narrow shelf along the bottom edge of a window

3. _____ mailbox   c. a metal wall around an area

4. _____ fence   d. mail is put in this

                                e. things like books are kept on this

B. Circle the correct word to complete each sentence.

1. I knew my dad already got the mail because the _____ was empty.

     a. shelf   b. fence   c. mailbox

2. The _____ was locked, so Olivia could not enter the garden.

     a. gate   b. mailbox   c. shelf

3. The _____ fell off the wall because there were too many books on it.

     a. fence   b. shelf   c. gate

4. Mandy has a _____ around her yard so that her dog doesn't run away.

     a. shelf   b. fence   c. gate

Challenge Words

Check (✔) the words you already know.

☐ curb   ☐ hedge   ☐ screen

☐ gutter   ☐ ledge   ☐ trellis

284. Furnishings and Decorations

Check (✔) the words you already know. Then, listen and repeat.

 Tracks 1–5

☐ **banner**

TR 1

Definitions

A **banner** is a long strip of cloth or plastic with something written on it.

A **carpet** is a thick, soft covering for the floor.

A **curtain** is a piece of material that hangs in front of or around a window.

A **rug** is a piece of thick cloth that you put on the floor. It is like a carpet but covers a smaller area.

A **vase** is a container that is used for holding flowers.

☐ **vase**

TR 3

☐ **curtain**

TR 2

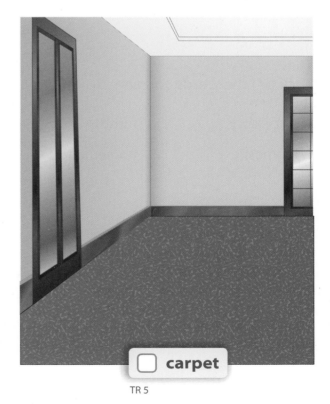

☐ **carpet**

TR 5

☐ **rug**

TR 4

Check Your Understanding

A. Match each word to the correct description. One description will not be used.

1. _____ vase
2. _____ banner
3. _____ rug
4. _____ curtain
5. _____ carpet

a. long strip of cloth or plastic with words on it

b. container for flowers

c. thick, soft floor covering

d. small, thick floor covering

e. a large piece of heavy cloth with a picture woven into it

f. material that hangs in front of a window

B. Answer the questions.

1. What goes in a vase? _____

2. What are banners made out of? _____

3. Where do curtains hang? _____

4. Where do you put a rug? _____

5. What does a carpet cover? _____

Challenge Words

Check (✔) the words you already know.

☐ accessory   ☐ furnish   ☐ tapestry   ☐ wreath

☐ domestic   ☐ homemade   ☐ wallpaper

93. Things You Travel On

Check (✔) the words you already know. Then, listen and repeat.

Tracks 1–18

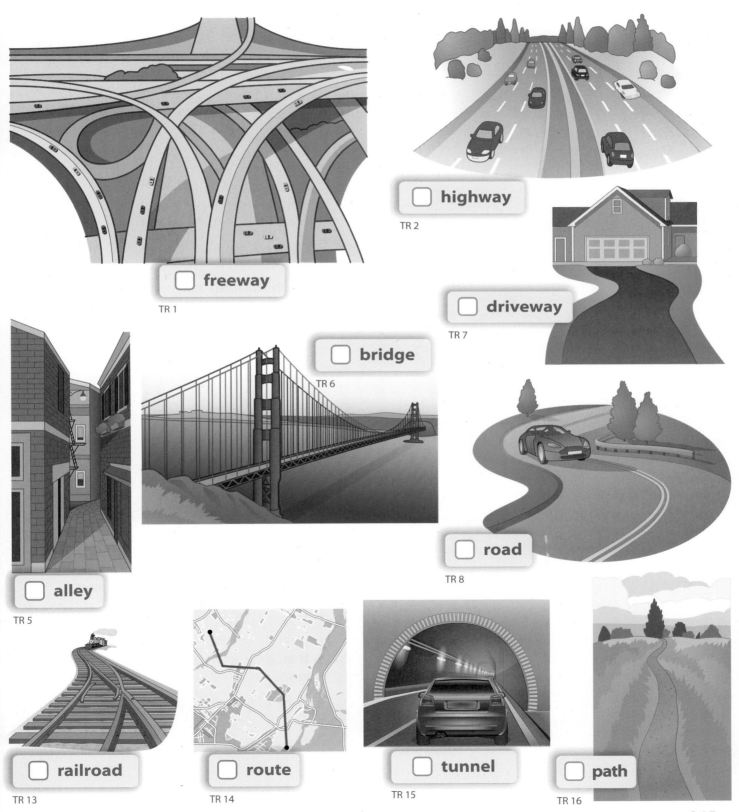

☐ **freeway**
TR 1

☐ **highway**
TR 2

☐ **driveway**
TR 7

☐ **bridge**
TR 6

☐ **road**
TR 8

☐ **alley**
TR 5

☐ **railroad**
TR 13

☐ **route**
TR 14

☐ **tunnel**
TR 15

☐ **path**
TR 16

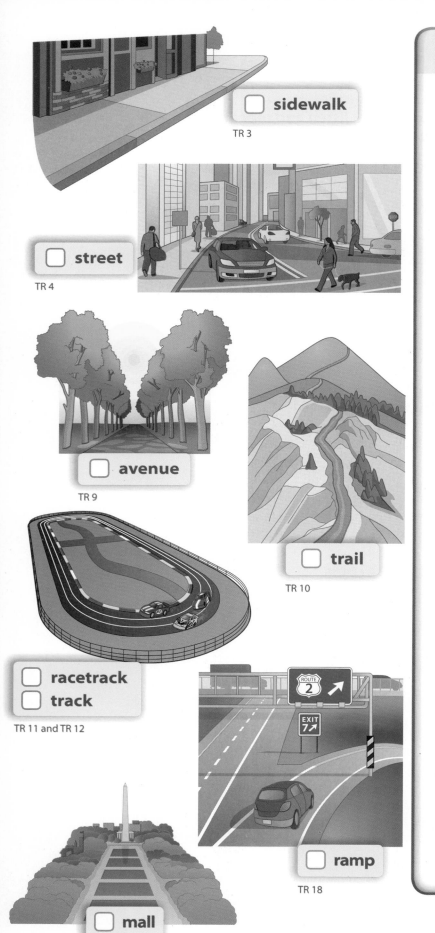

sidewalk
TR 3

street
TR 4

avenue
TR 9

trail
TR 10

racetrack
track
TR 11 and TR 12

ramp
TR 18

mall
TR 17

Definitions

An **alley** is a narrow street between the backs of buildings.

An **avenue** is a straight road, especially one with trees on either side.

A **bridge** is a structure that is built over a river or road so that people or vehicles can cross from one side to the other.

A **driveway** is a small road that leads from the street to the front of a building.

A **freeway** is a main road that has been specially built for fast travel over long distances.

A **highway** is a main road that connects towns or cities.

A **mall** is a paved or grassy area for people to take walks.

A **path** is a long, narrow piece of ground that people walk along.

A **racetrack** is a track for races between runners, horses, dogs, cars, or motorcycles.

A **railroad** is a route between two places that trains travel along on metal rails.

A **ramp** is a surface with a slope between two places that are at different levels.

A **road** is a long piece of hard ground that vehicles travel on.

A **route** is a way from one place to another.

A **sidewalk** is a walkway with a hard surface by the side of a road.

A **street** is a road in a city or a town.

A **track** is a piece of ground that is used for races.

A **trail** is a rough path usually used for hiking.

A **tunnel** is a long passage that has been made through a hill or under the sea.

Check Your Understanding

A. Fill in the blank with the correct word. The first letter for each word is provided.

1. Tom drove up the **r**＿＿＿＿＿＿＿ to get on the highway.

2. We followed a **t**＿＿＿＿＿＿＿ on our hike up the mountain.

3. I crossed the street and walked on the **s**＿＿＿＿＿＿＿ on my way to the grocery store.

4. Ana walked down the **a**＿＿＿＿＿＿＿ so she could enter the building through the back door.

5. The runners lined up on the **t**＿＿＿＿＿＿＿ to get ready to race.

6. We can't drive our car across the river because the **b**＿＿＿＿＿＿＿ is closed.

7. To get to work on time, Michael usually drives on the **f**＿＿＿＿＿＿＿.

8. Pat lives on a small country **r**＿＿＿＿＿＿＿.

9. Freddy drove through the **t**＿＿＿＿＿＿＿ and came out on the other side of the mountain.

10. The bus driver follows the same **r**＿＿＿＿＿＿＿ every day of the week.

11. The cars were going super fast as they went around the **r**＿＿＿＿＿＿＿.

12. There were many shops and beautiful trees along the **a**＿＿＿＿＿＿＿.

13. Jason pulled into the **d**＿＿＿＿＿＿＿ and parked his car.

14. Melanie lives on Bartlett **S**＿＿＿＿＿＿＿, behind the school.

15. Erica and Ali are going to take the **h**＿＿＿＿＿＿＿ to get to the party faster.

16. It was a beautiful day, so we took a walk on the **m**＿＿＿＿＿＿＿.

17. Marie watched the train going by on the **r**＿＿＿＿＿＿＿ tracks.

18. I followed the **p**＿＿＿＿＿＿＿ to the lake and went swimming.

B. Choose the sentence that correctly uses the underlined word.

1. a. I walked down my <u>driveway</u> to pick up the newspaper.

   b. She drove her <u>driveway</u> to work each day.

2. a. The bus waited on the <u>trail</u> to pick up the passengers.

   b. We hiked down the <u>trail</u> and saw some beautiful flowers.

3. a. As the cars zoomed around the <u>racetrack</u>, the people cheered loudly.

   b. The doctor traveled on the <u>racetrack</u> to get to the hospital.

4. a. I had a picnic with my friends on the <u>mall</u>.

   b. I wanted to swim in the <u>mall</u> before nightfall.

5. a. To deliver the newspaper each day, the man drove the same <u>route</u> from house to house.

   b. Every day for exercise, I <u>route</u> my dogs up and down the street.

6. a. In our town, the bank and <u>avenue</u> are on the same street.

   b. He watched as the trees along the <u>avenue</u> were being trimmed.

7. a. The <u>tunnel</u> lit up the sky at night.

   b. When we drove through the <u>tunnel</u>, we turned on our headlights so we could see better.

8. a. To cross the river, we walked over the <u>bridge</u>.

   b. The chef cooked rice and fish for the <u>bridge</u>.

9. a. The cars were parked on the <u>street</u>.

   b. The family met the <u>street</u> before eating dinner.

10. a. In the park, there was a shady <u>path</u> that led to a small lake.

    b. As the parade began, we listened to the <u>path</u> play marching music.

11. a. We decided the <u>freeway</u> was the best place to shop.

    b. After 4:00 p.m., the <u>freeway</u> has a lot of traffic.

12. a. The <u>railroad</u> goes through the mountains.

    b. After running, the <u>railroad</u> needed a shower to clean up.

13. a. Adam and Lisa were rollerblading on the <u>sidewalk</u>.

    b. The lady hung her jacket on the <u>sidewalk</u>.

14. a. To get ready for the party, Richard hung streamers and a <u>ramp</u>.

    b. Mr. Brown drove down the <u>ramp</u> to exit the highway.

15. a. My mom doesn't like driving on the <u>highway</u> because the cars go very fast.

    b. To maintain safety, the <u>highway</u> practiced parking on the street.

16. a. Laura's favorite hiking <u>trail</u> is in the mountains near Red River Valley.

    b. When Stephen passed his driving test, he drove his entire <u>trail</u> to lunch to celebrate.

17. a. The deliveryman went down the <u>alley</u> to enter the back of the building.

    b. As we entered the park, an <u>alley</u> jumped in front of us and yelled.

18. a. Before the race started, the workers cleared the <u>track</u> to be safe.

    b. The office workers drank coffee and ate doughnuts during their <u>track</u>.

Challenge Words

Check (✔) the words you already know.

- [ ] airstrip
- [ ] course
- [ ] detour
- [ ] passage
- [ ] chute
- [ ] crossroad
- [ ] intersection
- [ ] runway

97. Vehicles (Actions/Characteristics)

Check (✔) the words you already know. Then, listen and repeat.

Tracks 1–7

☐ **drive**

TR 1

☐ **ride**

TR 2

☐ **passenger**

TR 3

☐ **glide**

TR 4

Definitions

If a car, a ship, or an aircraft **cruises** somewhere, it moves at a steady, comfortable speed.

When you **drive**, you control the movement and direction of a car or other vehicle.

When something **glides**, it moves along smoothly.

A **passenger** in a vehicle, such as a bus, a boat, or a plane, is a person who is traveling in the vehicle, but is not driving it.

When you **ride** a bicycle or a horse, you sit on it, control it, and travel on it.

When you **row**, you make a boat move through the water by using oars.

A boat **sails** when it moves over water.

☐ **row**

TR 5

☐ **sail**

TR 6

☐ **cruise**

TR 7

Check Your Understanding

A. Circle the answer that best matches the meaning of the bolded phrase.

1. My dad let me use the oars to **move our boat through the water**.

   a. ride   b. row   c. fly

2. Sandy and her friends like to **drive at a steady, comfortable speed** down the street in her new car.

   a. cruise   b. skip   c. stop

3. Tom **travels on** his bike to the park to play soccer.

   a. walks   b. jumps   c. rides

4. The children threw their toy airplanes in the air, and then watched them **fly smoothly** through the air.

   a. glide   b. run   c. bounce

5. Sometimes I enjoy being a **person who is just riding** on the train instead of driving my car.

   a. passenger   b. visitor   c. driver

6. Charlie's dream was to **travel by water** on his boat around the world.

   a. ride   b. sail   c. drive

7. Miriam learned to **control a car** when she was sixteen years old.

   a. push   b. take   c. drive

B. Match each word to the correct definition. One definition will not be used.

1. _____ drive   a. to be carried in or on a vehicle
2. _____ passenger   b. to move across water in a boat
3. _____ ride   c. a person who travels in a vehicle
4. _____ row   d. to send into air or space
5. _____ sail   e. to move smoothly through the air
6. _____ cruise   f. to control the movement of a car
7. _____ glide   g. to move a boat through water using oars

                            h. to move at a steady, comfortable rate

Challenge Words

Check (✔) the words you already know.

- ☐ aerial
- ☐ aviation
- ☐ horsepower
- ☐ launch
- ☐ marine
- ☐ naval
- ☐ navigate
- ☐ transport

120. Vehicles (Air Transportation)

Check (✔) the words you already know. Then, listen and repeat.

Tracks 1–9

☐ **aircraft**

TR 1

☐ **airplane**
☐ **plane**

TR 2 and TR 3

☐ **airline**

TR 4

Definitions

An **aircraft** is an airplane or a helicopter.

An **airline** is a company that carries people or goods in airplanes.

An **airplane** or **plane** is a vehicle with wings that can fly through the air.

A **helicopter** is an aircraft with long blades on top that spin very fast. It is able to stay still in the air and to move straight upward or downward.

A **hot-air balloon** is for travel through the air in a basket suspended below a large balloon of heated air.

A **kite** is a toy that you fly in the wind at the end of a long string.

A **rocket** is a vehicle that people use to travel into outer space.

A **spacecraft** is a vehicle that can travel in space.

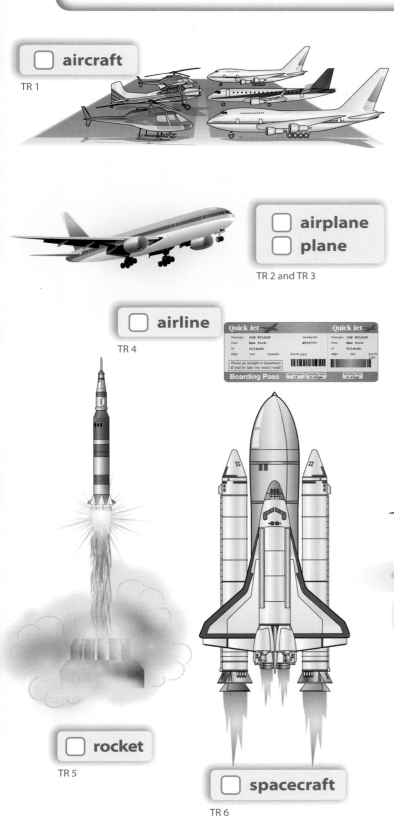

☐ **helicopter**

TR 7

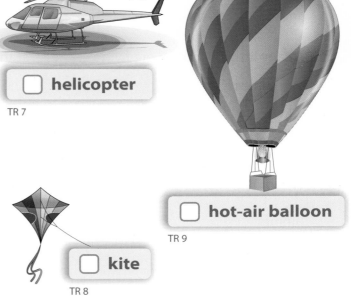

☐ **rocket**

TR 5

☐ **spacecraft**

TR 6

☐ **kite**

TR 8

☐ **hot-air balloon**

TR 9

251

Check Your Understanding

A. Circle the word in each group that does not belong.

1. hot-air balloon   kite   airplane

2. airline   plane   aircraft

3. rocket   helicopter   spacecraft

B. Circle the correct word to complete each sentence.

1. Rockets and satellites are examples of _____ that fly in outer space.

   a. hot-air balloons   b. rockets   c. spacecraft

2. Another word for plane is _____ .

   a. helicopter   b. airplane   c. airline

3. The _____ with the cheapest flights will probably have the most customers.

   a. airline   b. spacecraft   c. aircraft

4. I boarded the _____ and hoped the flight would be short.

   a. kite   b. airline   c. plane

5. Airplanes and helicopters are examples of _____ .

   a. spacecraft   b. aircraft   c. kites

6. When astronauts travel into outer space, they fly in a _____ .

   a. rocket   b. plane   c. helicopter

7. People enjoy floating in the air in the basket of a _____ .

   a. plane   b. hot-air balloon   c. kite

8. The rescue team used a _____ to save people on a sinking boat.

   a. rocket   b. airline   c. helicopter

9. Many little children were flying _____ at the park.

   a. airlines   b. kites   c. spacecraft

Challenge Words

Check (✔) the words you already know.

☐ airliner   ☐ blimp   ☐ jetliner

128. Transportation (Types)

Check (✔) the words you already know. Then, listen and repeat.

Tracks 1–20

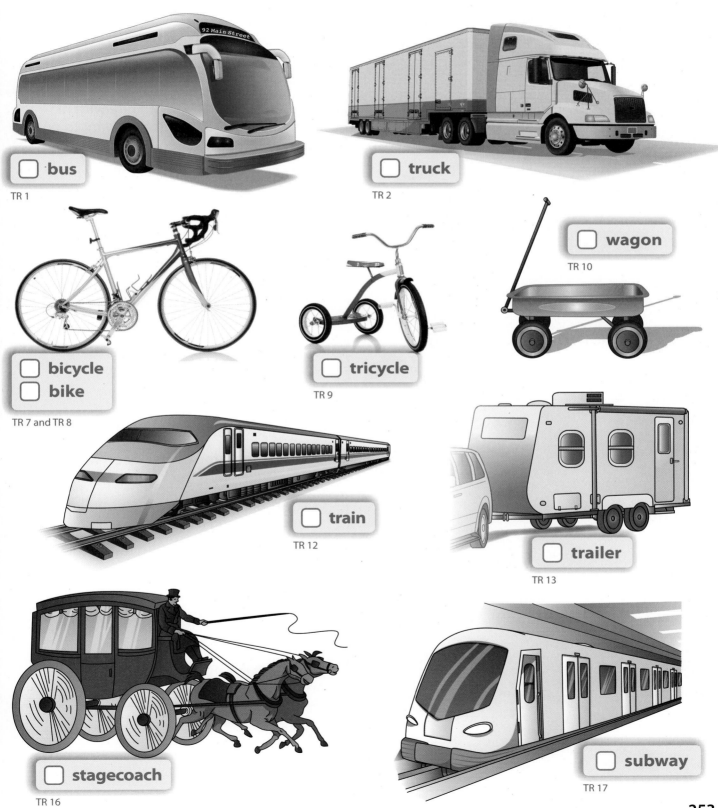

☐ **bus**

TR 1

☐ **truck**

TR 2

☐ **wagon**

TR 10

☐ **bicycle**
☐ **bike**

TR 7 and TR 8

☐ **tricycle**

TR 9

☐ **train**

TR 12

☐ **trailer**

TR 13

☐ **stagecoach**

TR 16

☐ **subway**

TR 17

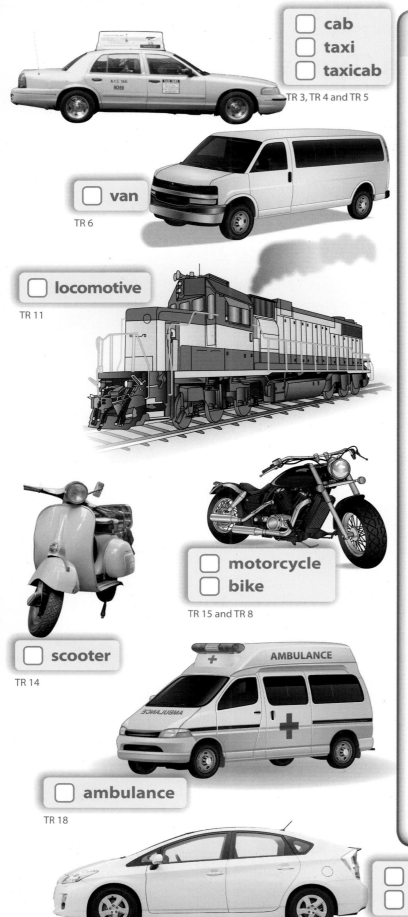

- [ ] cab
- [ ] taxi
- [ ] taxicab

TR 3, TR 4 and TR 5

- [ ] van

TR 6

- [ ] locomotive

TR 11

- [ ] motorcycle
- [ ] bike

TR 15 and TR 8

- [ ] scooter

TR 14

- [ ] ambulance

TR 18

- [ ] car
- [ ] automobile

TR 19 and TR 20

Definitions

An **ambulance** is a vehicle for taking people to the hospital.

A **bicycle** is a vehicle with two wheels. You ride it by sitting on it and using your legs to make the wheels turn.

A **bike** is a bicycle or a motorcycle.

A **bus** is a large motor vehicle that carries passengers.

A **cab** is a car that you can hire with its driver, to take you where you want to go. **Taxicab** and **taxi** are other words for **cab**.

A **car** or **automobile** is a motor vehicle with space for several people.

A **locomotive** is a large vehicle that pulls a train.

A **motorcycle** is a vehicle with two wheels and an engine.

A **scooter** is a small light motorcycle with a low seat.

In the past, **stagecoaches** were large vehicles pulled by horses that carried passengers and mail.

A **subway** is a railroad system that runs under the ground.

A **trailer** is a large container on wheels that is pulled by a truck or other vehicle.

A **train** is a long vehicle that is pulled by an engine along a railroad.

A **tricycle** is a bicycle with three wheels.

A **truck** is a large vehicle that is used for transporting goods by road.

A **van** is a vehicle with space for carrying things in the back.

A **wagon** is a small vehicle with four wheels that a child can pull to carry things.

254

Check Your Understanding

A. Circle the word in each group that does not belong.

1. taxi	ambulance	cab	taxicab
2. bicycle	bike	van	tricycle
3. scooter	automobile	car	truck
4. truck	van	wagon	scooter
5. locomotive	subway	motorcycle	train

B. Underline the correct word to complete each sentence.

1. The man called a (**trailer / taxicab**) to take him to the airport.

2. An (**ambulance / automobile**) rushed to the hospital with its siren screaming.

3. The (**stagecoach / bus**) was pulled by four strong horses.

4. Sammy rides his (**bicycle / tricycle**) to work every day.

5. The (**subway / wagon**) is a fast way to get around the city.

6. Many people enjoy driving a (**scooter / cab**) to save gas.

7. Jenny borrowed her dad's (**truck / car**) to move her furniture to her new apartment.

8. Mike rode his (**taxi / bike**) to baseball practice.

9. The (**train / van**) traveled through the tunnel on the railroad tracks.

10. The boy pulled his (**wagon / motorcycle**) down the street.

11. Another word for cab is (**truck / taxi**).

12. We hooked up the (**trailer / taxicab**) to our car and pulled it to Andrew's house.

13. A car that carries passengers for a fee is called a (**bicycle / cab**).

14. My little sister Emma loves riding her (**tricycle / train**) in the yard.

15. The (**subway / van**) was loaded with sports equipment for the soccer team.

16. Another word for car is (**wagon / automobile**).

17. The train was pulled by a (**locomotive / trailer**).

18. The policeman rode his (**subway / motorcycle**) down the street.

19. I had to buy four tires for my (**car / scooter**).

20. The city (**tricycle / bus**) took the passengers all over town.

Challenge Words

Check (✔) the words you already know.

- ☐ caboose
- ☐ chariot
- ☐ jeep
- ☐ pickup
- ☐ sedan
- ☐ streetcar
- ☐ trolley
- ☐ vehicle

159. Vehicles (Sea Transportation)

Check (✔) the words you already know. Then, listen and repeat.

Tracks 1–7

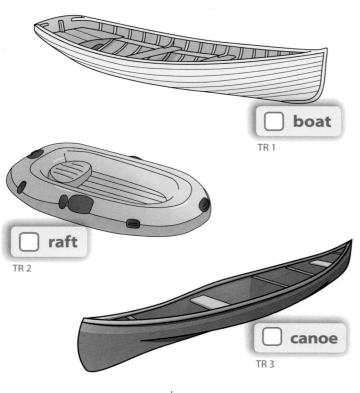

☐ **boat**

TR 1

☐ **raft**

TR 2

☐ **canoe**

TR 3

Definitions

A **boat** is something in which people can travel across water.

A **canoe** is a small, narrow boat that you move through the water using a paddle.

A **raft** is a floating structure that is made from wood, rubber, or plastic.

A **ship** is a large boat that carries people or goods.

A **submarine** is a type of ship that can travel below the surface of the ocean.

A **tugboat** is a small powerful boat that pulls large ships.

A **yacht** is a large boat with sails or a motor, used for racing or for pleasure trips.

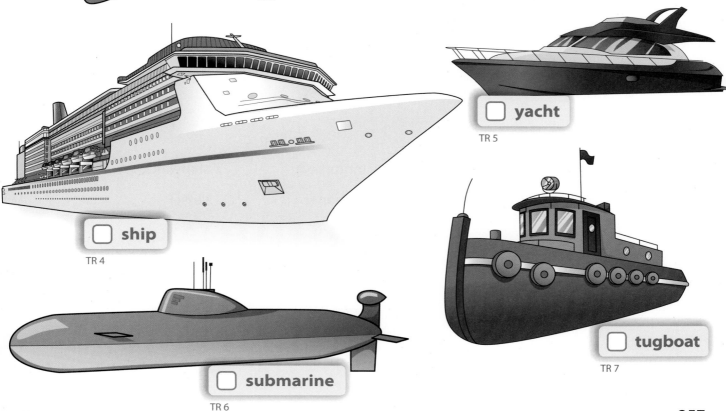

☐ **yacht**

TR 5

☐ **ship**

TR 4

☐ **tugboat**

TR 7

☐ **submarine**

TR 6

Check Your Understanding

A. Match the word with the correct definition. One definition will not be used.

1. _____ boat
2. _____ canoe
3. _____ ship
4. _____ raft
5. _____ submarine
6. _____ tugboat
7. _____ yacht

a. a small powerful boat that pulls or pushes other boats

b. an expensive boat used for racing or for fun

c. a type of ship that travels under water

d. a boat that is used to rescue people

e. a flat floating structure

f. a narrow boat that you paddle

g. something people travel across water in

h. a large boat

B. Underline the correct word to complete each sentence.

1. The (**raft / submarine**) floated slowly down the river.

2. Susan paddled her (**canoe / ship**) across the lake.

3. The (**raft / submarine**) traveled quickly below the surface of the ocean.

4. Large groups of people boarded the (**canoe / ship**) to take a cruise.

5. Dennis and his dad are racing their (**tugboat / yacht**) this Sunday afternoon.

6. Three (**tugboats / yachts**) pulled the ship out of the harbor.

7. At the lake, Randy's dad rented a (**submarine / boat**) to go fishing.

Challenge Words

Check (✔) the words you already know.

☐ barge ☐ kayak ☐ motorboat ☐ shipwreck

☐ battleship ☐ lifeboat ☐ schooner ☐ vessel

234. Parts of Vehicles

Check (✔) the words you already know. Then, listen and repeat.

Tracks 1–12

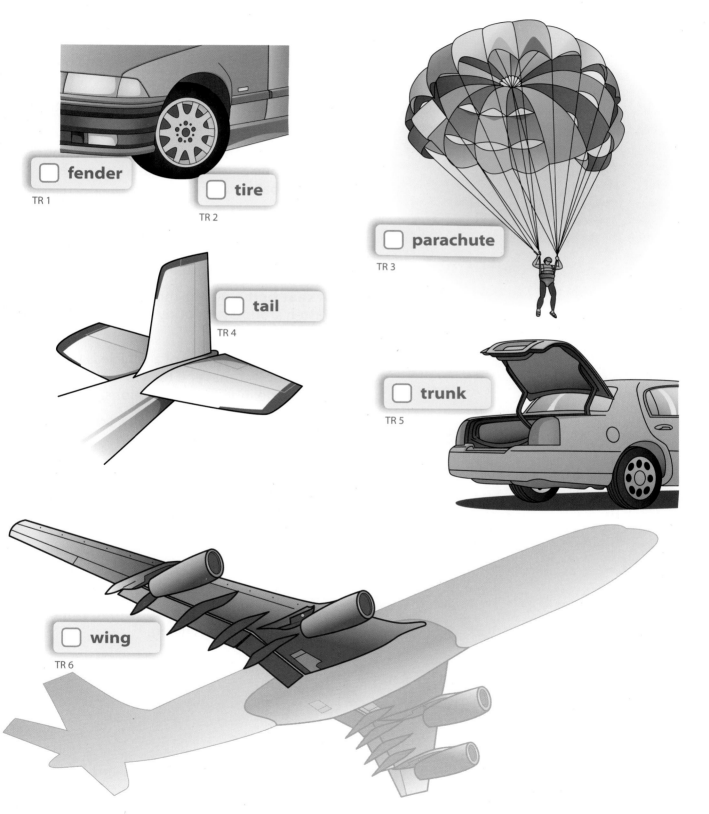

☐ fender
TR 1

☐ tire
TR 2

☐ parachute
TR 3

☐ tail
TR 4

☐ trunk
TR 5

☐ wing
TR 6

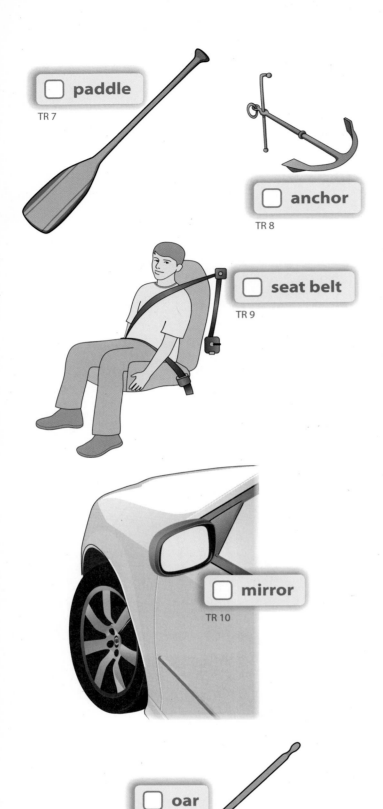

paddle
TR 7

anchor
TR 8

seat belt
TR 9

mirror
TR 10

oar
TR 11

steering wheel
TR 12

Definitions

An **anchor** is a heavy object that is dropped from a boat, into the water, to stop the boat from moving away.

The **fender** of a car is a bar at the front or back that protects the car if it bumps into something.

A **mirror** is a flat piece of glass that you can see yourself in.

An **oar** is a long pole with one flat end that is used for rowing a boat.

A **paddle** is a short pole with a wide, flat part at one or both ends, used to move a small boat through water.

A **parachute** is a large piece of thin cloth. People use a parachute when they jump from an aircraft. Parachutes help people float safely to the ground.

A **seat belt** is a long, thin strap that you fasten around your body in a vehicle to keep you safe.

The **steering wheel** of a vehicle is the round object that you turn to make the vehicle go in different directions.

A **tail** is the end or the back of something, especially something long and thin.

A **tire** is a thick, round piece of rubber that fits around each wheel of a car, bus, and bicycle.

The **trunk** of a car is a covered space at the back in which you put bags or other things.

The **wing** of an airplane is the long, flat part sticking out of each side that supports the plane while it is flying.

Check Your Understanding

A. Write the words in the correct column. Some words fit in more than one column.

anchor	oar	tail	tire
paddle	mirror	seat belt	wing
steering wheel	fender	parachute	trunk

AIRPLANES	CARS	BOATS

B. Underline the correct word to complete each sentence.

1. When his plane landed, James took off his (**anchor / seat belt**).

2. Suzy opened the (**trunk / fender**) of her car to unload the shopping bags.

3. Jay helped Marco change the flat (**tire / parachute**) on his car.

4. Carrie needs two (**oars / seat belts**) to row the boat.

5. Patrick looked in his (**tail / mirror**) to see who was behind his car.

6. I could see the airplane's (**paddles / wings**) from my seat by the window.

7. Amy watched as the (**tail / seat belt**) of the airplane disappeared in the clouds.

8. Mr. Winslow always keeps both of his hands on the (**steering wheel / trunk**) when he is driving.

9. Victor's (**parachute / wing**) opened and he safely floated to the ground.

10. Lana used a (**paddle / mirror**) to move her canoe through the water.

11. The truck smashed the car's front (**fender / wing**).

12. The sailor lowered the heavy (**wheel / anchor**) into the sea to keep the boat from moving.

Challenge Words

Check (✔) the words you already know.

☐ axle ☐ deck ☐ hub ☐ propeller ☐ rudder

☐ dashboard ☐ gangplank ☐ mast ☐ rotor ☐ windshield

318. Vehicles (Snow)

Check (✔) the words you already know. Then, listen and repeat.

Tracks 1–3

☐ **snowplow**

TR 1

Check Your Understanding

A. Fill in the chart.

	SLED	SLEIGH	SNOWPLOW
What is it used for?			
How does it move?			
Have you ever ridden one?			

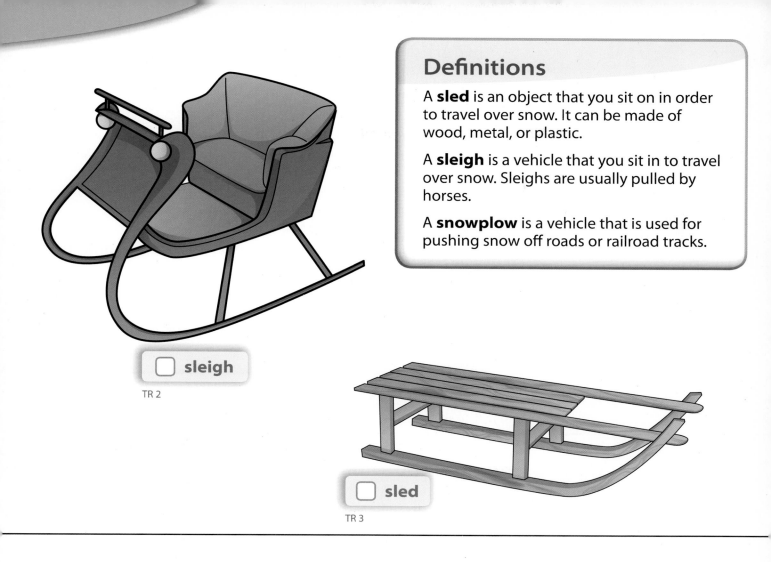

Definitions

A **sled** is an object that you sit on in order to travel over snow. It can be made of wood, metal, or plastic.

A **sleigh** is a vehicle that you sit in to travel over snow. Sleighs are usually pulled by horses.

A **snowplow** is a vehicle that is used for pushing snow off roads or railroad tracks.

☐ **sleigh**

TR 2

☐ **sled**

TR 3

B. Underline the correct word to complete each sentence.

1. The (**sleigh / snowplow**) cleared the streets so cars could drive safely.

2. The (**snowplow / sleigh**) was pulled by two brown horses.

3. Pam laughed as she rode her (**snowplow / sled**) down the hill.

4. The (**sled / snowplow**) pushed the snow off the railroad tracks so that the train could keep moving.

Challenge Words

Check (✔) the words you already know.

☐ bobsled   ☐ toboggan

331. Vehicles (Work-Related)

Check (✔) the words you already know. Then, listen and repeat.

Tracks 1–2

☐ **wheelbarrow**

TR 1

☐ **tractor**

TR 2

Definitions

A **tractor** is a vehicle that a farmer uses to pull farm machinery.

A **wheelbarrow** is a small open cart with one wheel and two handles that is used for moving things such as bricks, earth, or plants.

Check Your Understanding

A. Underline the correct word to complete each sentence.

1. The farmer repaired the engine on his (**wheelbarrow / tractor**) so he could plow the fields.

2. Sidney used the (**wheelbarrow / tractor**) to carry the bricks to the front of the house.

3. My mom asked us to put these plants in the (**tractor / wheelbarrow**) and bring them to the garden.

4. Peter works at a farm and drives a (**tractor / wheelbarrow**).

B. Write **T** for **true statements** and **F** for **false statements**.

1. _____ Wheelbarrows pull plows.

2. _____ A tractor has two handles.

3. _____ A wheelbarrow has one wheel.

4. _____ A tractor is used on farms.

Challenge Words

Check (✔) the words you already know.

☐ barrow   ☐ derrick   ☐ forklift   ☐ harrow

264

104. Money and Goods

Check (✔) the words you already know. Then, listen and repeat.

Track 1–12

☐ **dollar**
TR 1

☐ **penny**
☐ **cent**
TR 2 and TR 3

☐ **nickel**
TR 4

☐ **dime**
TR 5

☐ **quarter**
TR 6

☐ **coin**
TR 7

☐ **cash**
☐ **money**
TR 8 and TR 9

Definitions

Cash is money in the form of bills and coins.

A **cent** is a coin. There are 100 cents in a dollar.

A **check** is a printed form on which you write an amount of money and who it is to be paid to. Your bank then pays the money to that person from your account.

A **coin** is a small, round piece of metal money.

A **dime** is a U.S. coin worth ten cents.

The **dollar** ($) is the unit of money that is used in the U.S., Canada, and some other countries. There are one hundred cents in a dollar.

Money is the coins or bills that you use to buy things.

A **nickel** is a U.S. coin worth five cents.

A **penny** is one cent, or a coin worth one cent.

The **pound** (£) is the unit of money that is used in Great Britain.

A **quarter** is a U.S. coin worth 25 cents.

A **ticket** is a small piece of paper that shows that you have paid to go somewhere or to do something.

☐ **check**
TR 10

☐ **ticket**
TR 11

☐ **pound**
TR 12

Check Your Understanding

A. Answer the questions with a short answer.

1. What is money used for? _____

2. What form of money are bills and coins? _____

3. Where is the dollar used? _____

4. Where are pounds used? _____

5. What are coins made out of? _____

6. How much is a penny worth? _____

7. How much is a quarter worth? _____

8. What is a check used for? _____

9. How much is a dime worth? _____

10. How much is a nickel worth? _____

11. How many cents are in a dollar? _____

12. What is a ticket for? _____

B. Underline the correct word to complete each sentence.

1. My bicycle cost eighty-one dollars and sixty-five (**cents / quarters**).

2. Rick had to pay with a (**coin / check**) because he didn't have any cash.

3. When Ellen gets to England, she will exchange her U.S. dollars for British (**pounds / pennies**).

4. Quarters, nickels, and dimes are all (**dollars / coins**).

5. Melinda purchased a (**ticket / money**) to the concert on Thursday.

6. Annie gave Steve a (**dollar / dime**) because he needed ten more cents.

7. She didn't have enough (**tickets / cash**) in her wallet, so she went to an ATM.

8. Nicole found a (**penny / cash**) on the sidewalk.

9. Laurie put a (**dollar / quarter**) in the parking meter because it only accepted coins.

10. Kyle had plenty of (**money / pennies**) to buy his friend a gift.

11. My brother earns eight (**quarters / dollars**) an hour at his job.

12. I need five more cents. Do you have a (**nickel / quarter**)?

Challenge Words

Check (✔) the words you already know.

☐ capital   ☐ merchandise   ☐ receipt   ☐ stock

☐ finance   ☐ payroll   ☐ souvenir   ☐ wealth

109. Places Where Money/Goods Are Kept

Check (✔) the words you already know. Then, listen and repeat.

 Tracks 1–4

☐ **bank**

TR 1

☐ **purse**

TR 2

Check Your Understanding

A. Match each word to the correct description. One description will not be used.

1. _____ bank
2. _____ wallet
3. _____ safe
4. _____ purse

a. a strong, metal box with a lock where money and other valuable things are kept

b. a place where people can keep their money

c. a secure room where money and valuable things can be kept safely

d. a small bag that women use to carry money and other things

e. a small case that holds money and credit cards

B. Choose the sentence that correctly uses the underlined word.

1. a. Isaac put the $20 bill in his <u>wallet</u>.

   b. He went to the <u>wallet</u> to deposit money.

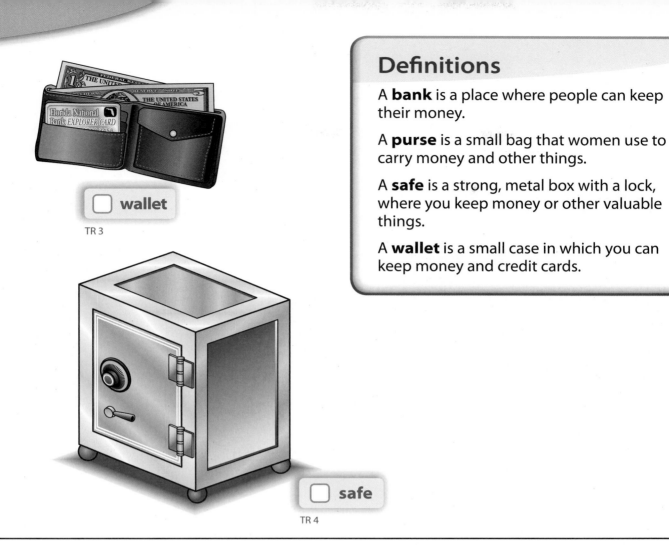

wallet

TR 3

safe

TR 4

Definitions

A **bank** is a place where people can keep their money.

A **purse** is a small bag that women use to carry money and other things.

A **safe** is a strong, metal box with a lock, where you keep money or other valuable things.

A **wallet** is a small case in which you can keep money and credit cards.

2. a. She put her diamond necklace in the <u>purse</u> and then locked it.

   b. Christine looked in her <u>purse</u> for the car keys.

3. a. Mario went to the <u>bank</u> and deposited his check.

   b. He keeps a <u>bank</u> in his back pocket.

4. a. The large, black <u>safe</u> was locked.

   b. Amy put her <u>safe</u> over her shoulder and left the house.

Challenge Words

Check (✔) the words you already know.

- [ ] account
- [ ] billfold
- [ ] commerce
- [ ] handbag
- [ ] mint
- [ ] pocketbook
- [ ] strongbox
- [ ] vault

116. Money-Related Characteristics

Check (✔) the words you already know. Then, listen and repeat.

Tracks 1–7

☐ **poverty**
TR 1

☐ **rich**
TR 3

☐ **broke**
TR 2

Check Your Understanding

A. Match each word to the correct description. One description will not be used.

1. _____ poverty

2. _____ expensive

3. _____ rich

4. _____ broke

5. _____ cheap

6. _____ free

7. _____ poor

a. a person who does not have a lot of money or possessions

b. something that doesn't cost a lot of money

c. the state of being very poor

d. a person who is not proud and doesn't think they are better than others

e. something that costs a lot of money

f. a person who has a lot of money and valuable possessions

g. someone who doesn't have any money

h. something that doesn't cost any money

B. Underline the word in parentheses that best fits in the sentence.

1. A (**rich / poor**) person cannot buy fancy clothes and other expensive things.

2. Charlie won a (**free / broke**) trip to Paris and didn't have to pay anything.

☐ poor
TR 4

☐ cheap
Only $50
TR 5

For sale
$180,000.⁰⁰

☐ expensive
TR 6

Definitions

If you are **broke**, you have no money.

Goods or services that are **cheap** cost little money or less than you expected.

If something is **expensive**, it costs a lot of money.

If something is **free**, you do not have to pay for it.

Someone who is **poor** has very little money and few possessions.

Poverty is the state of being very poor.

A **rich** person has a lot of money and valuable possessions.

☐ free
TR 7

3. The grocery store had a sale today, and all the fruit and vegetables were very (**cheap / rich**).

4. A lot of people lost their jobs and were living in (**poverty / cheap**).

5. I am (**free / broke**) because I have no more money.

6. Carrie knew that the camera she wanted would be very (**free / expensive**).

7. The Brown family was very (**expensive / rich**). They had a lot of money to buy nice things and went on many vacations together.

Challenge Words

Check (✔) the words you already know.

☐ costly   ☐ luxury   ☐ posh   ☐ wasteful

☐ humble   ☐ needy   ☐ royal

271

17 MONEY AND GOODS

122. Actions Related to Money / Goods

Check (✔) the words you already know. Then, listen and repeat.

Tracks 1–9

Here's $20.00 for mowing the lawn.

☐ **sale**
TR 3

☐ **spend**
TR 5

☐ **pay**
TR 2

SALE Was $50 **NOW** $20

I **bet** you a dollar I can hold my breath longer than you can!

☐ **earn**
TR 1

☐ **bet**
TR 4

Check Your Understanding

A. Write **T** for **true statements** and **F** for **false statements**.

1. _____ When you earn money, you receive money for no reason.

2. _____ If you owe someone money, you have to give that person money.

3. _____ When stores have a sale, they sell items for more money than they usually do.

4. _____ When you buy something, you get an item for free.

5. _____ Paying for an item involves giving money to someone for it.

6. _____ If a store sells an item, you can buy that item at the store.

7. _____ When you spend money, you use it on things you want or need.

8. _____ When you bet on something, you might win or lose money.

9. _____ Purchasing something is the same as buying something.

□ owe
TR 6

□ sell
TR 9

□ buy
□ purchase
TR 7 and TR 8

Definitions

When you **bet**, you risk losing something (usually money) if your guess about what will happen is wrong.

If you **buy** something, you get it by paying money for it.

If you **earn** money, you receive money for work that you do.

If you **owe** money to someone, you have to pay money to that person.

When you **pay** for something, you give someone an amount of money for it.

If you **purchase** something, you buy it.

A **sale** is a time when a store sells things at less than the normal price.

If a store **sells** a particular thing, it is available for people to buy there.

When you **spend** money, you pay money for things that you want or need.

B. Write the words from the word bank in the correct column. Some words can be used in more than one column.

pay	owe	bet
buy	sell	sale
earn	purchase	spend

YOU GIVE MONEY	YOU RECEIVE MONEY	YOU SAVE MONEY

Challenge Words

Check (✔) the words you already know.

□ afford   □ bargain   □ budget

273

201. Money/Goods (Received)

Check (✔) the words you already know. Then, listen and repeat.

Tracks 1–7

☐ **reward**

TR 1

☐ **award**

TR 2

☐ **gift**

TR 3

First Prize

☐ **prize**

TR 4

Check Your Understanding

A. Match each word to the correct example. One example will not be used.

1. _____ prize
2. _____ medal
3. _____ gift
4. _____ reward
5. _____ award
6. _____ savings
7. _____ treasure

a. a prize received for getting good grades in school

b. money saved in a bank account

c. a chest full of gold coins and jewels

d. money received for finding and returning a lost diamond necklace

e. money or a special object received for winning an essay contest

f. a birthday present

g. money received from an employer

h. a silver metal disk received for coming in second place in a race

☐ treasure

TR 5

☐ savings

TR 6

☐ medal

TR 7

Definitions

An **award** is a prize that a person receives for doing something well.

A **gift** is something that someone receives as a present.

A **medal** is a small metal disk that you receive as a prize for showing great skill or performing a brave or good act.

A **prize** is money or a special object that the person who wins a game, a race, or a competition receives.

A **reward** is something that a person receives for doing something good.

Your **savings** are the money that you have saved, especially in a bank.

In children's stories, **treasure** is a collection of valuable old objects, such as gold coins and jewelry.

B. Underline the correct word to complete each sentence.

1. There is a (**reward** / **gift**) for returning the stolen jewelry.

2. Angie gave a (**gift** / **treasure**) to her uncle to thank him for watching her cat.

3. The (**medal** / **prize**) for winning the game at the fair was a huge stuffed animal.

4. Mary hopes to win the gold (**gift** / **medal**) in the ice skating competition.

5. Edwin read his little brother a story about pirates searching for a buried (**gift** / **treasure**).

6. Jenna received an (**award** / **savings**) for not missing a single day of school.

7. Tyler had enough money in his (**treasure** / **savings**) to buy the new gaming system.

Challenge Words

Check (✔) the words you already know.

☐ allowance   ☐ fortune   ☐ insurance   ☐ refund

☐ credit   ☐ income   ☐ profit   ☐ salary

214. Money / Goods (Paid Out)

Check (✔) the words you already know. Then, listen and repeat.

Tracks 1–4

☐ rent

TR 1

Check Your Understanding

A. Write **T** for **true statements** and **F** for **false statements**.

1. _____ If you rent something, it belongs to you.

2. _____ The price of something is how much you have to pay in order to own it.

3. _____ A payment is money borrowed from someone.

4. _____ The cost of something tells you how much money you need to buy it.

$19.99

- [ ] price
- [ ] cost

TR 2 and TR 3

Definitions

The **cost** of something is the amount of money you need in order to buy, do, or make it.

A **payment** is an amount of money that is paid to someone.

The **price** of something is the amount of money that you have to pay in order to buy it.

Rent is the amount of money that you pay to use something that belongs to someone else.

- [ ] **payment**

TR 4

B. Circle the correct word to complete each sentence.

1. Justin worked hard to pay the _____ for his apartment.

   a. rent   b. price   c. payment

2. The original _____ of the refrigerator was $500.00.

   a. payment   b. rent   c. cost

3. Sylvia's monthly _____ for her new car is $215.00.

   a. price   b. payment   c. cost

4. Andrew couldn't find the _____ of the book, so he didn't know how much to pay.

   a. price   b. payment   c. rent

Challenge Words

Check (✔) the words you already know.

- [ ] debt
- [ ] fee
- [ ] levy
- [ ] mortgage
- [ ] product
- [ ] tariff
- [ ] tax
- [ ] tuition

63. Walking/Running

Check (✔) the words you already know. Then, listen and repeat.

 Tracks 1–12

☐ **dance**
TR 1

☐ **tiptoe**
TR 2

☐ **stumble**
☐ **trip**
TR 3 and TR 4

☐ **run**
TR 5

☐ **walk**
TR 7

☐ **hike**
TR 6

☐ **limp**
TR 10

☐ **skip**
TR 8

☐ **march**
TR 9

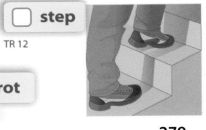

☐ **step**
TR 12

☐ **trot**
TR 11

Definitions

When you **dance**, you move your body to music.

If you **hike**, you go for a long walk.

If you **limp**, you walk with difficulty because you have hurt one of your legs or feet.

When you **march** somewhere, you walk there with regular steps, alone or in a group.

When you **run**, you move very quickly using your legs.

If you **skip** along, you move forward quickly, jumping from one foot to the other.

If you **step** on something, you put your foot on it.

If you **stumble**, you nearly fall down while you are walking or running.

If you **tiptoe** somewhere, you walk there very quietly on your toes.

If you **trip** when you are walking, you knock your foot against something and fall or nearly fall.

If you **trot** somewhere, you move at a speed between walking and running.

When you **walk**, you move forward by putting one foot in front of the other.

Check Your Understanding

A. Circle the correct word to complete each sentence.

1. After looking at the map, Paul decided to _____ to the farthest lake.

   a. hike   b. trip   c. dance

2. Marie happily _____ to her best friend's house.

   a. danced   b. skipped   c. tiptoed

3. The horse _____ across the field.

   a. trotted   b. hiked   c. tripped

4. Freddy will play his trumpet and _____ with the band in the parade.

   a. limp   b. hike   c. march

5. Olivia was so tired that she kept _____ as we walked to class.

   a. running   b. trotting   c. stumbling

6. We saw Maria _____ over the tree branch and fall down.

   a. skip   b. dance   c. trip

7. My grandfather and I _____ slowly through the park and looked at the flowers.

   a. walked   b. ran   c. marched

8. Pete _____ on the scale to see how much he weighed.

   a. skipped   b. stepped   c. walked

9. Ashley quietly _____ by her brother's room so she would not wake him up.

   a. marched   b. stumbled   c. tiptoed

10. The bus is going to leave, so we need to hurry and _____ to the station.

    a. run   b. dance   c. limp

11. Jason and Vanessa started to _____ when they heard the music.

    a. hike   b. stumble   c. dance

12. Maria hurt her foot and had to _____ home.

    a. trip   b. limp   c. trot

B. Match each word to the correct definition. One definition will not be used.

1. _____ march
2. _____ skip
3. _____ trip
4. _____ walk
5. _____ limp
6. _____ stumble
7. _____ hike
8. _____ step
9. _____ run
10. _____ trot
11. _____ dance
12. _____ tiptoe

a. to nearly fall down while walking or running

b. to move at a speed between walking and running

c. to walk somewhere very quietly on your toes

d. to walk with difficulty

e. to go for a long walk

f. to move slowly on your hands and knees

g. to fall or nearly fall while walking

h. to put your foot on something

i. to move forward quickly, jumping from one foot to the other

j. to move quickly on your legs

k. to walk formally with regular steps

l. to move your body to music

m. to move forward by putting one foot in front of the other

Challenge Words

Check (✔) the words you already know.

☐ amble   ☐ jog   ☐ saunter   ☐ swagger

☐ hobble   ☐ ramble   ☐ shuffle   ☐ tread

308. Jumping

Check (✔) the words you already know. Then, listen and repeat.

☐ **leap**

TR 1

☐ **hop**

TR 2

Check Your Understanding

A. Match each word to the correct description. One description will not be used.

1. _____ leap   a. move high into the air and cross a long distance

2. _____ hop   b. move quickly into the air by pushing off the ground with both feet

3. _____ jump   c. move by jumping toward someone and trying to take hold of them

                            d. move by jumping on one foot

B. Answer the questions.

1. How are *hop* and *jump* alike?

_____

_____

2. How are *hop* and *jump* different?

_____

_____

Definitions

When you **hop**, you move by jumping on one foot.

When you **jump**, you bend your knees, push against the ground with your feet, and move quickly upward into the air.

When you **leap**, you jump high in the air or you jump a long distance.

☐ **jump**

TR 3

3. How are *jump* and *leap* alike?

_____

_____

4. How are *jump* and *leap* different?

_____

_____

Challenge Words

Check (✔) the words you already know.

☐ bound   ☐ lunge   ☐ pounce

☐ coil   ☐ lurch   ☐ spring

339. Kicking Actions

Check (✔) the words you already know. Then, listen and repeat.

 Tracks 1–2

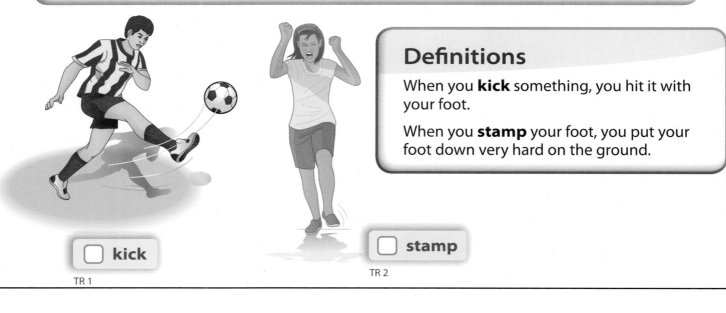

Definitions

When you **kick** something, you hit it with your foot.

When you **stamp** your foot, you put your foot down very hard on the ground.

☐ **kick**

TR 1

☐ **stamp**

TR 2

Check Your Understanding

A. Choose the sentence that correctly uses the underlined word.

1. a. Eddie tried to <u>kick</u> the ball into the goal.

   b. Nathan <u>kicked</u> his eyes and fell asleep.

2. a. My baby brother <u>stamped</u> his foot and started crying.

   b. We <u>stamped</u> the ball over to Joe.

3. a. Julie is <u>kicking</u> fruits and vegetables in the kitchen.

   b. Mark does not like playing soccer because he can't <u>kick</u> very far.

B. Write **T** for **true statements** and **F** for **false statements**.

1. _____ You kick with your hands.

2. _____ When you stamp your foot, it lands softly on the ground.

3. _____ If you stamp your foot, people might think you are angry.

Challenge Words

Check (✔) the words you already know.

☐ stomp   ☐ tramp

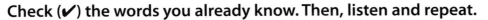

408. Creeping/Lurking Actions

Check (✔) the words you already know. Then, listen and repeat.

Track 1

TR 1

☐ **crawl**

> ### Definition
> When you **crawl**, you move on your hands and knees.

Check Your Understanding

A. Write T for true statements and F for false statements.

1. _____ Someone who crawls is close to the ground.

2. _____ Babies usually crawl because they do not know how to walk yet.

3. _____ You use your hands and knees to crawl.

4. _____ Adults usually crawl to work.

B. Choose the sentence that correctly uses the underlined word.

1. a. The large <u>crawl</u> moved slowly through the night.

   b. Paul had to <u>crawl</u> under the porch to rescue the kitten.

2. a. Cindy <u>crawled</u> under her desk when she heard the earthquake alarm.

   b. Mary <u>crawled</u> her mother on her cell phone.

3. a. Edgar <u>crawls</u> under the bed to hide.

   b. Monica <u>crawls</u> the car to work every day.

4. a. Bill <u>crawled</u> into the air to try to see over the tall fence.

   b. My baby cousin doesn't know how to walk yet, so she <u>crawls</u> everywhere.

Challenge Words

Check (✔) the words you already know.

☐ creep   ☐ prowl   ☐ slither

☐ lurk   ☐ slink   ☐ sneak

409. Standing/Stationary

Check (✔) the word you already know. Then, listen and repeat.

Track 1

☐ **stand**

TR 1

Definition

When you **stand**, you are on your feet.

Check Your Understanding

A. Write **T** for **true statements** and **F** for **false statements**.

1. _____ If your shoes hurt, you want to sit rather than stand.

2. _____ You stand on your knees.

3. _____ You stand when you sleep.

B. Choose the sentence that correctly uses the underlined word.

1. a. Because she was small, Teresa had to <u>stand</u> on a chair to see the parade pass by.

   b. Nick was <u>standing</u> because his car wouldn't start.

2. a. The sun was <u>standing</u> in the sky above us.

   b. Everyone <u>stood</u> when the president entered the room.

3. a. Tony <u>stood</u> his e-mails and ate his breakfast.

   b. Ellen <u>stood</u> and recited the Pledge of Allegiance.

Challenge Words

Check (✔) the words you already know.

☐ pose   ☐ posture   ☐ prone   ☐ recline   ☐ straddle

30. Attitudinals (Lack of Truth/Doubt)

Check (✔) the words you already know. Then, listen and repeat.

Maybe it's a necklace or **possibly** it's a watch!

Definition

You use **maybe** when you are uncertain about something that could happen.

You use **possibly** when something might happen, exist, or be true, but is not certain.

☐ maybe
☐ possibly

TR 1 and TR 2

Check Your Understanding

A. Write **T** for **true statements** and **F** for **false statements**.

1. _____ If something is possibly true, there's a chance it could be true.

2. _____ If something will possibly happen, it might not happen.

3. _____ If someone says, "Maybe it will rain," they are not sure that it will rain.

4. _____ If your mom says, "Maybe I will go to the library," she is certain that she will go to the library.

B. Write **C** if the speaker is **certain** and **U** if the speaker is **uncertain**.

1. _____ **Pete:** It is going to rain tomorrow.

2. _____ **Jeremy:** Maybe it will be sunny tomorrow.

3. _____ **Pete:** There could possibly be a thunderstorm.

4. _____ **Jeremy:** Maybe you are right.

Challenge Words

Check (✔) the words you already know.

☐ allegedly ☐ perhaps ☐ seemingly ☐ supposedly

31. Attitudinals (Other)

Check (✔) the words you already know. Then, listen and repeat.

Tracks 1–2

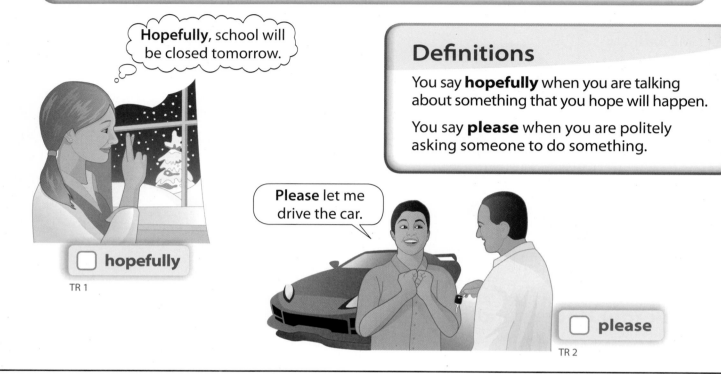

Hopefully, school will be closed tomorrow.

☐ **hopefully**

TR 1

Definitions

You say **hopefully** when you are talking about something that you hope will happen.

You say **please** when you are politely asking someone to do something.

Please let me drive the car.

☐ **please**

TR 2

Check Your Understanding

A. Fill in the blanks with *hopefully* or *please*.

1. After studying all day, I _____ will pass my test.

2. Would you _____ pass the salt?

3. _____ put your books away.

4. _____ we will get to the park in less than 10 minutes.

B. Write **T** for **true statements** and **F** for **false statements**.

1. _____ *Please* is a rude word.

2. _____ *Hopefully* is used to talk about something that you hope for.

3. _____ *Please* can be used to ask for something.

4. _____ *Hopefully* is used to talk about things you hope will not happen.

Challenge Words

Check (✔) the word you already know.

☐ preferably

285. Attitudinals (Truth)

Check (✔) the words you already know. Then, listen and repeat.

Tracks 1–6

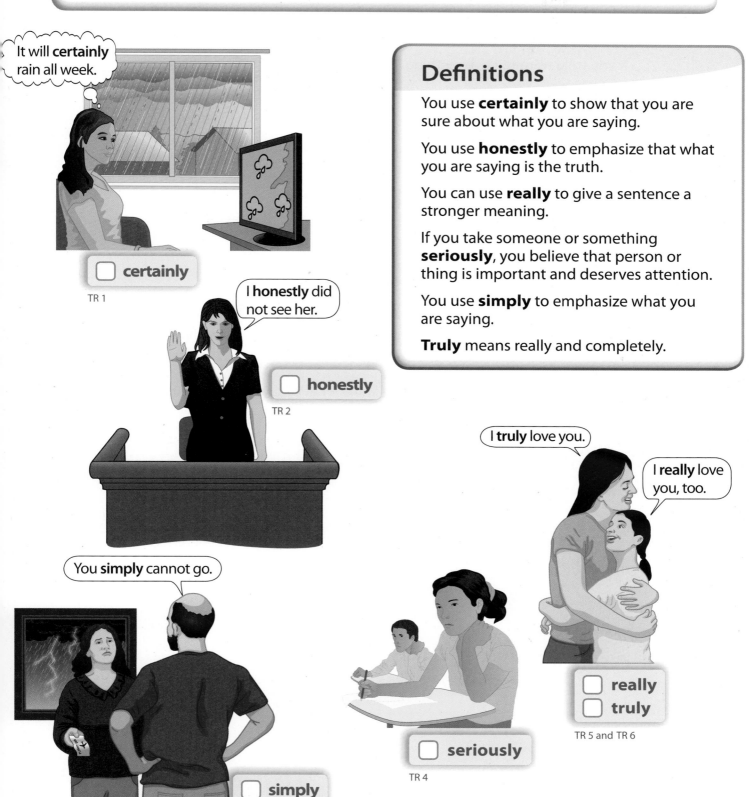

It will **certainly** rain all week.

☐ **certainly**

TR 1

I **honestly** did not see her.

☐ **honestly**

TR 2

Definitions

You use **certainly** to show that you are sure about what you are saying.

You use **honestly** to emphasize that what you are saying is the truth.

You can use **really** to give a sentence a stronger meaning.

If you take someone or something **seriously**, you believe that person or thing is important and deserves attention.

You use **simply** to emphasize what you are saying.

Truly means really and completely.

I **truly** love you.

I **really** love you, too.

You **simply** cannot go.

☐ **really**
☐ **truly**

TR 5 and TR 6

☐ **seriously**

TR 4

☐ **simply**

TR 3

Check Your Understanding

A. Write **T** for **true statements** and **F** for **false statements**.

1. _____ If you really want something, it means you want it a lot.

2. _____ If you use the word *honestly,* you are trying to show that you are telling the truth.

3. _____ If you truly want to do something, it means you do not really care if you do it.

4. _____ If you simply cannot go somewhere, it means that you are not sure if you will go.

5. _____ If you take someone seriously, you do not think that person is important.

6. _____ If you use the word *certainly,* you are trying to show that you are sure about what you are saying.

B. Unscramble the words in parentheses to complete each sentence.

1. People who are _____ (lyeral) happy smile all day.

2. We _____ (tylnercai) need to take a vacation soon.

3. Sarah _____ (misylp) wants to finish reading her book.

4. The family _____ (lytru) believed the firefighters saved their lives.

5. The store manager took the workers' suggestions _____ (slyriseou).

6. He _____ (lyteshon) did not know what to say about the problem.

Challenge Words

Check (✔) the words you already know.

☐ apparently ☐ clearly ☐ ideally ☐ surely

☐ basically ☐ definitely ☐ obviously ☐ undoubtedly

369. Attitudinals (Fortunate/Unfortunate)

Check (✔) the words you already know. Then, listen and repeat.

Tracks 1–2

Laundromat
Sorry!
CLOSED

☐ **unfortunately**

TR 1

☐ luckily

TR 2

Luckily, no one was hurt.

Definitions

You use **luckily** when you want to say that it is good that something happened.

You say **unfortunately** when you are sorry about something.

Check Your Understanding

A. Underline the correct word to complete each sentence.

1. (**Unfortunately** / **Luckily**), John had an umbrella to cover him when it started raining.

2. (**Unfortunately** / **Luckily**), Alex fell out of the tree and broke his arm.

3. (**Unfortunately** / **Luckily**), Sandy's dog escaped from her backyard.

4. (**Luckily** / **Unfortunately**), the movie had not yet started, although we arrived late.

B. Write **T** for **true statements** and **F** for **false statements**.

1. _____ The word *unfortunately* is used to talk about something that is very lucky.

2. _____ The word *luckily* is used to talk about something that is good.

3. _____ The word *unfortunately* is used to talk about something that you regret.

4. _____ The word *luckily* is used to talk about something you wish did not happen.

Challenge Words

Check (✔) the word you already know.

☐ happily

APPENDIX

Note: This Appendix provides information on how to find each cluster. To locate a specific <u>super cluster</u>, please refer to the Contents on pages v to vi.

PHOTO CREDITS